1514

D0830757

Advanced Project Management
Fourth Edition

Advanced Project Management

A Structured Approach

Fourth Edition

FREDERICK HARRISON and DENNIS LOCK

Published by
Gower Publishing Limited
Gower House
Croft Road
Aldershot
Hants GU11 3HR
England

Gower Publishing Company
Suite 420
101 Cherry Street
Burlington
VT 05401–4405
USA

Frederick Harrison and Dennis Lock have asserted their right under the Copyright, Designs and Patents Act, 1988 to be identified as the authors of this work.

British Library Cataloguing in Publication Data
Advanced project management: a structured approach. – 4th
   ed.
   1. Project management
   I. Harrison, F. L. (Frederick L.) II. Lock, Dennis, 1929–
   658.4'04

ISBN 0 566 07822 8

Library of Cataloging-in-Publication Data
Harrison, F. L.
   Advanced project management: a structured approach. -- 4th ed. / by Frederick Harrison
  and Dennis Lock
     p. cm.
   Includes bibliographical references and index.
   ISBN 0-566-07822-8
   1. Project management. I. Lock, Dennis. II. Title

   HD69.P75H37 2004
   658.4'04--dc22

2003056920

Typeset in 9 point Stone Serif by IML Typographers, Birkenhead, Merseyside and printed in Great Britain by MPG Books Ltd, Bodmin, Cornwall

Contents

List of Figures

List of Abbreviations

ACWP	actual cost of work performed
ADM	arrow diagram
APM	Assocation for Project Management
BAC	budget at completion
BCWP	budgeted cost for work performed (earned value)
BCWS	budgeted cost for work scheduled
BSI	British Standards Institution
CAD	computer-aided design
CBS	cost breakdown structure
CPI	cost performance index
CRT	cost–resource–time
EAC	estimate at completion
ECR	engineering change request
ETC	estimated costs to completion
FMEA	failure mode and effect analysis
FMECA	failure mode effect and criticality analysis
IPMA	International Project Management Association
IPMIS	integrated project management information system
ISO	International Standards Organization
NPV	net present value
OBS	organization breakdown structure
OD	organization development
PMIS	project management information system
PDM	precedence diagram
PERT	Programme Evaluation and Review Technique
PMI	Project Management Institute
PMIS	project management information system
PMP	Project Management Professional
SOW	statement of work
SPI	schedule performance index
WBS	work breakdown structure

Preface to the Fourth Edition

Fred Harrison's original work has won respect from a large volume of readers for its painstaking and logical approach to the structural aspects of projects. This approach includes topics that are difficult to explain and have thus been neglected in too many other project management books. I count myself among the many earlier admirers of this work, and have over the years recommended it to those of my students showing a desire to progress beyond the usual basic syllabus and, especially, explore in greater depth the mysteries that relate the work breakdown structure and organizational breakdown structure. It was, therefore, a privilege to be asked to assist in the preparation of this fourth edition. Mr Harrison and I have known each other for many years and this collaboration has been particularly easy, because we both share very similar views on the nature and purpose of project management and have had no disagreement at all on the content and format of this fourth edition.

This edition is considerably changed from its predecessors. Most of the original chapters remain, either substantially intact or redistributed throughout the new text. All the illustrations have been reviewed, redrawn and augmented with new illustrations where appropriate. The third edition comprised 12 chapters, and this edition has 21. It is immediately apparent, therefore, that a considerable body of new material has been added. The following topics are among those that are either new to this book or which have been given greater emphasis:

- Project definition and appraisal
- Procurement and the supply chain
- Concurrent engineering
- Cost and management accounting
- Quality management
- More detailed explanations of critical path analysis, now predominately using the precedence system
- Increased treatment of resource scheduling
- Planning with multiple calendars
- Planning within fixed time constraints, using crashing and fast-tracking methods
- Standard networks, modules and templates
- Risk management.

References and further reading lists have been thoroughly reviewed and updated. We have also found and corrected a few minor errors that crept into the text and diagrams of the third edition. The result is a completely updated and substantially enhanced book that we expect at least to uphold the high reputation gained by the previous editions.

Dennis Lock
St Albans
2004

PART 1

Setting the Scene

1 *Introduction to Project Management*

Project management is probably the fastest growing profession in today's world. This is apparent in at least two ways:

1 Recognition, at least by enlightened senior managers, that a project management approach can be applied with profit to a wide range of business development and change endeavours far removed from the traditional concepts of commercial and industrial projects. Such projects can include, for example, internal management projects created to drive through an organizational change, to acquire and install some new capital asset or to manage a company relocation.
2 Rapid and continuous increase in individual membership of professional organizations. Indeed, those new to project management could do no better than contact one of the professional associations, such as the Project Management Institute (PMI) or a local national affiliate of the International Project Management Association (IPMA). More details are given at the end of Chapter 3.

The purpose of project management

Projects, as new endeavours, are often carried out in unfamiliar or even hostile environments. They require the use of untried designs and work processes, might have complex organizations, and must accomplish demanding requirements within strict time and cost boundaries. It is not surprising that many projects fail to achieve all their objectives, sometimes by wide margins. In other words, projects are prone to damage through risk.

The purpose of project management, and the principal role of the project manager, is to achieve all the set project objectives in spite of the risks.

Measurement of a project's success or failure can be viewed from two different perspectives. First there are the primary objectives of the project manager, usually working for a group or organization that is committed to achieving closely defined performance, cost and time objectives. These primary project management objectives align with the objectives agreed between the customer (or client) and the project contractor.

We must allow the terms 'customer' and 'contractor' wide meaning in this context. In addition to its application in the familiar sense of business between two companies, we also consider as a contractor any group or company department that carries out an internal management project on the instructions.of the company's own senior management. In that case the corporate body becomes, in effect, the customer or client for its own project.

Then there are the wider measures of a project's success or failure, as perceived by stakeholders not only within the contractor–client relationship, but also in the more diverse business and public environment.

THE THREE PRIMARY OBJECTIVES

Most projects are set up with firm objectives in mind. The only obvious exception is a project for pure research, which might lead either to no conclusive result or to some unexpected but important scientific discovery. We can describe the three primary objectives under the headings of specification, delivery date and cost.

Specification

A specification should define what outcome is expected from the project – the project deliverables in the current jargon. It must set out in unambiguous terms (and, where relevant, measurable quantities) the benefits that the project customer can expect in return for the investment or price paid. The specification should certainly include the scope of supply in a clear statement of what the contractor is committed to do.

Delivery date

Delivery date is the time when the project is completed and handed over in a state that satisfies the reasonable expectations of the customer. Much of the project management task is concerned with identifying the many activities needed to complete the project, placing them in a logical sequence, estimating the time required and allocating resources. A practicable plan, made in appropriate detail, is the main benchmark for controlling progress towards completion on time.

Delivery promises often have to be made to the customer early in the life of the project, at the proposal stage, when no serious thought can be given to detailed schedules. Then, when work is eventually authorized, the contractor's project manager must attempt to devise a plan that can meet the preordained completion date.

Delivering a project on time is an extremely important objective, not only for the customer, because any project that runs late is at risk of being skimped in respect of quality and reliability, and late running almost always leads to spending over budget.

Cost

Although many project contractors are in business to make profits, by no means all projects are conducted for profit. Many internal management projects, projects carried out by charities and other not-for-profit organizations have no direct profit objective. In general terms, therefore, it is best to regard cost objectives in terms of authorized budgets.

BALANCING THE PRIMARY OBJECTIVES

The three primary objectives are dependent one upon another. Extend the project scope or enhance the specification, and it is clear that the time and budget limits must be extended to suit.

Some writers portray the three primary objectives as the corners of a triangle (see, for example, Chapter 1 in Lock, 2003). They argue that high-level decisions dictate which of the three primary objectives should be considered most important for project success, and which should be subjected to the greatest degree of management control. We prefer to regard this balancing decision as shown in Figure 1.1, where a project is portrayed as having three primary inputs that contribute to the final outcome or project deliverables:

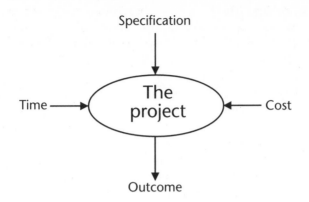

Figure 1.1   Balancing the three primary project objectives

1 Specification: the nature and scope of what has to be achieved.
2 Time: the time span allocated to the project.
3 Cost: the amount of money and cost-consuming resources that can be expended on the project.

Many organizations manage their projects without making any conscious decision to distinguish between the primary objectives or to balance them. Yet most will have a corporate culture that emphasizes some attribute of their product or service. This might be quality (standard of specification and fitness for purpose) or customer service. It is possible to list circumstances where one of the primary objectives should assume greatest importance. Here are some examples:

• Projects where specification should have high priority: nuclear energy, petrochemical plants, aerospace and defence. Safety, reliability and the standard of performance in these projects should be paramount.
• Projects where time is especially important: preparation for any event where the date has been announced, such as a trade exhibition, public festival, stage show and so on. Product development where time-to-market is critical. Projects set up in emergencies to deal with natural disasters where lives are at risk also have to be carried out as quickly as possible.
• Projects where budget limits are especially important: some organizations need to be particularly economical with their spending plans – for example, when their funding is derived from public subscription or charitable donations, or in any other case where funds are scarce.

WIDER CONCERNS OF STAKEHOLDERS

From the project manager's and contractor's point of view, it is probable that any project which completely satisfies the three primary objectives will be viewed as an unqualified success. But these criteria might not determine the wider, longer-term view of project success or failure as seen by the entire body of stakeholders. A property developer that builds a high-rise office block to good specification, attracting desirable tenants who pay high rents, might consider the project to be a great success. Local shopkeepers and traders (secondary stakeholders of the project) could welcome the attraction of additional trade. Nearby residents who lives are blighted by increased road traffic, reduced natural light, noise and interrupted views would not see the project as such a great success.

People living near a new manufacturing plant will be more concerned about the specification (safety, levels of pollution, noise, and so on) than about the cost of the project or the length of time taken to build it. The local authority, emergency services, employment agencies, suppliers of raw materials and many other stakeholders would each have their own perception of what makes the project a success or failure.

Suppose that contractors build a new tollbridge over a Scottish loch that cuts 25 kilometres from the average journeys of road traffic drivers. If the project cost twice the budget and bankrupted the first contractor, that contractor and its workers might consider it as a terrible failure. The project owner might also be considerably upset in those circumstances, having to find another contractor, lose some sunk costs, and wait for far longer than anticipated before receiving toll revenues. The travelling public, however, might be very satisfied and grateful for the eventual outcome of the project.

Hundreds of examples can be visualized where true project success or failure cannot be measured simply by the three primary objectives alone. Thus each group of stakeholders will probably hold a different view of the way in which the objectives of a project should be valued and balanced. Hartman (2000) claims that a successful project is one that makes all the stakeholders happy. Although that ideal might not always be attainable, Hartman's point is a good one that should be borne in mind by all who commission new projects.

The nature of project management

Project management can be defined as the achievement of project objectives through people and involving the organization, planning and control of resources assigned to the project. It requires the development of constructive human relations with and between all those concerned, both in the contracting company and in all the other organizations that might be involved. Projects demand specialized, information systems, scheduling and control techniques. They need managers who are skilled in dealing with human resource problems that arise because of the particular characteristics of projects and the specialized nature of project organizations.

Project management has evolved to become a general management-oriented and integrative activity, usually operating below board and top management levels. Effective project management integrates the various people and groups into one organization. It develops teamworking and commitment to project objectives. It is generally accepted that project management is essential for large, complex undertakings and that the effectiveness or otherwise of project management will have a profound effect on the cost of a project and the time taken to complete it.

PROJECT MANAGEMENT AS AN ADVANCED, SPECIALIZED BRANCH OF MANAGEMENT

Project management might be considered as a branch or specialized form of management, similar to production management, marketing management and so on. It does have its own range of special methods, systems and techniques, particularly for planning and control. These in themselves would be sufficient to distinguish project management as a special branch of management. However, project management is far more than that, not least because of its particular organizational, human relations and cultural factors.

Organizational factors

Project organization structures are specialized. They are often complex and designed to handle multi-discipline, multi-company undertakings. These structures often break many of the traditional rules of organization theory, which include the following:

- The organization will have a hierarchical structure.
- Authority must be based on the superior–subordinate concept.
- A subordinate can have only one superior (the principle of unity of command).
- There is a clear division of labour based on task specialization.
- A manager's span of control must be kept within certain limits.
- People are divided into staff and line management.
- There must be parity between a manager's responsibility and his or her authority.

Any or all of the above rules can be violated in project management.

Human relations

The problems and challenges which face the project manager when dealing with people might at first be thought no different from those facing most managers. But in project management human relations problems are accentuated and accelerated. Project managers do not always work in the traditional superior–subordinate hierarchy and their responsibility typically exceeds their authority. Yet they are often expected to manage people who are not directly responsible to them and may even be outside their own company. They must be able to build teams quickly, or at least establish cooperative working relationships. They must also be able to deal with conflict, which is generally held to be endemic in project work.

Culture

Culture, as much as anything, distinguishes project management from many other branches of management. Project management has a culture all of its own, which includes the following:

- thinking globally, not just parochially about one's own commitment
- a total commitment to goals, which includes being:
  - results-oriented
  - cost- and time-conscious
- accepting change as a way of life
- dealing with:
  - flexibility
  - uncertainty
  - complexity
  - indefinite and inadequate authority
  - temporary situations and relationships
- having a high level of imagination.

The project manager

Functional department managers often direct their time and effort to the technical success of a project rather than to a holistic consideration of time, cost and technical performance. Functional managers, not surprisingly, tend to concentrate their efforts, understanding and enthusiasm within their own departments. This often leads to a kind of tunnel vision, in that they view a project within the narrow scope of their own specialist function and cannot exercise judgement on the project as a whole.

Without a project manager, no one in the traditional departmental organization can be entirely responsible for a project and manage it throughout its life. The only common superior of the various groups, departments and organizational units of the principal company involved in a project is otherwise one of the senior general managers, who is not usually trained or free to carry out this project management role.

Projects of significant size, value and complexity require to have accountability and responsibility for integrating the management functions and activities of the many organizational units involved vested in one individual (the project manager). Otherwise there can be no effective management, leadership or integration of all those involved in the project. This need becomes even greater when more than one project is being handled at the same time. In multi-company projects, where individual companies might or might not have their own project managers, the following points are often true:

1 There is no single-point accountability and responsibility for the overall project. No individual, group or even company is accountable for all the organizational units contributing to the project throughout its life cycle.
2 Thus no individual, group or company attempts to integrate the work and the people from all the companies.

For example, in a building project the owner is unlikely to have all the skills and resources needed to manage the overall project. At the same time, the architect and the building contractor may be concerned only with their own spheres or activities. Thus there is a requirement in such multi-company projects for an overall or supreme project manager.

The foregoing discussion has revealed the need for three different levels of project management, which we might call stage 1, stage 2 and stage 3. This is a simplification, and many variations can be expected in practice, but it is convenient to summarize these three stages here as follows:

- Stage 1 project managers: managers of single projects carried out by single companies.
- Stage 2 project managers: managers responsible for integrating multiple projects carried out within individual companies. These might be called 'project directors' or 'programme directors' and have several project managers reporting to them.
- Stage 3 project managers: managers who integrate the work of project managers and other managers spread over a project organization containing several or even many different companies.

Each project manager is responsible for the success of the sub-project, project or group of projects under his or her control. In the widest context at stage 3 level, the project manager must provide the management and leadership necessary to bind the people and groups from different departments and many companies working on the project into one managerial organization and team. Every project manager, at any level, must produce the drive necessary to ensure project or sub-project completion on time and within budget.

Project planning and control

In routine operations (such as in a factory) people carry out the same functions week in and week out. Such repetitive work generates an effective learning curve. Budgetary control consists of straightforward periodic measurements of variables that might change only slightly from one month to the next. Operational management can be viewed, at least in the short term, as taking place in a relatively unchanging situation. Although day-to-day fluctuations and occasional emergencies can be expected, the underlying concept is that of a static organization carrying out work that is largely routine and repetitive. Planning and control are, of course, important in the management of operations, but these relate to a relatively stable labour force using fixed production facilities.

None of this applies to project management. A project is, by definition, a unique non-repetitive undertaking. Everything has to be started from scratch. The scope of the project has to be defined, responsibilities must be allocated, and work scheduled, resourced and budgeted uniquely. There is a limited learning curve, as a project manager might repeat various project stages only once every few months or even years. Moreover, mistakes, errors, omissions, wrong or late decisions cannot be fully compensated for in the lifetime of a single project. People's functions and roles are in a constant state of flux and are never the same, week in and week out. Interpersonal relationships have to be established anew for each project and will vary throughout the life of the project. Project information systems have to be uniquely designed and established for each project. Budgetary control must cope with variables that change considerably from month to month. Thus a project is in a constant state of change, and project management never deals with a static situation.

A project can be a large, complex, ever-changing entity, and it is difficult for a mere human being to envisage all parts of it and to know what is happening everywhere and at all times. Projects are usually difficult to coordinate and subject to many changes. Effective planning and control are critical to their success or failure. Many projects have suffered delays and overexpenditure because of inadequate planning and control. Yet planning and control are difficult functions, owing to such factors as the large numbers of activities, groups and companies involved.

Although attention is often centred on the use of critical path network techniques, more emphasis has to be placed on the wider context of the methodologies and systems in which these are applied. The planning techniques form only one of the subsystems of total project management. Effective planning and project control involves many information systems and includes the functions of work definition, estimating, materials management, design control, quality assurance and many others.

All these systems must be taken into account or involved in planning, and particularly in controlling, a project. It is critical that these systems are integrated into a single system, so that a change in one part of the whole system is communicated to all other relevant parts of the system. This integration must extend to include the schedule, resource and expenditure budgets, organization and the human system. Integration is essential for project control.

Those who plan and control today's projects are increasingly looking beyond the data provided by the initial schedules to predict what lies ahead for the project. There are at least three different approaches to these forecasting aspects:

1 a formalized approach to risk identification and management
2 probability analysis, similar to PERT but relying on the computers to conduct modelling using Monte Carlo analyses
3 earned value analysis to monitor and periodically predict the probable outcome of the project in terms of time and costs.

People in projects

The project manager has to operate in a complex organization that includes people from different professions, different departments, different companies and other organizations. Even in the best circumstances, managing a project can be a difficult task. The project manager has to plan, organize, coordinate, communicate, lead and motivate all the participants to achieve a successful project outcome.

A project manager's task is made more difficult because he or she acts as a junior general manager, usually with ill-defined authority. Lines of authority or influence are grafted on to the existing pyramid structure, cutting across the normal lines of command and department boundaries. Project managers do not carry out all their work in the useful superior–subordinate relationships but must manage all project participants, including their peers, juniors and superiors in other departments and companies. Many participants will find themselves working for two managers, namely the project manager and their own parent department or company manager.

In the typical project organization, all these people must work together, but many will have no direct line responsibility to the project manager. The project manager is not responsible for their performance assessments, coaching and development, promotions, pay increases, welfare and other line relationships. Project personnel have different loyalties and objectives, have probably never worked together before, and might never work together again. The one thing that binds them all together is the project organization structure. The project manager must, therefore, deal with the human problems of developing a project team out of the diverse groups working on the project. This involves complex relationships with managers in many departments and companies, not all of whom will be directly employed on the project.

The temporary nature of project organizations allows insufficient time for interpersonal relationships to reach the static state possible in routine operations management. Good group performance is necessary from the beginning of a project, because it is difficult or even impossible to recover from mistakes made and time lost at the start. Also, the total management group on a project changes frequently, with new members joining and the roles of others diminishing as the project proceeds through its life cycle. In spite of all these disruptions and difficulties, project managers must work under pressure to deliver their time, cost and performance targets, which can require the application of pressure or other motivational measures on the people and groups involved.

Thus the project manager has a particularly difficult task and must exercise special skills in handling all the human problems that can arise. Some management principles, such as 'authority must equal responsibility' and 'a subordinate must have only one superior' must be disregarded. There is a particular need for the project manager to be skilled in the following areas:

- leadership, directed to achieving the project objectives
- achieving power in difficult and changing circumstances
- motivating individuals and groups
- developing teams and teamwork
- managing conflict – many projects fail through conflict.

Project culture

Organizational culture distinguishes project management in several ways from other branches of management. Project managers have to be concerned with the activities of all who contribute to their project. They cannot think parochially of only their own department or company's contribution. They must instead think globally about all the departments and companies working on the project, and accept responsibility for all their work. This is a significant culture change for many people.

Everybody involved in the project must learn to think in terms of the project's global organization. The client, consultants, design organization, purchasing department, manufacturing or construction department, subcontractors, suppliers and so on must all be seen as belonging to one project organization. The project manager must learn to manage across organizational boundaries and to think of, and integrate, the people involved from all the companies and departments as part of a single project organization.

The project manager and everyone else involved should have a total commitment and loyalty to the project. The project can become almost a living entity that unites people in achieving its successful completion. People should develop loyalties to the project and its team as well as, or even instead of, their parent organizations. This therefore means adopting an attitude of mind that subordinates their own and their parent organization's interests to the demands and targets of the project.

Project people must become goal-oriented rather than operations-oriented. The project goals must be broken down into individual and group goals. Such a results orientation, with a highly developed consciousness of time and costs, often requires a significant change in culture and outlook for those who have been accustomed only to day-to-day operations.

The project manager and people involved must accept change as a way of life. Nothing ever remains static in project work, and the personnel live in a world filled with uncertainty and complexity where nothing exists in a permanent state. People must therefore be flexible in everything that they undertake.

Project management is concerned largely with the management of change; there is no such thing as the status quo. This is quite disruptive to some people. Not only is the project manager concerned with implementing change, but also the project is itself a dynamic, ever-changing entity. The project personnel must adapt to living in a world where nothing remains the same from one day to the next, neither the work nor the human inter-relationships involved in carrying out the work.

The project manager has often to manage without clear-cut superior–subordinate authority over all those involved. His or her authority is often uncertain, usually inadequate to match the responsibility and partly based on contractual arrangements. The project manager must learn to gain power through any means available, rather than through the usual positional authority.

Accountability and responsibility for parts of the project are delegated to all the managers involved. Thus everyone, not simply the project manager, must accept this accountability and responsibility for project results. This requires acceptance and adoption by all managers of 'the buck stops here; there can be no excuses, only success or failure' attitude.

All those involved in a project must also accept a commitment to planning and control as a key component of management. Planning must be viewed both as a tool that allows decision-making, task-sequencing, establishment of priorities, resource allocation and as providing a sound basis for control and work measurement. Managers and supervisors must also be committed to controlling progress, which means keeping work in step with the plan and taking action to resolve difficulties or correct deviations from it.

When a project involves many people, groups and companies, these organizational entities interact and are interdependent. Project performance depends on cooperation and teamwork, which involves the following:

- mutual support
- open communication
- trust
- respect.

When crossing organizational boundaries with inadequate authority, the project manager must manage by participation, not confrontation, with the other managers involved. The prime example of this is when the client and the principal contractor each have their own internal project manager for the same project. They are bound together by contractual lines of power and a joint commitment to the project, and must work together in a participative manner for full effectiveness.

Not only must the project manager have a commitment to teamwork and participation, he or she must also exert leadership and drive. Teamwork and participation can lead to a contented project group, but not necessarily to the highest possible performance. Project managers must be strong leaders, and drive themselves (and others when necessary) to achieve the results that count. Teamwork, participation, drive and leadership are not incompatible, and the best results are obtained when they are combined.

Finally, the project manager needs a strong imagination to take a project from its initial concept or authorization to arrive at a successful completion, which might not be reached until considerable resources and billions of pound have been spent. All this demands a culture very different from the regular management of routine operations. It is not surprising that many people find the adjustment to project management difficult.

Integrated and structured project management

The three critical functions or systems of project management (organization, planning and control, and human systems) are not separate parts of management. They interact and are interdependent. They must therefore be treated as an integrated whole, not in isolation one from another. Here are some examples of the ways in which these systems can interact with each other:

- The project organization is one determinant of the project management information systems (PMIS), including planning and control.
- In turn, effectiveness of the PMIS will strongly influence the effectiveness of the project organization structure.
- The form of organization structure used can strongly influence human behaviour, including individual and group motivation, team development and the extent of conflict. The size of groups, effectiveness of integration, patterns of authority, 'tallness' of the organization hierarchy, and the tendency for organic or bureaucratic working (all discussed in Part 2) are factors that influence the management of people.
- The planning and control system can influence teamwork and the motivation of individuals and groups. Achievement motivation, goal theory and feedback on performance are intimately connected with the planning and control system, which can be one of the project manager's most powerful manual tools.
- A suitably designed planning and control system can facilitate the use of different organization structures (the federal organization, for instance).
- The needs of the human behaviour system or man-management can influence the design and effectiveness of both the organization used and the project information system.

To manage a project successfully, it is necessary to integrate not only the PMISs, but also to take a 'total' integrated approach to the management of projects. Thus the organization structure, the PMISs, including the planning and control system, and the human system must be viewed and combined as one integrated system. This is the essence of the advanced approach to project management implied by structured project management. When all these subsystems are structured as one totally integrated system, each contributes to the other and synergy results: that is, the sum of the individual systems when integrated is greater than their individual worth.

CHAPTER

2 *Project Definition and Appraisal*

Project definition is a continuous process. It begins when a project is nothing more than a gleam in the eye of a project's progenitor. When the original concept has been refined, definition can be more precise and lead to proposals for the project. If the project is eventually authorized, definition will continue throughout the project's active life cycle, taking account of design and changes so that finally, when the project is handed over to its owner, the project can be defined by drawings and other documents that record the 'as-built' project condition. Accurate project definition in the early stages is often very difficult because of the number of unknown factors to be investigated.

This chapter will concentrate on the early aspects of project definition, taking the process to the stage where a financial case can be made to help the investor decide on a course of action. We have based our discussion on the definition and appraisal process for large, expensive projects where the prospects and justification for investment are not always clear-cut. A project feasibility study of this kind begins with fact-gathering, usually involves a degree of forecasting or speculation, can uncover alternative strategies, and requires risk assessment and financial appraisal. The more important stages are shown in Figure 2.1, which will serve as a route map for the remainder of this chapter.

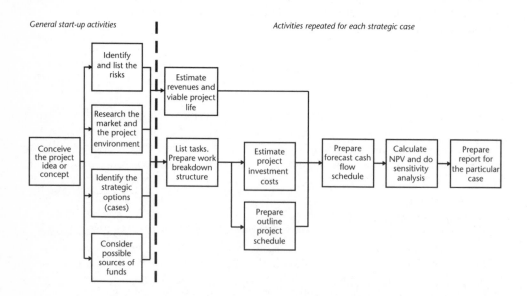

Figure 2.1 Some activities in feasibility studies and project appraisal

Early stages

FACT-GATHERING

The title of this section is not entirely appropriate because facts are hard to come by during the conceptual stages of a project and much of the information collected must be based on forecasts and speculation. It is also a sobering thought that some well-publicized projects would never have been started if their initial appraisals had been based on more accurate forecasts.

Identifying and listing the risks

No project can be entirely free of risk and uncertainty. Forecasting the possible risks, the probability of their occurrence and the severity of their impact should always be an important part of a project feasibility study. There will, of course, be occasions when the perceived risks are so great that the wisest decision would be not to proceed with the new project. Risk management is dealt with at greater length in Chapter 13.

Market research and forecasts

Most project parameters identified in checklists or brainstorming sessions should be quantifiable by investigation, site visits and technical surveying. However, the ultimate business outcome of many projects must depend on the economic and market conditions that will apply several years after initial definition and appraisal. The developer of a copper mining complex requires the best possible forecasts of what world markets in copper will be doing, not just in the present, but for many years ahead. An entrepreneur building a leisure complex needs to know how many visitors can be expected and how much they will be prepared to spend.

There have been many well-reported instances of projects that failed because their original market forecasts were wildly optimistic. Thus a project feasibility study must contain some form of analysis that tests the sensibility of revenues and profits to inaccuracies in market forecasts.

Defining the project environment

Many companies are faced with projects that must be delivered to (or built in) parts of the world where they have no previous experience. Whilst these companies might be completely familiar with all the regulations, engineering standards, political issues, climate and other factors affecting projects built in their own countries, new challenges abroad bring special difficulties and uncertainties. Companies that habitually pursue projects overseas will develop checklists of information that must be gathered before a business case can be made. Here are just a few of the many areas that might have to be examined before a project can be defined:

- Physical conditions at the project site:
    - availability of services such as clean water, power
    - access to the site for people
    - access to the site for plant and heavy goods deliveries
    - communications facilities
    - climatic and seismic conditions
    - ground and soil characteristics

- local availability of hire plant
- local availability of supplies
- for mining, minerals and oil projects, estimated size and quality of the reserves.

- Conditions for project workers:
  - accommodation for imported labour
  - availability of local workers
  - local employment regulations
  - local pay rates
  - trades unions and industrial relations
  - local amenities and other facilities
  - local endemic diseases.

- Political environment:
  - stability of government
  - relationship with neighbouring states
  - any special regulations
  - fiscal policy
  - availability of financial grants or incentives
  - security, crime rates, terrorist or bandit threats.

- Commercial issues:
  - capabilities of local subcontractors
  - creditworthiness of local companies
  - expected terms of payment
  - insurances required
  - trade tariffs, special import/export regulations.

And so on.

Sources of funds

Even the most promising project, where all the signs point to great success, will fail to get off the ground or will collapse if sufficient funds cannot be raised. Both project customers and contractors need to be concerned with the availability of funds – the customer (owner) for paying the contractor's bills and the contractor for funding work in progress. However, at this project appraisal stage the contractor has yet to be appointed and funding is a question solely for the project owner.

There are many possible sources of funds, including (for instance) cash reserves, a bank loan, sale of assets, mortgaging and lease back of real estate, issue of new stocks or shares and more. Whatever the preferred source, however, the investor will need to know not only how much money must be provided but also when it will be needed. This requires the calculation of a net cash flow forecast. No cash flow forecast can be made without two principal inputs, which are:

1 a cost estimate, to establish the amounts of money needed
2 an outline project schedule, to forecast when the money will be needed.

Cash flow scheduling is discussed in more detail later in this chapter.

STRATEGIC OPTIONS (CASES)

Once an idea for a project has been conceived there are often several different possible strategic approaches. As an example, consider an established international company that has discovered and laid claim to rich deposits of copper ore in an undeveloped part of the world. The company might consider several strategic options for mining and processing the ore, which might include the following:

1 Mine the ore and ship it 1000 miles to an existing but underutilized processing plant already owned by the company.
2 Mine the ore and carry out local crushing and concentrating, and then ship the concentrate to an existing smelter and refinery plant 1000 miles away.
3 Mine the ore and build a plant locally to produce crude copper bars, then ship the copper bars 1000 miles to an existing refinery.
4 Build all the processing plant to produce refined copper at the mine.
5 Build not only the basic processing plant at the mine, but also include plant and machinery to produce semi-finished or finished product (such as copper wire or rods).

A large international company, with mines and processing plants in many different countries, would probably be able to identify and consider many different business strategies for dealing with newly discovered ore deposits. When each of these different strategies is analysed in depth it is clear that each of them will result in a different business case.

A lengthy feasibility study can result in some of the distinctions between the different strategies being confused. Thus it is important, right from the start, to give each different strategic option a unique identifying code or case number. Then, if a decision is made to proceed with the project there should be no doubt about which case has been chosen.

Assembling time and cost data for each strategic case

The area to the right of the vertical broken line in Figure 2.1 shows some of the activities to be followed in evaluating each of the possible strategic cases. In practice many technical, environmental, political, human and operational factors would have to be considered, but we have concentrated here on the commercial and financial aspects leading to a financial appraisal

TASK LIST AND WORK BREAKDOWN

An important step in project definition is to decide and document exactly what will have to be done before the project can be declared finished. This means defining the scope of the project, noting that it is almost as important to list what is not included in the scope as what is included.

The tasks must be arranged into a hierarchical family tree, with the project at the head and the smallest known tasks at the lowest level. This is the work breakdown structure (WBS). A carefully designed and coded WBS is usually the supporting framework for all significant project management functions, such as cost estimating, budgeting, cost collection, cost control, planning, document numbering, reports and so on. The role and design of the WBS is covered more fully in Chapter 8.

ESTIMATES FOR CASH INFLOWS

Each strategic case must be supported by an estimate of the cash inflows that the project can be expected to earn. These might be forecasts either of actual revenues or of notional revenues and cost savings. Examples include:

- sales of commodities, such as chemicals, fuels or minerals from a new processing plant
- sales of produce resulting from investment in a farming project
- sales of a new consumer product, developed by the project
- savings in process costs or other operational costs made possible as a result of the project
- savings in organizational administration costs made possible by a management change project
- any government grants, special incentive payments or allowances available to offset the investment.

Monies expected to be raised from banks, investors and other creditors can be shown as cash inflows provided, of course, that the eventual repayments of principals and interest appear later as cash outflows.

Whatever the project case it is usually necessary to declare some limit on the expected operational life of the project, and then estimate the cash flows for each year of that life.

ESTIMATING CASH OUTFLOWS

Cash outflows must be considered for the whole life of the project, and will include at least the following:

- project development costs (all the costs leading to project handover and operation)
- operation and maintenance costs for the expected operational life of the project
- taxes, other duties and expenses
- repayments to banks and other creditors.

Project development cost estimates must be made for all aspects of the project design, construction and commissioning, for which the tasks in the WBS should provide the principal checklist. Many tasks in the lower levels of the WBS cannot be defined in any detail (or even known) at this early stage, so the project development cost estimates will necessarily have to be made on a ballpark basis. This is top-down estimating, rather than the more detailed bottom-up estimating that cannot take place until some of the actual design has been accomplished.

OUTLINE PROJECT SCHEDULE

Tasks, or at least the major work packages from the WBS, must be set out on a summary timescale. This provisional schedule will forecast the period of project development investment and the time when the project can be expected to start generating cash inflows.

A detailed critical path network is not usually possible at this stage, and a carefully considered bar chart (Gantt chart) will probably be the best that can be achieved. The plan should, however, be as realistic as possible because key dates in the programme will greatly influence the outcomes of subsequent net cash flow forecasting and financial appraisal. The summary schedule should therefore predict all foreseeable project milestones.

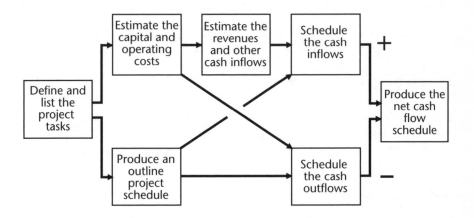

Figure 2.2   Steps towards creating a project net cash flow schedule

Project name: This case number:																	All figures are £000s
Item	2006				2007				2008				2009				Item totals
	1	2	3	4	1	2	3	4	1	2	3	4	1	2	3	4	
Outflows Engineering Construction Commissioning Operating cost Loan repayments Taxation																	
Total outflows																	
Inflows Loans Grants Sales revenues																	
Total inflows																	
Net period flows																	
Cumulative balance																	

Figure 2.3   General format for a project net cash flow schedule

REVIEWING THE ESTIMATES

All prudent managers will question every cost and time estimate for any errors and omissions, even though these estimates might have been made on broad assumptions and forecasts rather than on a more precise basis. Any company with sufficient experience should be able to refer to data from past projects and make comparisons, at least to ensure that the new project data fall within the right ballpark.

COMPILING THE NET CASH FLOW FORECAST

When the cash outflows, cash inflows and key timings have all been estimated, a net cash flow schedule can be prepared. The steps leading to a net cash flow schedule are summarized in Figure 2.2 and a suggested general format is shown in Figure 2.3.

Net cash flow schedules serve at least two valuable purposes:

1 They provide the project's financial managers with the amounts and timings of any provisions that must be made to raise funds.
2 They are the principal input for calculations leading to financial project appraisal.

Financial appraisal

An example will demonstrate two methods commonly used for financial project appraisal. All names and figures used are fictitious and no reference or resemblance to any existing company is intended. We have ignored taxation and loan finance for simplicity.

Cuprosity Inc. is a company engaged in winning minerals and non-ferrous metals from natural sources. It has discovered large deposits of rich copper-bearing ore near the town of Copperville that can be recovered by open cast mining. Company policy is to always aim for an annual return on investment of at least 8 per cent.

It is estimated that the price of copper will continue at $1600 per metric tonne and that, whatever strategy is followed, 20 000 metric tonnes of copper bars can be produced and sold per annum, giving a projected annual sales revenue of £32 million.

The company has an existing processing plant with spare capacity at another mine which is 400 miles distant at Groundwealth. The old plant is relatively inefficient, with high operating and maintenance costs. Groundwealth is only ten miles inland from the seaport of Shippit, which Cuprosity Inc. uses as its main export outlet. A good railroad connects Groundwealth and Copperville, and it would be easy to construct the short rail link needed to serve the new mine.

Several different strategic cases have been identified for exploiting the newly discovered orebody, but we shall consider just two of these, which we have labelled as Case 1 and Case 2.

1 In Case 1, the company would develop the mine and its associated administration offices and then transport all the ore, as untreated lumps of rock, in rail ore wagons to Groundwealth for processing before onward transit to the port of Shippit.
2 In Case 2, the company would develop the mine and also build a modern, cost-efficient processing plant at the mine site, allowing copper bars to be produced and sent by rail direct to Shippit for export.

DATA FOR CASE 1

Case 1 initial project development

The following tasks and costs have been identified for the development project of Case 1:

- Develop the open cast site (which includes constructing roads, offices, other administrative and service buildings and a short railroad link) taking one year to complete at a cost of $10 million.
- Purchase heavy plant and other equipment for mining operations at a cost of $5 million.
- Purchase ore wagons for transporting the mined ore to Groundwealth at a cost of $10 million.

Thus, for Case 1, the total development costs are expected to be $25 million, all to be incurred in the first year.

Case 1 operations

The annual production operations costs for Case 1 are expected to be as follows:

- mining operations, $10 million
- ore transport by rail from Copperville to Groundwealth, $7 million
- processing costs at Groundwealth, $12 million
- copper bar transport by rail from Groundwealth to Shippit, $1 million.

Thus, for Case 1, production will start after one year of development and construction (on 1 January) at an annual cost of $30 million.

DATA FOR CASE 2

Case 2 initial project development

The following tasks and costs have been identified for the development project of Case 2:

- Develop the open cast site (which includes constructing roads, offices, other adminis-trative and service buildings and a short railroad link), together with processing plant for producing copper bars, taking two years to complete at a total cost of $100 million.
- Purchase heavy plant and other equipment for mining operations at a cost of $5 million.
- Purchase flat rail wagons for transporting copper bars to Shippit at a cost of $2 million.

Thus, for Case 2, the development costs are expected to be $107 million, spread over two years.

Case 2 operations

The annual production operations costs for Case 2 are expected to be as follows:

- mining operations, $10 million
- processing operations, $8 million
- copper bar transport by rail direct from Copperville to Shippit, $2 million.

Thus, for Case 2, copper bar production and shipping will cost $20 million each year, beginning on 1 January two years after the start of the development and construction project.

COMPARISON OF CASES 1 AND 2 USING SIMPLE PAYBACK CALCULATIONS

The summarized data from Cases 1 and 2 are set out in net cash flow tabulations in Figure 2.4. The cumulative cash flow totals in the right-hand columns show that the projected revenues should repay the initial cost of investment by year 14 for Case 1 and by year 11 for Case 2. Thus the strategy of Case 2 should allow the project to become profitable about three years earlier than the Case 1 option would allow.

Project name: Copperville mine development				All figures are $000s
Case 1				
Year	Cash outflows	Cash inflows	Net cash inflows (outflows)	Cumulative cash flow
1	25 000	—	(25 000)	(25 000)
2	—	2 000	2 000	(23 000)
3	—	2 000	2 000	(21 000)
4	—	2 000	2 000	(19 000)
5	—	2 000	2 000	(17 000)
6	—	2 000	2 000	(15 000)
7	—	2 000	2 000	(13 000)
8	—	2 000	2 000	(11 000)
9	—	2 000	2 000	(9 000)
10	—	2 000	2 000	(7 000)
11	—	2 000	2 000	(5 000)
12	—	2 000	2 000	(3 000)
13	—	2 000	2 000	(1 000)
14	—	2 000	2 000	1 000

Project name: Copperville mine development				All figures are $000s
Case 2				
Year	Cash outflows	Cash inflows	Net cash inflows (outflows)	Cumulative cash flow
1	53 500	—	(53 500)	(53 500)
2	53 500	—	(53 500)	(107 000)
3	—	12 000	12 000	(95 000)
4	—	12 000	12 000	(83 000)
5	—	12 000	12 000	(71 000)
6	—	12 000	12 000	(59 000)
7	—	12 000	12 000	(47 000)
8	—	12 000	12 000	(35 000)
9	—	12 000	12 000	(23 000)
10	—	12 000	12 000	(11 000)
11	—	12 000	12 000	1 000

Figure 2.4   Simple cash flow schedules for the mining project, Cases 1 and 2

DISCOUNTING THE CASH FLOWS

The payback calculations just illustrated for the mining project in Figure 2.4 are valid as far as they go, but they do not take into account the effect of time on monetary values or the requirement of the Cuprosity company to earn at the minimum rate of 8 per cent per annum on the original investment. It is clear that no project requiring heavy investment will earn that kind of return in its first year.

In a project requiring substantial investment, any projected net cash amount forecast to be earned (or spent) in the future must be gauged against what that same amount of money would be worth in today's values if it could have been invested instead in a bank for an interest rate of 8 per cent. In other words, would the company have been better advised to place its money in a non-risk deposit account rather than proceed with the project at all?

Suppose that Cuprosity could invest $100 million dollars with a bank and receive 8 per cent interest, so that the initial amount would be worth $108 million dollars in one year's time. We can say that $100 million is the *net present value* (NPV) of the future $108 million.

Because it is the declared intention of Cuprosity to earn at least 8 per cent on all its investments, we have to view the cash flow examples of Figure 2.4 in a different light. Every amount spent or earned in the future must be discounted to bring it to its NPV.

Remember that the ore reserves for this project are expected to run out after 20 years of mining, so that the cumulative NPVs of this project, discounted at 8 per cent per annum, must reach the amount of the initial investment before those 20 operational years have

Project name: Mine development at Copperville				All figures are $000s
Year	Cash outflows	Cash inflows	Net cash inflows (outflows)	Discount factor (8%)	Net present value
0	25 000	—	(25 000)	1.000	(25 000)
1	—	2 000	2 000	0.926	1 852
2	—	2 000	2 000	0.857	1 714
3	—	2 000	2 000	0.794	1 588
4	—	2 000	2 000	0.735	1 470
5	—	2 000	2 000	0.681	1 362
6	—	2 000	2 000	0.630	1 260
7	—	2 000	2 000	0.583	1 166
8	—	2 000	2 000	0.540	1 080
9	—	2 000	2 000	0.500	1 000
10	—	2 000	2 000	0.463	926
11	—	2 000	2 000	0.429	858
12	—	2 000	2 000	0.397	794
13	—	2 000	2 000	0.368	736
14	—	2 000	2 000	0.340	680
15	—	2 000	2 000	0.315	630
16	—	2 000	2 000	0.292	584
17	—	2 000	2 000	0.270	540
18	—	2 000	2 000	0.250	500
19	—	2 000	2 000	0.232	464
20	—	2 000	2 000	0.214	428
			Project net present value for this case		(5 368)

Figure 2.5 Net present value calculation for the mining project, Case 1

| Project name: Mine development at Copperville | | | | All figures are $000s |
| Case 2 | | | | |
Year	Cash outflows	Cash inflows	Net cash inflows (outflows)	Discount factor (8%)	Net present value
0	53 500	—	(53 500)	1.000	(53 500)
1	53 500	—	(53 500)	0.926	(49 541)
2	—	12 000	12 000	0.857	10 284
3	—	12 000	12 000	0.794	9 528
4	—	12 000	12 000	0.735	8 820
5	—	12 000	12 000	0.681	8 175
6	—	12 000	12 000	0.630	7 560
7	—	12 000	12 000	0.583	6 996
8	—	12 000	12 000	0.540	6 480
9	—	12 000	12 000	0.500	6 000
10	—	12 000	12 000	0.463	5 556
11	—	12 000	12 000	0.429	5 148
12	—	12 000	12 000	0.397	4 764
13	—	12 000	12 000	0.368	4 416
14	—	12 000	12 000	0.340	4 080
15	—	12 000	12 000	0.315	3 780
16	—	12 000	12 000	0.292	3 500
17	—	12 000	12 000	0.270	3 240
18	—	12 000	12 000	0.250	3 000
19	—	12 000	12 000	0.232	2 784
20	—	12 000	12 000	0.214	2 568
21	—	12 000	12 000	0.199	2 388
			Project net present value for this case		6 026

Figure 2.6   Net present value calculation for the mining project, Case 2

passed. So the cash flows must be viewed over the expected life of this project, they must be discounted, and the cumulative NPV must be positive if the company is to earn its 8 per cent return.

The discounted cash flows for Case 1 are set out in Figure 2.5. The 8 per cent discounting factor for year 1 is 0.926, found by dividing 1 by 1.08. Discount factors for subsequent years are calculated by repeated division by 1.08, which is easily performed with a pocket calculator. Computer programs are available that can perform the complete NPV calculations, or the discount factors can be looked up in published tables. If the calculations are (as here) to be performed manually, then it is important to set out all the cash flows in a consistent and formal manner to avoid confusion and mistakes.

The NPV of Case 1 is minus $5.368 million. This negative result means that the project strategy of Case 1 will not produce the required rate of return of 8 per cent. If the calculation is reiterated with a range of discount factors, starting with 7.9, 7.8, 7.7 per cent and so on, a discounting rate should be found that produces a NPV of zero, and that is the rate of return that can be expected.

The discounted cash flow calculation for Case 2 is shown in Figure 2.6. Here the positive NPV is a clear indication in favour of this case.

Sensitivity analysis

Because most project feasibility studies are carried out with a considerable proportion of estimated data, any result from project financial appraisal must be viewed with some circumspection. Whenever there is any lack of confidence in one or more of the parameters used, sensitivity analysis can be used to gain some understanding of how critical any estimating errors might prove if the project is allowed to go ahead.

Sensitivity analysis means repeating the initial financial appraisal calculations using stepped variations in the values of one or more parameters. This will determine how sensitive the original result is to any forecasting error in the parameters tested.

Conclusion

In the mining project example illustrated above, the positive NPV result for Case 2 gave a clear indication that, subject to sensitivity analysis and an appraisal of possible risks, Cuprosity would be right in going ahead with the project. Financial appraisal can, therefore, be an important factor in deciding whether or not to go ahead with a single project proposal or in choosing between two or more different project strategies. Financial appraisal is, however, not always the deciding factor.

Although financial appraisal is usually central to a project feasibility study, some projects are authorized to proceed when there is no hope of any direct return on the money invested. Obvious examples are projects that are reactions to various crises, such as wars or natural disasters. Many other projects are conducted with no thought for financial gain, even within industrial companies that normally expect to make profits on all their activities. Consider, for instance, a company compelled to spend £500 000 on building improvements ordered by the local authority for reasons of health and safety or fire regulations. Although that project must be carried out for no direct financial return, failure to authorize the work could result in successful legal action to close the company down.

So, a project feasibility study is a mix of careful investigation and definition, consideration of different strategic options, risk appraisal and, usually, an appraisal of the financial outcome.

3 Associated Disciplines

This chapter considers a few related activities that, although not usually considered as part of mainstream project management, can none the less have a considerable impact on project success or failure.

Procurement and the supply chain

Purchased materials, equipment and bought-out services account for over half the cost of many projects. Further, project work can be seriously delayed if the necessary materials are not in the right place at the right time. So it is relevant to describe some elements of purchasing and the supply chain here.

THE PURCHASING CYCLE

The acquisition of a piece of equipment or batch of materials can be considered as a cyclic process, beginning with the contractor's realization that the goods will be needed and ending with delivery of the goods to a place chosen by the contractor. The complexity of the cycle will depend on the nature of the goods being purchased and their value. Simple items of stationery might be purchased against petty case vouchers, for example. So, it is convenient here to describe the purchase of a high-cost good, recognizing that, for lower-cost items, some of the stages described can be omitted. Figure 3.1 depicts the cycle.

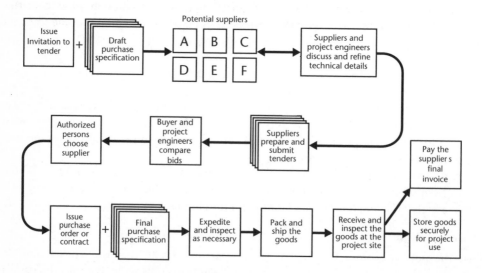

Figure 3.1   Outline activities for a high-cost project purchase

Draft specification

The first step in the cycle is to specify the requirement, which usually means that the project engineer or deputy must prepare a draft purchase specification. At this stage, the document will probably be called an enquiry specification. To save time and effort in this process it is usually possible to store blank standard specifications in a computer system for commonly ordered items such as pumps and motors: the engineer then has only to enter the particular technical characteristics needed for the current project.

Enquiries and tenders

Next it is necessary to identify possible suppliers. Conflict sometimes rages on this issue between the purchasing department and the engineers, the engineers having their preferred choice whilst the purchasing department has its own favourites. The ideal, as in many aspects of project management, is cooperation and partnership, with engineers and buyers contributing to the list and agreeing jointly which suppliers should be approached.

For European public sector projects, one of the European directives on public sector purchasing will apply for goods or services that exceed certain contract values. There is a limited range of exemptions (for example to protect secrecy and national security). These price limits are changed from time to time and so are not given here. The UK Inland Revenue has a very informative website giving full and up-to-date details at http://www.inlandrevenue.gov.uk/manuals/pummanual/specificguidance/pum4070.htm.   One important feature of these directives is that relevant opportunities for suppliers and contractors must be advertised in advance in *The European Journal*, so that bidding is not restricted to one or a few suppliers favoured by the contractor.

During the preparation of proposals by potential suppliers, especially for large items of equipment such as machinery, cranes and locomotives, the contractor's project engineers and the suppliers' engineers might have technical discussions that could result in specification amendments, usually with the intention of achieving mutual benefit for the supplier and customer.

When the tenders have been received they must be compared on a like-for-like basis that removes the effects of different proposal structures and different currencies. This process (often called a bid summary or bid analysis procedure) must be based on the total cost and time estimated to get the goods to the project site. Tenders submitted after the purchaser's given deadline are usually disqualified.

A process known as the two packaged sealed bid procedure is sometimes used for high-value bids. Each tender document comprises two sealed packages, one containing the technical details, whilst the other sets out the proposed price and commercial terms. The technical packages are opened first, and the project engineer can rule out proposals that fail to satisfy the project's physical requirements. Suppliers thus excluded are informed and their commercial packs are returned unopened.

The project engineer and the purchasing department jointly approve and recommend the choice of supplier. The final choice, depending on the value of the contract, might be made at a high level, and it is not uncommon for the client to be consulted.

The order stage

When the purchase order is issued it is necessary to ensure that the original enquiry specification is revised to take account of any changes made during pre-contract discussions with suppliers. Thenceforth the specification becomes known as the purchase specification.

The purchase order and specification will set out not only the technical and commercial requirements, but will also give details of packaging standards, pack marking and delivery arrangements.

A binding contract will exist once an order has been issued and accepted by the supplier. Once the order has been committed it will be too late to rectify any spending over budget. Cost control can only be exercised before this stage: afterwards it will be too late. It is also necessary to avoid subsequent amendments as far as possible, because every change provides an opportunity for the supplier to increase the original price in a one-to-one relationship where competition for supply no longer exists.

Final stages

If goods have to be manufactured specially against the purchase order, the contractor should monitor progress, which might mean arranging inspection and expediting visits to the supplier's premises. It is common for inspection and expediting reports to be prepared for the project manager after each such visit.

After the goods have been received and checked for freedom from damage, deficiencies and non-conformances, payment of the supplier's final invoice can be released.

PURCHASING ORGANIZATION AND ROLES

There are probably as many variations in purchasing organizations as there are projects, but Figure 3.2 shows a fairly complex organization used by an international engineering company with worldwide projects. In this example the purchasing department is directly responsible to the project manager, but in many cases the purchasing department has a

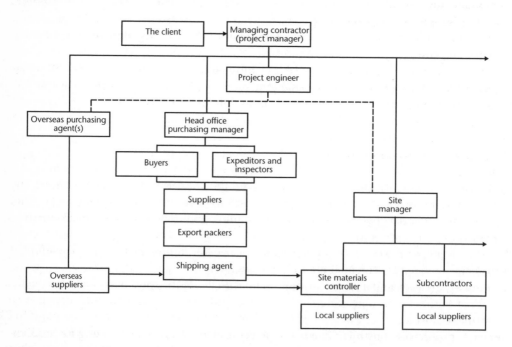

Figure 3.2   A purchasing organization for a large project

different reporting line and acts only as a service department to the project manager. This organization is best described by considering each of the roles.

The project engineer is responsible to the project manager for all the purchase specifications, technical decisions and instructions.

The head office purchasing manager heads a department in which buyers prepare invitations to tender and purchase orders. In this international example, where some high-value purchases are to be made overseas, the head office department concentrates on orders to be placed with inland suppliers, although the purchasing manager will be involved in collating and analysing tenders received from all sources.

The purchasing department will also contain people for following up suppliers during manufacture of the goods. These people, known as expeditors, sometimes also combine the role of inspectors and visit suppliers' premises to view progress and check quality at first hand.

When the goods are to be sent to a project site overseas, some suppliers will use specialist export packing companies to protect the goods in transit.

A freight forwarding or shipping agent fulfils an important function in the supply chain by arranging all aspects of transportation (by air, sea, road or rail) from the suppliers' premises to the project site. Another function of freight forwarders is load consolidation: they are able to organize bulk container loads to achieve economical shipping charges. Freight forwarding agents have worldwide agency links that monitor all stages of the journey and help to get the goods smoothly through international borders and port and customs authorities.

Where purchases are to be made from foreign suppliers, local purchasing agents can be engaged whose relative proximity to the suppliers enables them to deal with enquiries, purchase order issues, expediting and inspections. The local knowledge of overseas purchasing agents is often invaluable.

The final links in the supply chain are found at the project site. Here the site materials controller is the key person, being responsible for the receipt, inspection, safe storage and issue of materials and equipment. Project site organizations usually carry out some purchasing themselves (such as bulk building materials) that can be obtained cheaply and quickly from local suppliers.

Concurrent engineering

We have stressed in various chapters throughout this book the need for cooperation and partnership. Known also as simultaneous engineering, concurrent engineering is, perhaps, the supreme example of partnership towards attaining mutual benefits. The process involves people from different departments or different companies working together to achieve a design solution that is both economic and practicable for the contractor to build and for the project owner or end user to maintain and operate.

The simplest example of concurrent engineering is seen when different departments working within the same company cooperate to develop a combined design and construction strategy that will result in the lowest possible overall costs for the company and the most practicable construction or manufacturing methods. This might mean, for instance, accepting greater design effort and higher design costs to produce a result that has minimum overall cost and production difficulty.

In its widest and most useful context, concurrent engineering will also involve the customer. Every stage of design will be discussed and agreed with the customer, who will be prepared also to modify project requirements to achieve the most satisfactory mutual result. An example is a manufacturer of special purchase heavy machine tools, built specifically for the customer to use in high-volume machining of a particular component. If the component is, for instance, an automobile engine cylinder block, the machine will carry out all milling, drilling, boring, reaming, tapping and probing operations to convert the raw casting into an accurately machined component. Concurrent engineering in this case would mean that the machine tool designers work with the customer's engineers to arrive at a solution in which the machine design and component design are developed together, to achieve best machining reliability and accuracy for minimum component cost.

Concurrent engineering can pose particular problems of planning and control for the project manager, since both the contractor's and customer's engineers must work together on design tasks that run in parallel with each other and whose time and costs can be relatively difficult to estimate. Also, there is no superior–subordinate relationship with the customer's engineers.

Cost and management accounting

Most engineers and other project staff have little knowledge and even less interest in accounting practice. Many might take the work of accountants for granted but, quite apart from the essential contribution they make to corporate financial management, accountants also play a vital support role for project managers. Their most obvious function in this respect is measuring, analysing and reporting project costs but they also support project management in several other ways. For example, they can compile and store records that help in future comparative cost estimating. Earned value analysis (see Chapter 16) would not be possible without a reliable accounts department.

In return for the services that project managers expect from accountants, they should ensure that essential cost information is passed to the accounts department promptly and regularly for inclusion in the relevant ledgers and reports. A common aspect of this is the collection of labour times on staff timesheets. All managers have a duty to ensure that their departmental staff timesheets are compiled, checked and passed to the accounts department with maximum accuracy and minimum delay. Project timesheet data are now often collected using direct entry into project management software, but the project manager remains responsible for accuracy and the prevention of false time bookings.

Some sensible practices for maintaining time sheet accuracy include the following:

- ensuring that everyone is aware of the job cost codes for the work they are doing
- managing the authorization and closure of projects to prevent people booking time to projects that are unauthorized or finished
- encouraging staff to enter idle or waiting time and other non-productive time without fear of reprisal – statistics compiled from such time bookings provide valuable management information, so if inefficiencies are hidden by false accounting there can be no hope of preventive action

- checking timesheets regularly to prevent misbookings – especially important where timesheet data are the basis for billing clients in cost-reimbursable contract payment arrangements.

Project managers should also be familiar with their company's standard code of accounts and should, wherever possible, structure the project cost coding system to agree with the standard code or at least to be compatible with it.

Every person with any responsibility for project cost estimating or cost control should also have at least an elementary knowledge of accounting terms. A few of these are given below, but a more comprehensive and authoritative source will be found in CIMA (1996).

DEFINITIONS OF SOME COMMON TERMS USED IN COST AND MANAGEMENT ACCOUNTING

Below-the-line-costs: a collective name for the various allowances that are added once a total basic cost estimate has been made. These include allowances for cost escalation, exchange rate fluctuation and other contingencies.

Cost escalation: the increase in any element of project costs caused by wage and salary awards and inflationary pressures on prices paid for materials and purchased components. Cost escalation is usually expressed as an annual rate per cent.

Direct costs: costs which can be attributed and booked directly to a job or project task.

Fixed costs: costs are said to be fixed when they are not dependent on the rate of working. They continue to be incurred even when no work is taking place at all. These costs typically include management and administrative salaries, rent, business rates, heating, insurance, buildings maintenance and so on. Fixed costs usually form the biggest component of a company's indirect or overhead costs.

Indirect costs (overhead costs or overheads): many facilities and services (such as accommodation, management, personnel and welfare services, training, general administration, heating, lighting and general maintenance) give rise to costs that must generally be incurred in running a business. The overhead salaries, expenses and materials costs of an entire organization cannot be allocated directly to one job or project and they are therefore termed indirect costs (often called overhead costs, or simply 'overheads'). The provision of facilities at the site of a construction project that would be classed as indirect back at the home office can be classed as direct costs because they are easily identified solely with the project and can be charged directly to it.

Labour burden: an amount, usually expressed as a percentage of wages or salaries, added to the basic hourly or weekly rate for employees to allow for non-working time and various additional expenses. The constituents of a typical labour burden might be the cost of paid holidays, illness or other absence, and per capita amounts payable by the employer as employee benefits, either voluntarily or as a requirement of the national legislation. In the UK, for example, these would include employers' National Insurance contributions.

Materials burden: materials purchased specifically for a project (direct materials) are typically marked up by contractors to recover their administrative and handling costs. These mark-ups generally range from 15 per cent (or less) for very large costly items shipped directly to site to 25 per cent or even more on small low-cost items that have high handling and administration costs relative to their value.

Overhead costs: see **Indirect costs.**

Overhead recovery: most costing systems work on the basis of charging direct labour costs as time recorded on the job multiplied by the standard hourly cost applicable to the grade. An amount can then be added to this labour cost (usually as a rate per cent) to recover the company's indirect, overhead costs. If the planned direct workload should fail to materialize for any reason, the amount of direct labour costs that can be allocated to jobs and charged out in invoices will be less than that forecast. Then the proportion of revenue received to pay for the overheads will also fall below plan. This condition is called overhead underrecovery. Conversely, overhead overrecovery will occur if workload and direct labour billings exceed expectations.

Clients for large capital projects who insist on delving into the cost structures of their projects can be very critical of high overhead rates chargeable to their projects. They might ask for explanations of what the overhead costs are intended to include.

Standard costing: a system in which cost estimates and budgets are composed using average costs for materials and various grades of labour derived from experience. In project costing, these standards are used both in cost estimating and in subsequent cost collection from timesheets and material requisitions. At regular intervals the accountants compare actual cost rates with the standard rates in use. Any significant differences (variances) indicate that the standard cost rates in use have become outdated and must be corrected.

Standard labour costs: these are used in standard costing. When estimating, budgeting, accounting and cost reporting for any job or project, it would be tedious and impracticable to attempt to use all the different rates of pay earned by individuals. Two engineers with similar capabilities and identical job titles might, for example, be earning quite different salaries. The cost estimator cannot possibly name the individuals who will be engaged on jobs that might not be started for months, or even years, after the estimates are made. There is also the need to keep confidential the actual salaries earned by individual members of staff. Allocating standard salary costs for the various management and workforce grades solves these problems.

Standard materials costs: these can be devised for commonly stocked materials and purchased components, but apply more commonly to routine manufacturing operations than to projects where all materials are specially purchased. The standards are calculated as averages based on unit costs in suppliers' invoices.

Variable costs: costs incurred at a rate depending on the level of work activity. They are typically confined to the direct costs, but may have a small indirect content.

Variance: a variance is any deviation measured between a planned or budgeted quantity and the quantity actually used on the project. Variances usually apply to cost differences, although they can also describe differences between scheduled and achieved times. Variances highlight errors and satisfy the principle of management by exception.

Quality management and engineering standards

Perceptions of quality management have undergone great change in the recent past. Quality management was once regarded as something applying only to manufacturing processes, with reliance on inspection and testing to discover non-conformances before components or assemblies could be released for use. Engineering standards were used as guidelines for various design disciplines and work practices, but these were not necessarily integrated into any quality culture. Standards engineering, reliability engineering and quality management were separate functions in many companies.

Now quality is seen as a subject to be taken seriously by all who work in the provision of services, products and projects in every branch of commerce and industry. Led by gurus such as Crosby (1979), Deming (1986) and Juran (1988), the whole attitude to quality changed. Their message was heeded first in Japan but has now been embraced internationally. The ISO 9000 series of quality standards sets out a structured approach to achieving a quality culture in an industrial or service organization, which must start with a quality statement from top management and continue down through the organization as a series of document quality systems and procedures. Quality is now seen as something that should be uppermost in the minds of all who work on projects, not simply a practice that can be left to inspectors and test engineers. Certification to the ISO 1900 series of quality standards is usually desirable and may be obligatory in some contract conditions.

The range of engineering and general quality standards is extensive. Many cover practices and procedures particularly relevant to project managers. BS 6079-1: 2002, *Project Management – Guide to Project Management* and BS 6079-2: 2000, *Project Management Vocabulary* are obvious examples.

To take another important example, ISO 14001 – *Environment* sets out the responsibilities for project managers and workers in protecting the environment. Publicity from the BSI for this standard states:

The primary aim of an Environmental Management System is to protect our increasingly fragile environment, but it does much more besides. Organizations that take environmental issues seriously are less likely to incur significant liabilities or expose themselves to damaging publicity. Compliance with ISO 14001 helps you to identify problems before they happen and demonstrate to all stakeholders that you are an environmentally responsible organization.

The leading body in the development, issue and use of all these standards is the BSI. For a full catalogue of standards, membership details, and related publications and services, contact the BSI headquarters at the following address:

BSI
389 Chiswick High Road   Telephone; +44 (0)20 8996 9000
London   Email: Info@bsi-global.com
W4 4AL   Website: www.bsi-global.com

Project management associations

THE INTERNATIONAL PROJECT MANAGEMENT ASSOCIATION (IPMA)

The profession of project management is represented in many countries by member associations of the International Association of Project Management. The corporate member of the IPMA in the UK is the Association for Project Management (APM), and further information is available from their secretariat at:

The Association for Project Management
Thornton House
150 West Wycombe Road
High Wycombe
Buckinghamshire
HP12 3AE
Telephone +44 (0)1494 440090
Email: secretariat@apm-uk.demon.co.uk
Website: www.apm.org.uk

The Association arranges seminars and meetings through a network of local branches and publishes the monthly journal *Project*. Membership of the association is a good way for project managers and all others involved in project management to meet and to maintain current awareness of modern techniques, practices and computer systems.

Membership starts at student level and rises through various grades to full member (MAPM) and fellow (FAPM). The Association's basic qualification, which depends on suitable experience and written examinations, is the APMP. This is a professional qualification that recognizes an individual's baseline knowledge and experience in project management. It is regarded by the Association as the benchmark qualification in the project management profession and is the first step towards certification.

The Association has a well-established certification procedure for project managers, who must already be full members. As evidence of competence, certification has obvious advantages for the project manager, and will increasingly be demanded as mandatory by some project purchasers. Certification provides employers with a useful measure when recruiting or assessing staff, and the company that can claim to employ certificated project managers will benefit from an enhanced professional image. Certification has also relevance for project clients. It helps them assess a project manager's competence by providing clear proof that the individual concerned has gained peer recognition of his or her ability to manage projects.

THE PROJECT MANAGEMENT INSTITUTE (PMI)

Founded in the US in 1969, the PMI is the world's leading not-for-profit organization of choice for individuals around the globe who work, or are interested, in project management. The PMI develops recognized standards, not least of which is the widely respected project management body of knowledge guide, commonly known by its abbreviated title, the *PMBOK Guide*.

The PMI publications include the monthly professional magazine *PM Network*, the monthly newsletter *PMI Today* and the quarterly *Project Management Journal*.

In addition to its many research and education activities, the PMI has (since 1984) been dedicated to developing and maintaining a rigorous, examination-based professional certification programme to advance the project management profession and recognize the achievements of individual professionals. The PMI claims that its Project Management Professional (PMP) certification is the world's most recognized professional credential for project management practitioners and others in the profession.

The Institute has chapters in many countries worldwide that provide local activities and events for the Institute's 100 000 members. For more information, contact the PMI at:

PMI Headquarters
Four Campus Boulevard
Newtown Square
PA 19073-3299
USA
Telephone: +610-356-4600
Email: pmihq@pmi.org
Website: www.pmi.org

References and Further Reading for Part 1

Backhouse, C.J. and Brookes, N.J. (eds), (1996), *Concurrent Engineering*, Aldershot: Gower (in association with The Design Council).

Capper, R. (1998), *A Project-by-Project Approach to Quality*, Aldershot: Gower.

Cavatino, J.L. and Kaufman, R.G. (eds) (2000), *The Purchasing Handbook: A Guide for the Purchasing and Supply Professional*, 6th edn, New York: McGraw-Hill.

Chartered Institute of Management Accountants (CIMA) (1996), *Management Accounting Official Terminology*, 3rd edn, London: CIMA.

Cox, A. (1998), *Strategic Procurement in Construction*, London: Thomas Telford.

Crosby, P.B. (1979), *Quality is Free: The Art of Making Quality Certain*, New York: McGraw-Hill.

Deming, W.E. (1986), *Out of the Crisis*, Cambridge, MA: MIT Press.

Drury, Colin (2000), *Management and Cost Accounting*, 5th edn, London: Thomson Learning.

Erridge, A., Fee, R. and McIlroy, J. (2001), *Best Practice Procurement*, Aldershot: Gower (in association with IPSERA).

Farmer, D. and van Weele, A.J. (eds) (1995), *Gower Handbook of Purchasing Management*, 2nd edn, Aldershot: Gower.

Hartman, F.T. (2000), *Don't Park Your Brain Outside*, Newtown Square, PA: Project Management Institute.

Juran, J.M. (1988), *Juran on Planning for Quality*, New York: Free Press.

Leenders, M.R. (2001), *Purchasing and Supply Management*, Maidenhead: McGraw-Hill.

Lock, D. (2003), *Project Management*, 8th edn, Aldershot: Gower.

Oakland, J. (1993), *Total Quality Management*, 2nd edn, Oxford: Butterworth-Heinemann.

Stevens, M. (ed.) (2002), *Project Management Pathways*, High Wycombe: The Association for Project Management. A comprehensive book structured on the APM Body of Knowledge.

2 *Project Organization*

4 Introduction to Project Organization

Project success or failure depends not only on the performance of the individual people involved but also on the following important factors:

- how well people communicate with each other
- how well people work within groups or teams
- how well all the groups, larger units and companies involved in the overall project organization work together to achieve the set objectives.

Significant differences in the performance of the same people and companies can be produced by adopting different forms of organization. The chosen organization structure, as well as influencing how well the work is carried out as a system, will have a strong effect on the motivation of people and groups, and on the extent of teamworking, conflict and politics.

The elements of organization design structure

In a small project employing only a handful of people, the very simple organization structure means that the project manager can manage all the people directly, usually as one mixed group. However, most projects require more than a handful of people and there are practical limits to the number of people that any manager should be asked to supervise directly. This is usually known as the manager's 'span of control'. Graicunas (1933) set out to prove that no manager could control adequately more than six direct subordinate managers and he recommended a maximum span of five. This is sometimes called the 'rule of five'. Today, the actual number will depend on circumstances and debate. In most cases it will be fewer than ten, but there are exceptions.

Management in the project setting, as in any other, involves many functions including the following:

- organization
- planning
- directing
- controlling
- decision-making
- integration
- coordination
- leadership

- motivation
- teambuilding
- conflict management
- welfare
- administration
- communication.

In a large project employing many people, no manager can single-handedly carry out all these functions for everyone involved. As soon as the number of people involved increases beyond a reasonable span of control for the manager, the people must be divided into functional groups, each with its own manager. Authority and responsibility for management functions must then be delegated from the senior or project manager to the managers of these groups.

As project size increases, involving more people, so will the number of groups increase. Again, there are limitations on the number of groups that one manager can manage directly. The same delegation process must be repeated, possibly several times. Thus, for many larger projects, people are formed into groups and then these groups are consolidated into bigger units. The basis of this grouping can be in one of two ways:

1 People, or groups of the same function, profession or specialism may be grouped together (for example in functional departments).
2 People and groups of different functions, professions and specialisms who work together on one task or other division of the project, and who interact and are interdependent, are grouped together. These groupings tend to be semi-independent, self-contained mixed 'organizational units'.

Thus the people from the companies engaged on a project are formed into groups, functional departments and organizational units. One of the first steps in project organization design is to break down all the required work into divisions and subdivisions of a size suitable for allocation to these individuals, groups, departments, organizational units and companies. Thereafter, because the work of the various groups requires considerable interaction, the groups are interdependent and the work and those carrying it out have to be integrated. In other words, the structure of the authority, coordination and communication relationships between all the groups, departments, organizational units and companies must be established and defined.

In projects of significant size these larger groupings are consolidated into the overall project organization with a managerial hierarchy or 'organizational superstructure'. The number of managerial levels in this hierarchy depends not only on the number of people involved, but also on the mode of operation or managerial philosophy.

A large number of management levels (a 'tall' superstructure) is generally associated with centralized decision-making and close control or supervision of the people involved. A small number of levels (a 'flat' superstructure) is generally associated with decentralized decision-making, with more delegation of accountability and less supervision from the centre. A wider span of control is possible in a flat organization compared with a tall structure.

The complexity of this project organization structure, with its groups, functional departments, organizational units and an organizational superstructure, is compounded by the fact that some of the people and groups may also belong to organizations that are external to the actual project organization (the 'parent' functional departments and/or companies). This can mean that individuals in a project group may also belong to different external organizations. Similarly, groups in a project organizational unit, and even whole organizational units, could also belong to different external organizations. Thus not only must the internal project organization be designed, but also the form of the relationships with these external organizations must be determined.

Thus the design of the project organization structure involves decisions on the following factors:

1 how the work involved in the project is broken down into divisions and subdivisions that are of such a size that they can be allocated to the individuals, groups, functional departments, organizational units and companies involved in the project;
2 how the people involved, principally managers, professionals and technical staff (who may be from several external organizations) are grouped together at the lower, middle and higher levels – that is:
   • how individuals are grouped together to form the 'basic' working groups
   • how these groups are consolidated into larger groups, such as functional departments and organizational units;
   • how these groups, departments and organizational units are linked together into an overall project organization with a managerial hierarchy or superstructure;
3 what relationships exist between these components of the structure and the external organizations to which some of them might belong (in other words, identifying the 'global' project organization);
4 what the basis of this grouping is at the various levels of the organization – for example, does a typical group contain people of the same function or do the groups each contain people of different functions (mixed groups)?
5 how the work of the people is integrated, which includes coordination, communication, reporting and information systems, teambuilding and conflict management;
6 how authority, decision-making and responsibility are delegated, which includes decisions about the degree of centralization or decentralization and whether the organizational superstructure is tall or flat.

The basic building blocks of the organization structure

The first action required when thinking about a new organization design is to sketch an organization chart (sometimes called an organigram). The conventional elements of an organigram are shown in Figure 4.1. A chart depicting a traditional functionally arranged organization, with a hierarchical pyramid structure, is shown in Figure 4.2. Organizations with this structure pattern have been common in industry for hundreds of years, and can be traced back for far longer in the churches and in military formations.

Organigrams are sometimes considered to be an inadequate method for representing an organization but they do define the main elements (building blocks) of the organization's design. They show:

• how people (managers, professionals and other staff) are grouped to form the basic 'foundation block' groups of the organization structure;

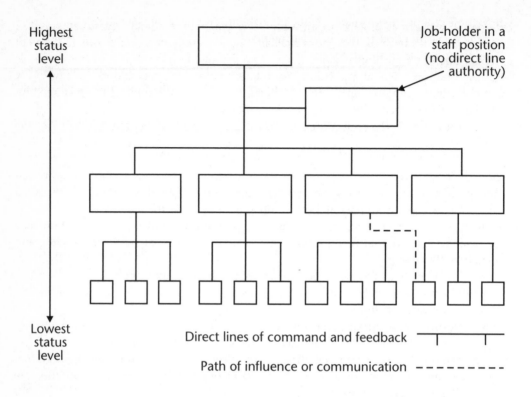

Figure 4.1   Organigram conventions

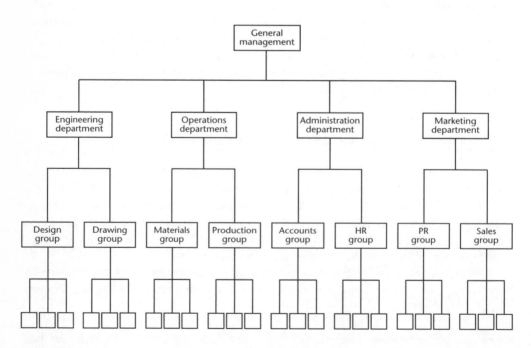

Figure 4.2   A functionally organized, hierarchical pyramid organization

- how these groups are consolidated into larger organizational groups such as:
  - large single function groups or 'departments'
  - mixed function organizational units;
- how these groups, large functional departments and organizational units are consolidated into the total company or project organization – that is, defining the organizational hierarchy or superstructure;
- the division of labour into specialist functions (such as finance, production, marketing and so on);
- how the work of these groups, functional departments and organizational units is integrated;
- the level of authority of people shown on the chart and the superior–subordinate relationships;
- the managers' spans of control.

Before describing the specialized forms of project organization structures it is worthwhile examining these basic building blocks of any organization, and the importance of functional specialization and integration.

BASIC MANAGERIAL GROUPS

Groups exist at all levels in the management hierarchy but the foundation blocks of the hierarchical organization chart are the basic managerial, professional and staff groups. The subordinate members of these groups may be foremen, but are more generally the first-level managers, or specialists such as accountants, engineers and software analysts. The managers of these basic management groups are individuals who have progressed to the first rung of the hierarchical tree.

GROUP STRUCTURE

In this three-tiered organization structure of basic groups, functional departments/organizational units and organizational superstructure, the organization structure of the basic groups can include four forms, which are:

1 functional
2 mixed
3 matrix
4 horizontal (informal).

The first three of these forms can be recognized in organigrams, but it is not usually possible to chart all the informal horizontal relationships, although dotted lines can be used for a few most significant relationships.

Functional groups
Functional groups contain individuals of a common functional, technical or professional specialism. Examples are production, marketing and finance. Other examples (on a different scale) include design, construction, planning, software engineering, electrical work and so

on. This specialization by function leads to an efficient division of labour and utilization of resources. Figure 4.2 is an example of this form of organization structure.

Mixed groups

Mixed groups, as their name implies, are made up of individuals from different functional, technical or professional backgrounds. This form of group is used for the smaller organizational unit, which might consist of only one mixed group. Examples of mixed groups include task forces, product groups and regional or geographical groups. Each group tends to contain all the resources and skills needed to complete its assigned tasks. Mixed groups facilitate teamworking in the organizational unit and lead to less conflict and undesirable politics. However, they do not use resources as efficiently as functional groups.

Matrix groups

The matrix group is an organization form that attempts to combine the efficient use of people (associated with functional groups) with the higher potential for teamworking and goal achievement (associated with mixed groups). It is a secondary form of organization in which people from different functional groups are integrated into a mixed group under its own separate matrix manager. Figure 4.3 shows the addition of a matrix group to the conventional pyramid structure. In our context, the matrix manager is the project manager, whose role is to integrate the individuals noted as 'A' in the organigram to work together on the project for which the matrix manager is responsible. The functional or parent groups remain intact. The matrix group members thus belong to two groups and each reports to two superiors; that is, there is dual subordination.

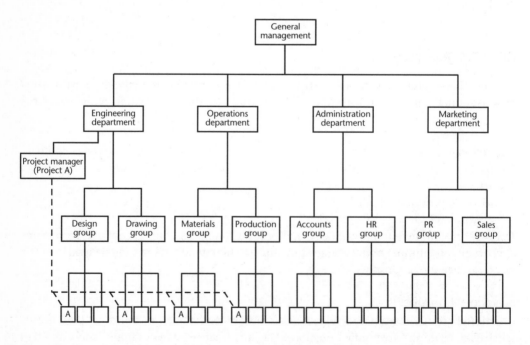

Figure 4.3   A matrix organization, in this case for a single project

Horizontal groups

It is generally necessary for individuals in functional groups to work with people from other groups. No organigram can show all these necessary cross relationships that are usual between peers and near-peers in the different functional groups.

These relationships create a secondary or horizontal group, which exists as a 'ghost organization group' or collateral organization. This group is ill-defined, and is without clear superior or superior–subordinate relationships. In many ways it is similar to a weak form of matrix group, but with no integrating superior and no group identity. For example, if the individuals noted as 'A' in the functional groups in the pyramid organization of Figure 4.3 have to work together on a project, they form a horizontal group with only the general manager as the common integrating superior. Any integration that can be achieved is through mutual adjustment of the planning systems. There is no single manager who is totally responsible for the project. Thus this kind of organization does not handle projects effectively.

LARGER GROUPS

Whenever there is more than a handful of groups in an organization it becomes necessary to consolidate them into larger groups, each with its own manager. These larger groups can take two forms:

1 functional departments
2 organizational units.

Functional departments

Functional departments consist of two or more basic groups of the same or similar expertise. They are grouped together (for reasons that will be outlined later) under one manager who will normally have the same technical background. Most companies have one or more such functional departments, such as design, marketing, finance, purchasing, construction or production, and so on. A functional department does not, by itself, form a complete organizational entity, but must react and be interdependent with other functional departments to carry out the organization's mission.

Organizational units

The term 'organizational unit' has a very different meaning from the total company organization. It is defined as the total collection of individuals and/or groups that have the following characteristics:

1 They interact and are interdependent.
2 They work towards common goals.
3 They have relationships (formal and/or informal) determined by a certain structure.

However, the senior manager of any such organizational unit will normally belong to a senior management group; that is, the organization superstructure or corporate group.

An organizational unit can thus carry out its assigned tasks without support from outside functional departments or groups. It contains all the expertise and resources needed to achieve its objectives. In military terms it is a self-contained combat group. In management terms it is similar to a division of the company, a subsidiary company, a factory or a dedicated project group.

A small project might need only one such organizational unit, which is the project itself. A large project might be made up of several, or even many, organizational units, some or all of which may cross company boundaries. The significant factor is that, except for the senior manager of the unit, individuals and groups within an organizational unit interact principally with other individuals and groups within that organizational unit. They are largely or wholly independent of individuals and groups outside the organizational unit. It is thus almost a self-contained entity, independent as far as conflict, power, politics and teamwork are concerned.

Size and structure of the organizational unit

Organizational units can be of any size. They might be:

- small, composed of individuals who form just one basic group
- medium, with two or more basic groups contained within the organizational unit
- large, containing two or more big groups, each of which might have two or more basic groups. A large organizational unit can range upwards in size to one that contains small, medium and large groups from a number of different companies.

The structure of the small organizational unit is that of the single group making up the unit, which might be functional, mixed or matrix.

The structure of medium and large organizational units can be as follows:

1 Single function: all the groups in the unit comprise people of the same or similar function. This is typically found in professional organizations such as accountants, architects or quantity surveyors.
2 Functionally organized: each contained group is a single-function group.
3 Matrix-based: single-function groups drawn from their parent large groups or departments are organized into one unit under a matrix group manager (as shown in Figure 4.3).
4 Mixed: each group in the organization unit is a mixed, all-function group. In such cases, interactions and interdependencies tend to be of a pooled or sequential nature.

ORGANIZATIONAL SUPERSTRUCTURE

Because medium to large project organizations contain a number of organizational units, there will, in most organizations, be an organizational superstructure or management hierarchy. In very large organizations there may be multiple layers of such groups. This superstructure is deemed necessary to manage, control, coordinate or integrate the various organizational units. The subordinate managers of this superstructure are thus generally the senior managers responsible for the organizational units.

There will typically be a management hierarchy within each functional department and each organizational unit. In a large project, with a number of organizational units, a senior management hierarchy or superstructure will exist to manage, control, coordinate and integrate the units. Thus a large project organization will have a number of management hierarchy levels. In some projects the number of such levels has even reached double figures.

Functionalization

Functionalization, or the specialization of managerial and professional labour, is the placing of people of the same function or expertise into groups. This could be termed the conventional or classical organization design. Despite its widespread use, the amount of functionalization used can be a strong indicator of the possibility of conflict in an organization. Nevertheless, functionalization is widespread and has many advantages, among which are the following:

1 It promotes the efficient use of resources.
2 It allows functional expertise to develop.
3 It allows specialists to be managed by specialists.
4 It allows coordination of the functional policies and systems.
5 It provides a home base and a clear career path for each functional specialist.
6 It tends to have a stable existence, with power to survive.

In a mixed group or divisional organizational unit, the workload for each function within the group can vary to the extent that the mixed group may sometimes be understaffed for some functions at times, yet overstaffed at other times. A single-function group, on the other hand, is more flexible. It allows people within the group to be switched between different tasks and the unit size can be varied to suit the changing workload. Functional grouping therefore promotes a more efficient use of resources. This is particularly apparent in projects, where the workload for any particular function can change greatly during the life of a project. A functional organization can resource a stream or portfolio of projects more efficiently than can a divisional or mixed group organization.

Functionalization is also very beneficial to the continuing development of each specialism and the functional skills of the people involved. An isolated specialist, divorced from contact and interaction with professional colleagues, is more at risk of lagging behind developments in his or her specialism. Specialists in a same-function group should, on the other hand, enjoy productive interaction and mutual support with their professional colleagues, exchanging ideas and keeping up to date. There should be more opportunity for effective training and personal development. An additional advantage is that the concentrated grouping of people of one specialism allows a fund of knowledge to be built up within the group, both mentally and in data stores, so that the group as a whole develops competence in its specialism and becomes a greater asset to the overall organization.

The person in charge of a functional group will usually come from the same professional background as the other members of the group. This manager should, therefore, be in a position to empathize with the group members and, through his or her greater experience and expertise, be able to help them overcome difficulties or problems. He or she should be able more effectively to control work output and technical standards than a manager lacking familiarity with the group speciality. Thus the function will be managed more effectively than if it were diluted in a mixed group.

A functional group also provides a home base for each professional specialist, who can work in a relatively stable organizational environment and has a clear superior–subordinate relationship with someone of the same professional background. In addition, one of the most important characteristics of a large functional group, at least as perceived by its members, is that it gives each functional specialist a career path possibility that does not exist in a mixed group.

Most organizations will probably have a degree of functionalization in their structure. Functionalism is indeed traditional, the established norm. The heads of the functional departments can wield considerable power and they will probably resist any change that is seen likely to reduce that power. Thus functionalization is the most common form of specialization in organizations. Unfortunately, specialization by function is also a principal contributor to the accentuation of politics and conflict in an organization, both directly and indirectly. This is principally because functionalization leads to the following:

- a functional orientation
- problems relating to the different cultures formed
- problems with the integration of these functional groups.

FUNCTIONAL ORIENTATION

Grouping people into functional groups leads them to be oriented to the goals of their functions rather than to the goals of the project. These people tend to think in terms of their own specializations rather than taking a more holistic view. For example, people working in design, production, construction, accounts and so on are oriented more to these functions than to the combined working of their organizational unit or to the complete project. Thus they tend to be introverted. Their loyalty is given to their function rather than to the project. All this inhibits teamwork between different functional groups and the project manager, and encourages conflict.

PROBLEMS RELATING TO THE DIFFERENT CULTURES FORMED

Each individual group (irrespective of its size), company and organization unit is as distinctive and unique as the people in it. Each has its own personality, character, core values, norms, attitudes and sometimes language that influence how people conduct them-selves, work together and even think. This uniqueness is termed 'culture'. Culture evolves over time and is not easily changed. It reflects the deeply held beliefs – even subconscious feelings – of the people in the group.

Functionalization draws into one group people of the same skills, background and outlook. Such groups therefore tend to have their own highly developed and specialized cultures. Culture is particular to the actual function involved so that groups of one specialism or profession from different companies will have a culture more in common with each other than with groups of different specialisms or professions in their own companies.

Differences in culture between groups can lead to conflict in many different ways. Different cultures tend to lead to incompatible objectives in functional or professional groups. For example, a group of competent designers will instinctively strive for a design of the highest reliability and technical standards – one that will be a monument to their expertise and, perhaps, to their egos. The operations group will want a production plant that is easy to operate, has many available spares, capacity for expansion and a high standard of amenities. The purchasing group might have a bias towards obtaining goods from its preferred suppliers, regardless of the wishes of people in the design and production groups. The project group will want to balance time, cost and technical standards. When these groups work together there will always be a risk of conflict over incompatible objectives.

Even given goodwill between groups with different cultures, they might draw different conclusions, make different decisions and take different courses of action – all based on the same information – simply because of their different cultures. Culture differences go far deeper than factors such as core values. They lead to people thinking, feeling and behaving differently. All too often these differences lead to dysfunctional conflict without any obvious intent or self-interests being involved.

Thus functionalization tends to promote strong, specialized professional cultures, and differences between these cultures can lead to conflict between professional groups.

Integration

Hand-in-hand with the division of labour implicit in the functional form must go the integration of that labour. This includes coordination, communication, reporting relationships and information systems. When individuals and groups are interdependent and must interact to achieve the organization's objectives, an important factor in the organization's performance is how well they are integrated.

Lawrence and Lorsch (1967) found that, with increasing size and complexity of organizations, there is an increasing need for both greater differentiation and tighter integration. The greater the size of a project and of the specialization within it, the more critical is the need for this integration, the more difficult it will be to achieve, and the more likely it is to be ineffective.

Integration involves more than just the coordination of work to achieve the organization's goals. It must also have a large emphasis on managing individual people and groups. Therefore integration has two roles in design organization:

1 an operational management role, to integrate the work of individuals and groups so that this contributes to the organization's effort
2 a human- and group-management role in:
   • managing and resolving conflict
   • reducing the amount of political activity
   • developing a team, or at the very least establishing a cooperative working relationship between individuals, groups and companies working on the project.

The need for integration varies with the degree of interdependency. Thompson (1967) identified three types of interdependency:

1 pooled interdependency, essentially 'A + B' – for example, two excavators working together to dig one hole
2 sequential interdependency, essentially 'A → B' – for example, an excavator digging a trench ahead of a machine laying a pipeline
3 reciprocal interdependency, essentially 'A ↔ B'.

Integration difficulties are fewer with pooled resources and sequential interdependencies. Unfortunately, project work usually involves reciprocal integration, so that integration tends to be a problem. In projects there is thus a critical need to integrate individuals, groups of various kinds, functional departments, organizational units and companies. The following outline describes the methods of integration open to the traditional functionally organized firm, and then looks at the development of project organization structures to achieve integration, namely:

- key integrating superiors
- management systems
- mutual adjustment
- coordination committees
- liaison positions
- task forces, working groups, special teams or project groups
- matrix organization.

KEY INTEGRATING SUPERIORS

The primary integrator in any group, department, organizational unit, project or company should be the senior manager in charge of it. This manager is the common superior to everyone involved, and it is his or her managerial function to see that their work is integrated, that coordination and communication exist, to build teamwork and to manage any conflict that might arise between the subordinates. The senior manager's actions and leadership, together with the 'tightness' of the organization structure and authority, are critical to achieving these results.

However, for projects in a functionally organized company with a departmental structure, the common key integrating superior is often ineffective because he or she is normally a senior manager with many diverse responsibilities and is too remote from the scene of the project action. The further away (in hierarchical terms) the common superior is, the more ineffective he or she will be in carrying out the integration function. If conflict should erupt between individuals or groups on the project, the integrating superior will not be fully aware of it until too late. He or she might have to deal with it through one or more levels of intermediate subordinate managers, who may or may not be directly involved or might not be averse to conflict occurring. This is where the mixed group structure is better, where the superior is nearer the scene of the action and can deal with the problem quickly and directly.

Thus projects carried out using the functional organization cannot rely on the usual key integrating superior to integrate the work and the people. Other integration methods must be found.

MANAGEMENT SYSTEMS

One method of integrating project work is through the use of its management systems, particularly the planning and control systems. The organization of both the work and the people assigned to a project is carried out in the planning phase, where the integration of the work of the various groups, departments, organizational units and the complete project should be explicitly detailed. Planning techniques or methodologies such as work breakdown structures (WBS) and organization breakdown structures (OBS) ensure the integration of organization, work and plan. Control systems emphasize communication channels and links to maintain the integration of work as it progresses. Thus the integration of organization with planning and control can be used to integrate effectively the work on a project.

However, these systems do not by themselves meet the person- and group-management needs of integration in terms of developing teamwork and managing conflict. Also, unless the organization has well-developed project-oriented systems, and these are backed up by a key integrating superior, they will tend to be less than effective in integrating the work.

MUTUAL ADJUSTMENT

The need for integration is often not formally recognized or not spelled out explicitly: individuals and groups are implicitly expected to work together to achieve results. This they often do – in spite of the organization or lack of it – particularly on smaller projects. This can work provided that conflict is absent.

This method of integration is implicitly assumed in horizontal groups in a functional organization. Horizontal groups are expected to work together by the 'system', with no defined close common integrating superior. This often works satisfactorily, and an organic group or team is formed, sometimes uniting its component members against their own vertical group superiors. This mutual adjustment involves individuals (at both lower and higher levels in the organization) achieving integration by processes of informal communications, give and take, or mutual adjustment. If this did not work in practice, all organizations would soon grind to a halt, but it cannot deal with cases of conflict.

Often, however, no group identity is established, loyalty can remain totally with the parent functional groups, and any cooperation that does exist tends to be neutral or coldly formal. There is no recognized accepted key integrating superior who can lead the group to teamwork and manage differences before they escalate into conflict. In such cases, unless an organic team forms naturally, it is worthwhile naming one person as the group leader or coordinator.

COORDINATION COMMITTEES

Often, when a functionally organized firm is handling projects, one or more special coordination committees are formed. Each consists of a group of specialists or senior managers and acts as the common integrating superior. Although a coordination committee can, to a limited extent, perform a general liaison and supervisory function for the project, it is usually totally ineffective on the human side of project management. It can do little or nothing to build teamwork or manage conflict.

These coordination committees are composed of what might be termed 'political players', each with his or her own vested interests. They can, themselves, be arenas where conflict and politics flourish. Such a senior management group is generally totally ineffective in managing conflict. The subordinates have little option but to resort to politics when working with this group of superiors. Individuals or factions in the superior group have to be influenced by political actions, and are unlikely to knock heads together or take any other action to manage conflict or minimize politics.

LIAISON POSITIONS

When there is a certain amount of interaction between groups, one individual may be assigned to a liaison position, to facilitate communication and coordination (integration). This individual is essentially a weak coordinator, with little or no formal authority. Any power that such liaison people have is based on their centrality, access to the ear of senior management and the information channels that they control.

An extension of this liaison position is where the individual concerned may have some authority over the decision-making process, but not over the people who form the different groups and departments involved in the project. He or she therefore has to influence, persuade and be a supplicant to people over whom he or she has no direct authority. He or she cannot give direct instructions. Thus, when a conflict or political problem arises, the person in the liaison role is placed in a very difficult situation.

TASK FORCES, WORKING GROUPS, SPECIAL TEAMS OR PROJECT GROUPS

Task forces provide a single, short-term mission, mixed group to perform a particular task. Special mixed teams are similar, but these deal with regularly recurring problems. The fullest extension of this concept is the formal project group, where the individuals and groups involved in a particular project are formed into a separate mixed organizational unit under a project manager. This project manager is appointed as the group's key integrating superior, with partial or full line authority over the people involved.

These arrangements are usually intended to last only for the duration of the particular task or project and so are temporary, but the project manager can, in some instances, remain in place for a period of years. Although temporary, they do involve an actual change in the organization structure, from a purely functional organization to some type of mixed organizational unit.

MATRIX ORGANIZATION

The matrix organization attempts to combine the advantages of the functional organization with those of the mixed group organization by creating a dual reporting responsibility. It can integrate both work and people but also creates many problems of its own.

The matrix does have an integrating superior and can therefore increase the potential for teamwork. However, the functional group managers may resent this invasion of their territories, so the matrix can also increase the potential for conflict between each functional manager and the project manager. Nevertheless, in the matrix organization there is a defined group entity and key integrating superior and leader, although his or her authority is limited and there are problems with dual subordination.

SUMMING UP

The most effective method of integration is that carried out by a close key integrating superior supported by effective management systems. However, this can rarely be achieved in functionally organized firms. Reliance on informal or weak methods of integration may go some limited way to integrating project work, but does little for the human side of integration. Liaison positions, task forces, project teams and the matrix organization involve restructuring the organization (to varying extents) into a project-oriented organization. Thus the need to integrate multi-disciplinary work has tended to be one of the main reasons for the adoption of project management and project organization structures.

5 *Basic Project Organization Structures*

This chapter will introduce some basic forms of project organization that can be clearly identified and labelled in small and medium-sized projects. Chapter 6 will extend the discussion into organizations that are more complex or apply generally to larger projects.

Identifying different forms of project organization

Project organization forms can be considered on two levels, which are:

1 *The external or global project organization.* This is the structure of the relationships between individuals and groups involved in the project with their parent functional departments and companies.
2 *The internal project organization.* This is the structure of the relationships between the individuals and groups involved in the project. This structure is considered independently of the external relationships of these organizational elements with their parent organizations in the external or global project organization. The internal structure is of particular importance in larger projects.

Thus the internal project organization exists within the external structure. These external and internal forms can be outlined as follows:

1 Basic external organizational forms:
   • dedicated project team (including task force)
   • matrix:
     – functional matrix
     – balanced matrix
     – project matrix
     – contract matrix
   • hybrid structures
   • modular network structures.

2 Larger project organizations and the internal structure (discussed in Chapter 6):
   • internal functionalization
   • divisionalization
   • internal matrix
   • the 'federal' organization
   • central and decentralized forms of the larger organization.

Dedicated project team organizations

The task force, working group, special team or (in project terms) the dedicated project team is much the preferred form of organization when considered only from the project manager's point of view. People, groups and other assets are allocated completely to the project organization for as long as they are needed to complete the project. The project manager has full line authority over all these resources. This is, in effect, setting up a separate goal-oriented division of the company, with its own functional departments.

The project manager still has the problem of managing and integrating other companies and external organizations contributing to the project, but has full mastery over all the people and groups working on the project within his or her company. However, this does mean that the true dedicated project team can exist only within an individual company. In multi-company projects, therefore, the dedicated team can form only one part of the overall project organization.

This goal-oriented organization makes planning, control and general project manage-ment simpler and easier than with other forms of organization. There can be much better integration of all those involved on the project and communication between them (formal and informal) is faster, more direct and more frequent. Teamwork is much easier to develop and, consequently, there is more commitment to the project objectives. Conflict is likely to be less than in other project organization forms and, if it should arise, can more easily be resolved. Project teams, therefore, tend to maximize the probability of completing projects on time, within budget and to specification.

Unfortunately, teams are not the most flexible way in which to use company resources. If more than one team exists in the same company, it becomes necessary to increase the numbers of specialists on the payroll because each specialist (or group of specialists) must be allocated wholly to each project team for much of the project's life. It is usually difficult to switch specialists from one project to another to take account of day-to-day fluctuations in workload. Functional groups allocated to a number of project teams in a company will each be smaller than pooled functional groups would be in a functionalized organization handling the same total amount of project work. Division of labour within functions is therefore more difficult, so that a dedicated project team might have to make do with a generalist in a function where a specialist would be preferred.

Therefore, although the dedicated project team (or separate divisional form of project organization) enables projects to be managed more effectively than the functional organiz-ation and, although it avoids some of the problems of more complex organization forms, it can generally be used only on larger projects capable of sustaining bigger functionalist groups within the team. The team structure is appropriate, therefore, when a company is handling a single important project, or where one project is so very much more important than the others that it justifies setting up a completely separate company division. The size of the project and the volume of work should be great enough to provide full-time activity for each of the functional specialists or groups assigned to the project organization.

Dedicated project teams cannot generally be used where a company is handling several relatively small projects simultaneously on a continuing basis, because they would splinter up the functional resources. This splintering inhibits the transfer of personnel between projects according to demand and reduces the number of projects that a company can handle for a given number of staff. Also, there are many good reasons for maintaining these specialist or functional departments intact.

All project teams are temporary organizations. Their life equates with project duration. Although teams, especially in the early and middle stages of a project, tend to motivate people towards achieving the project objectives, things change as the project end comes into view. Then the team begins to diminish in size as people are no longer needed and released. The end of project life can be unsettling for the remaining team members. The same close contact with team colleagues that engendered a team spirit now can become a breeding ground for the spread of gloom and despondency, unless the company can assure all concerned that there will be new work for them as soon as they are no longer needed on the team.

Another aspect of dedicated project teams is that they are more easily contained within a given accommodation unit. Other forms of organization can be more physically dispersed. Containment is important when the project involves work of a secret or confidential nature. The case for secrecy is clear in projects for national defence. Proprietorial confidentiality is often needed in projects for the development of new products, such as automobiles. Even management projects, perhaps when investigating possible mergers and acquisitions, or looking at potential new locations for a company, have to be conducted (at least in their initial stages) in an atmosphere of some secrecy. So dedicated project teams or task forces are indicated where project work has to be hidden from the public or even from unauthorized staff in the same company.

TASK FORCE ORGANIZATION

A task force is a special form of dedicated project team. Its name implies that it has been assembled to concentrate all its energies on performing a particular task. Military task forces are a common example. In the world of commerce and industry a task force is a hyper-dedicated project team, oblivious to non-project distractions, motivated only to achieving the project goals. Two examples where a task force must be the preferred organization structure follow.

Task force for a management project

Some management projects must be started in complete secrecy for a variety of commercial and other reasons. Consider, for example, a large insurance company that wishes to relocate from the centre of London to a provincial town or semi-rural location. Much of the early work will consist of finding possible new locations and researching their attributes for work, communications, local amenities, available labour, climate and environment, and so on. This insurance company has a functional organization, in the form of a hierarchical pyramid. Many functions in the organization will have to contribute to all the initial plans and feasibility studies, yet much of this work must be kept secret from the main body of staff if unfounded rumours are not to proliferate. Certainly the plans must be communicated to staff, and there will probably have to be counselling and negotiations later in the project. But the preliminary objectives must first be decided.

A task force organization is ideal for carrying out the initial studies and, later, for implementing the agreed move. To preserve confidentiality this task force must be given its own secure offices, or at least provision for locking away all the information generated during the initial studies. Yet, whilst the study should take place behind closed doors, most functions of the company must be consulted for their requirements, ideas and reactions if the new project schedules and accommodation plans are to be developed into a

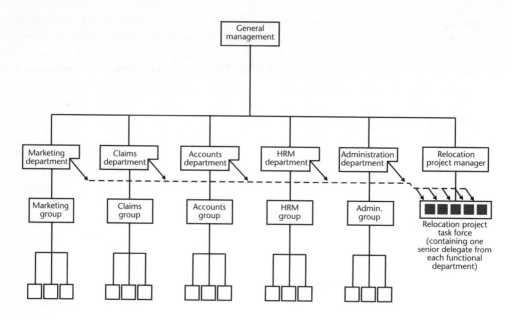

Figure 5.1   Task force for an insurance company relocation project

comprehensive, workable and practicable solution. Figure 5.1 shows how this might be organized. Under a project manager (who might be a specially engaged consultant or a member of the existing staff) senior delegates are assigned to the task force from all the significant functional departments of work. Only these delegates and their functional managers need to know the information from the initial studies. By removing these delegates from their normal workplaces and placing them in the project office there is a better chance of teamwork within secrecy. Each delegate is sufficiently senior to have enough authority for making day-to-day decisions on behalf of his or her functional manager. More difficult decisions can be referred discreetly back to the functional managers by their delegates.

Task force for rescuing an ailing project

Suppose that a project is running so late that all concerned have lost faith in the schedules. There is no effective plan, no credible system of project priorities and the customer keeps asking for assurances that the project will be delivered on time. One solution is to create a task force dedicated to rescuing the project from disaster.

The first step is to decide who shall lead the task force. If no suitable person exists within the company, there will be no time to train anyone in the necessary project management skills and it will probably be prudent to import a suitably qualified consultant. Then, a senior delegate must be chosen from each functional group in the company that has work remaining on the project. In a manufacturing project (for example) this might include representatives from the design, purchasing, production engineering, manufacturing and quality functions.

Accommodation (sometimes called a 'war room') must be set aside for the task force's exclusive use, where they can meet, plan, coordinate and control the remaining project work.

Once the remaining work has been identified, planned and prioritized, each member of the task force can issue instructions to his or her functional group to ensure that the project work gets the priority that it needs to see the project through to a successful conclusion.

Meanwhile, the expert project manager must oversee the progress of the project and report accordingly to senior management. As a secondary but important role, this manager, especially if imported as a temporary consultant, should (through both personal example and formal training sessions) make certain that when he or she departs there will be at least two people from the company's original staff who can plan and control any future project.

Another role for the consultant is to 'educate' senior management, so that they understand the value of project management and recognize that some special work needs to be treated and managed as projects, not just as a continuation of the company's routine work.

SUMMARY

A dedicated team organization has the advantage of a relatively simple structure in which superior–subordinate roles can be well defined and the lines of communication are generally direct and short. People in a team should identify more easily with the project and its objectives. It is far easier to develop a team spirit when a team actually exists. Thus a dedicated project team would seem to be the obvious choice of organization for meeting the project objectives. The alternative functional form of organization is, however, more efficient and flexible than a dedicated team in the use of resources. What is often required in project work is an organization that both uses resources efficiently and is effective in achieving the project objectives. This is what the matrix organization (described in the following pages) attempts to do, but at the expense of increased organizational complexity.

Matrix organizations

The matrix form of organization became fashionable for projects during the 1970s and 1980s. Its use has since spread to more general management because of its flexibility and ability to cope with complex organizational needs. Although at one time promoted too strongly by project management experts, matrix organization forms undoubtedly provide a valuable solution in appropriate cases, especially for companies that need to pass a continuous succession of projects through a relatively stable company organization.

In fact, the complexity implicit in the matrix organization of lines of authority (different from the simple superior–subordinate relationship and creating duality of command) exists in most organizations. Whenever there is a horizontal group, an embryonic relationship exists outside the conventional vertical lines of command. There is also an implicit matrix relationship whenever strong central functional groups (finance, for example) claim some authority over functional members of the company's divisions or operating groups.

The matrix organization is used very commonly. A matrix or project manager is appointed to manage and integrate the work and people on the project, but the functional groups are retained intact beyond the life of the project. Lines of authority and responsibility, communication and coordination exist horizontally and diagonally, as well as in the conventional vertical pyramid form. Individuals working on the project are responsible to two managers, their parent group functional manager and the project manager.

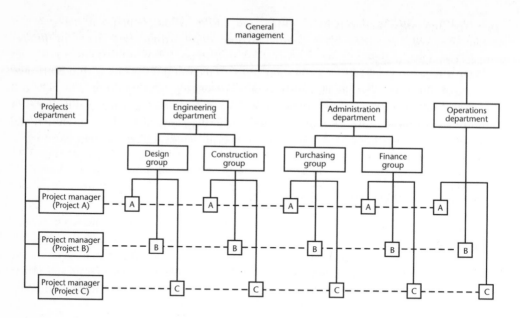

Figure 5.2   A company with a matrix organization

Because authority in most forms of matrix management is shared between the project manager and the functional managers, the project manager cannot be the complete master of decisions affecting the project but must operate in a decision-making matrix. The project manager's authority or influence cuts across the traditional vertical lines of command and leads to a matrix or network of authority relationships.

A typical organigram for a matrix project organization is shown in Figure 5.2. Each project manager in this matrix acts as a junior general manager, and the in-company project work is undertaken by the relevant functional departments (such as design, manufacture and assembly).

Some functions, such as marketing, accounts and general administration often fall outside the matrix structure because they are not engaged directly in project work and the project manager has no reason to control or influence them. One can often observe that the matrix project organization includes all those functions that add value to the project but excludes those that add cost without value.

The matrix maintains the functional departments intact, as projects come and go, and facilitates the transfer of staff between different projects. Departmental members can be allocated to one project for its life, or for just a part (or parts) of its life. Allocation can be on a full-time or part-time basis, as required. All these people remain part of their parent functional departments, under the management of their relevant functional department managers. At the same time, however, the project relationship integrates them on the project dimension, provides a means of communication and coordination, management and leadership, facilitates planning and control, and gains their commitment to meeting the project's objectives. Making each individual a member of both a functional and a goal-oriented organization attempts to obtain the advantages of both.

The project manager must rely on support and services from the functional departments, and determines, in consultation with the departmental managers, what is required and when. The functional managers then control how and by whom. Functional managers can allocate their own departmental personnel to jobs more satisfactorily than any project manager could, because they know the capabilities of their people and the resources available.

The functional managers are also responsible for technical decisions within their own areas of specialism. The project manager can bring pressure to bear regarding schedules and budgets, and may ask for a review of alternatives when there are problems or differences of opinion. Nevertheless, responsibility for technical decisions lies with the functional managers, because they know their own areas of specialism best and will be held accountable for the technical outcome.

FORMS OF THE MATRIX ORGANIZATION

Matrix organizations can be set up with different balances of power between project managers and functional department managers. At one extreme, in weak matrix organizations, the functional managers enjoy far more power than the project managers. At the other extreme, in strong matrix organizations, the project managers have far greater power than the functional managers and can enforce many decisions. The more commonly recognized matrix forms are as follows:

1 functional matrix (the weakest form)
2 balanced matrix
3 project matrix (a very strong form).

The above-listed forms often share the same kind of organigram, because organigrams are not, by themselves, usually able to show how power and authority are apportioned between project managers and managers of the functional departments.

There is also a quite different form of multi-company matrix organization, used for example in large construction projects. This form is sometimes termed a 'contract matrix'. This will be described in the following chapter (see Figure 6.6).

Functional matrix

The functional matrix is the weakest form of matrix project organization. The project manager is principally a coordinator and integrator, rather than a line manager. He or she acts as a focal point for information on the project, but with limited authority, status and seniority. The functional managers retain responsibility and authority for their specific segments of the project. The project manager can only monitor progress, practise a weak form of coordination, and depend on the goodwill of the functional managers for success. He or she is, in effect, in the position of a supplicant to the managers of the functional departments.

The project manager in a functional matrix must persuade others from a position of weakness and will often find the job difficult. When evidence of an adverse trend is slight or inconclusive, the project manager may find it difficult to generate corrective action. It is only when adverse trends are patently obvious that the project manager can implement change, and he or she must usually do this by bringing down the support of higher management through the line (by which time it is often too late).

Thus this form of the matrix organization can achieve integration of the work but loses many of the advantages of the project management concept. It is only suited to smaller projects, for handling occasional projects in a non-project oriented firm, or when functional departments are strong and unassailable.

Balanced matrix

In the balanced (or overlay) matrix, the project manager shares responsibility and authority for completing the project with the functional managers. Project managers and functional managers jointly direct many workflow segments and jointly approve many decisions. This is the classical form of the matrix organization.

Project matrix

In the project matrix the project manager has primary responsibility for managing project activities and ensuring that the project is completed successfully, meeting all the set objectives. The functional managers are expected to act in a supporting role, making personnel and technical expertise available when the project manager calls for them. The project matrix itself can exist in different strengths, the strongest of which is the *secondment matrix*. Here, nominated members from the functional departments are assigned to work on the project, sometimes even being asked to relocate temporarily to accommodation set aside for the project.

The project matrix, especially in its secondment matrix form, approximates to the dedicated project team organization. It is, therefore, the form of matrix most preferred by project managers and most disliked by the functional managers. It is generally applied only in project-oriented companies, whose principal business is projects, and which recognize that project managers are their new line managers.

In these stronger forms of the matrix organization the organigrams can be rotated, as shown in Figure 5.3, to denote that the functional departments are, in essence, service departments to projects.

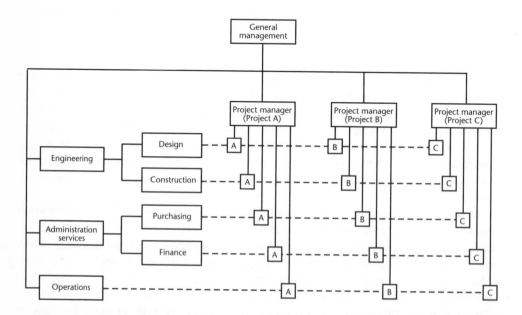

Figure 5.3   The project/rotated matrix

The project manager's position in the matrix organization

The project manager's position or 'grade' in the hierarchy of the company, the question of to whom he or she should report, and whether there is to be an overall project manager or projects director for groups or projects are topics subject to considerable debate and 'power politics' in many organizations. If the company handles multiple projects there will invariably be interactions between projects, if only in the claims for scarce resources from the functional departments. Someone then has to 'integrate' the project managers.

The grade of the project manager in a matrix organization depends on the size, complexity and importance of the project, the form of matrix organization adopted, and the distribution of power in the organization. The higher the grade, the more likely the project manager is to be effective and vice versa.

Figure 4.3, in the previous chapter, showed the matrix group, or the project manager, responsible to the engineering department manager, which is a common arrangement. The project manager is placed at a level in the organigram below that of the group functional managers but above the level of their subordinates, which symbolically indicates the project manager's grade or organizational status. As such, this organigram is likely to represent a functional matrix organization.

Figure 5.2 shows a separate projects department, the manager of which reports directly to the general manager. This manager (called the projects director in some companies) is shown on a level with the functional department managers. By implication, the project managers are on the same grade as the functional group managers in this balanced matrix.

Figure 5.3 shows the project managers as the principal line managers in a project matrix, each reporting directly to general management. Here they are on a par with, or perhaps are graded above, the functional department heads.

There are many permutations and combinations of these arrangements in practice. The seniority of project managers and the organizational level of the person to whom they report are significant factors in effective project management in any company.

ADVANTAGES OF THE MATRIX CONCEPT

The matrix organization underlies most project organizations, whether in its basic form, its hybrid adaptations or its global form. Although the dedicated project team is the most effective in achieving project objectives, it tends not to use resources efficiently and flexibly unless the project is very large. Also, the dedicated project team cannot extend to cover the multi-company global organization, where the matrix is the only practicable alternative.

Although there are many problems with the matrix organization (which will be discussed later) it does have many advantages:

- It permits the integration of individuals, groups, organizational units and companies across formal organizational boundaries into a single organization.
- It is a very flexible arrangement that can be used to organize a small mixed-function group, but is just as appropriate for linking together and integrating hundreds of groups, departments and companies on a large project.
- The matrix establishes a group or organization identity, which is essential to the management of the group, the organization and the project itself. In this respect it makes it possible to:

- have a matrix group leader or project manager who can provide the leadership needed to achieve the project objectives
- develop teamwork and manage conflict
- establish communication, coordination and management information systems
- motivate the matrix members and build commitment to the project and its objectives.

Thus the matrix group can be developed into a goal-oriented organization that facilitates achievement of the project objectives.

At the same time as creating a project group identity, the matrix organization retains the functional groups, departments or companies intact and thus can have all the advantages of a functional organization. For example, a matrix organization can create a small mixed-function project group or organizational unit from a company organized into functional departments, without disruption to these departments. The matrix organization can therefore combine the efficient use of resources with the project orientation essential to achieving the project objectives.

PROBLEMS WITH MATRIX ORGANIZATIONS

Unfortunately, although the matrix organization can achieve results and facilitate teamwork, it also creates many human relations problems. To manage a project effectively, the project manager must understand and be able to deal with these problems.

The matrix form of project organization conflicts with traditional organization theory in many ways. Inherent in it are dual subordination, division of authority and responsibility, without corresponding authority and with a disregard for the so-called hierarchical principles. These contravened principles are no more than generalizations about what has been seen to work in the past. They derive from experience and, as such, must be subject to revision in the light of new experience and circumstances. It can be as foolish to be totally bound by past experience as it is to ignore it. Nevertheless, disregard for these principles does mean that the matrix has organizational complexity, with an inherent tendency for conflict. In project work, where different functional departments and companies have to be integrated across formal organizational boundaries, there is a new set of circumstances. To bind these diverse elements into one organization, committed to managing a project so that it achieves all its objectives, a new set of ground rules has had to be evolved.

It is wrong to blame the matrix form of project organization for all the problems that can arise. The complexities and ambiguities that do occur are not so much a result of the matrix but are instead the basic reasons for adopting it. The traditional hierarchical pyramid simply cannot handle the number of different groups and complexities involved in a project of any size, leaving little alternative to using some form of the matrix organization. This is especially true in multi-company organizations.

The principal reasons for the problems in matrix organizations can be listed as follows:

- The matrix brings the project manager and the functional departmental or other company managers into direct confrontation.
- Project managers' authority does not match their responsibility: there is an 'authority gap'.
- The matrix creates dual subordination and divided authority. Members of the organization find themselves responsible to two managers, the project manager and their functional or company manager, which violates the principle of unity of command.
- The matrix organization structure can be complex and ambiguous.

Confrontation

The matrix project organization sets the project manager and the functional managers as protagonists in an arena. These managers might hold very different points of view. There is often a great difference in cultures and objectives between these protagonists, yet they are interdependent and must interact to achieve results. Each person's performance will be strongly influenced by the other's. In addition, the common superior to the project and its functional managers is likely to be very remote, if such a superior exists at all.

The project manager's authority gap

In theory, in the traditional pyramid organization, formal positional authority flows from the chief executive to the next level of manager, and cascades down to the lowest level of management. All superior–subordinate relationships and the spans of control are defined. Looked at from the bottom up, the individuals in this organization are split into groups, each with its superior, who in turn belongs to a higher-level group, which in turn has its superior. The concept extends upwards, defining higher-level groups until the top management group is reached, where the chief executive is the superior.

Authority patterns in the traditional pyramid structure are thus primarily vertical. The superior–subordinate relationships are close, unambiguous and more or less permanent. When different groups work together, they theoretically have a common superior somewhere in the hierarchy who has a superior–subordinate relationship with the group managers and can thus integrate the groups.

Whilst this may be the theory, the practice is far more ambiguous. Responsibility, accountability and authority are often unclear or indefinite. Relationships are not always clearly defined. Organizations rarely work as shown in their organigrams. Even if an organization chart did happen to portray the true relationships and authority patterns when it was drawn, it is likely to become inaccurate within days.

A common ambiguity is that authority or power is dispersed, ill-defined, inadequate or does not match the responsibilities of the manager. When the power structure is weak, or uncertain, or the position-holders are weak, power is 'up for grabs'. Decisions will then be made by political processes, and there is competition for power. All this leads to conflict and politics. Individuals and groups will question why they should follow the instructions of a project manager. In a condition of uncertainty, some will act assertively, assuming power that, in the eyes of others, they do not have. Those who are more defensive and cautious will resent their more assertive colleagues.

This weakness in authority or power is what makes the liaison or coordinator methods of integration ineffective. It leads to many of the matrix organization's problems with what is termed the project manager's 'authority gap'. This is also commonly known as responsibility without power. In a military context, this might be likened to ordering an infantry commander to wipe out an enemy armoured division.

The matrix organization structure is far more complex than the traditional pyramid. Authority patterns can be vertical, horizontal, diagonal and multi-dimensional. Project managers in such a matrix must try to manage across departmental boundaries in their own company (and across company boundaries when other companies are involved) to integrate all the parties and achieve the project objectives. Even in the dedicated project team, no project manager can have direct superior–subordinate authority across all the departmental and company interfaces. What authority they do have will be subject to constraints and is usually limited to some degree.

Thus the matrix organization contravenes the principle that management responsibility should be coupled with corresponding authority. This lack of formal authority makes it difficult for a project manager to persuade people in the many functional groups to do what is needed when it is needed. This, in turn, leads to the project manager becoming frustrated and using political means to achieve power. There is then a great danger of conflict.

Conversely, if the project manager is given the formal authority or power (in a strong form of the matrix) functional managers may resent this power. Such resentment may extend beyond these functional managers to their subordinates and even to their superiors. They may consider that their authority and positions are being undermined. This in turn will lead to resentment, hostility, conflict and withdrawal of support. Thus there is almost a no-win situation in the matrix organization.

Dual subordination

A significant characteristic of the matrix organization, especially in its balanced form, is the existence of dual subordination. This violates the classic principle of unity of command: a person working in a functional group might receive conflicting instructions from the project manager and his or her own functional manager. Dual subordination is not unique to matrix organizations but it is more clearly recognized here than in traditional hierarchical organizations. Most experienced managers recognize that the classical unity of command concept, with authority and responsibility packaged within neat boundaries in a conventional organigram, seldom portrays reality. Managers, whatever the organization structure, are usually subject to several sources of power or influence.

Dual subordination in project management matrix structures creates a complex psychological problem and puts a stress on all three classes of people involved (the project manager, the functional managers and their subordinates). Subordinates are often expected to abandon their 'permanent home', old friends and loyalties for a set of temporary loyalties and relationships, causing them to feel insecure. The project manager will want everyone working on the project to have their loyalties totally committed to the project, the project group and the project objectives. The project manager will tend to resent the subordinates' residual loyalty to their functional homes. Any intervention by the functional managers might be seen as interference. The functional managers, on the other hand, will tend to resent loss of power over their subordinates and pressures from the project manager. Too often, dual subordination is a struggle for power over the subordinates, leading to unproductive conflict.

Although dual subordination is a weakness of the matrix organization in theory, it can be made to work. An individual can accept and work to instructions from two managers provided that these instructions do not conflict with each other. This is the case where the project manager determines what must be done and when, whilst the functional manager is concerned with the technical issues and, perhaps, choosing the person best able to perform each particular task.

When differences in instructions do occur, clearly one of the managers must clearly be recognized as the one who should initially be obeyed. Any remaining differences then have to be resolved by the two managers (not by the subordinates) before conflict arises. Dual subordination therefore requires good relationships between the project and functional managers and a willingness to compromise. The functional managers must be willing to relinquish some control over their subordinates. The project manager must recognize and accept the old ties of the functional managers and their subordinates. Open communication, trust, respect and mutual support are essential.

Complex, ambiguous and uncertain structures

When an organization structure is complex, ambiguous and uncertain (not to say also temporary) the authority and responsibility of its members will be correspondingly uncertain. Integration might be ineffective or non-existent, groups may not be defined, and relationships will be indefinite. All this can occur in any form of organization, particularly with large endeavours, but it is marked in project work and in the matrix form of organization. A project typically involves more than one company, each with two or more functional groups. In a large matrix organization there might be many groups, departments, organizations and even a hundred or more different companies.

In such cases it is unfair to blame the matrix organization for all the problems that arise through this organizational complexity. The complexities that arise here are not caused by using a matrix organization, but could instead be considered as the basic reason for adopting the matrix. The traditional hierarchical pyramid simply cannot handle the number of groups, the need to cross organizational boundaries, and the complexities that are unavoidable in a large project organization or when managing multi-projects. There are then few alternatives, if any, to the matrix organization.

One of the problems is that often senior managers do not face up to the difficulties and the possible conflicts involved in clarifying authority, responsibility and reporting relationships. Management is sometimes unaware of the need to deal positively with these issues or prefers to avoid the unpleasantness or fights that firm rulings might cause. As a result, organization relationships, authority and responsibilities are often uncertain. More often, they are not understood by the people involved, even when they are defined. Thus an important point is people's awareness or perception of the organization. If people do not understand the structure of which they are a part then, again, there is ambiguity and uncertainty. This uncertainty itself contributes to many interpersonal and intergroup problems, and thus to conflict.

A special problem with project work is that the organization is temporary. Projects are temporary entities with lives typically ranging from three months to a few years. This means that those involved work together for limited periods, often leaving insufficient time for interpersonal relationships and teamwork to develop as they can in relatively stable line management. There is also less time in which to resolve interpersonal and intergroup conflicts.

Technical problems can almost always be solved, given enough skills, time and money. But 'people' problems are far more difficult, if not impossible, to overcome within the life span of a project. The problem is compounded because the composition of the organization and its constituent groups is usually undergoing continuous change, with new members joining, others leaving as their jobs are done, and with the roles of some members changing in importance as the project progresses. Relationships and dependencies are, therefore, constantly changing in a project organization.

Despite all these problems, the matrix organization can be effective in facilitating achievement of the project objectives. Its use is unavoidable in many projects – for example, where several companies are involved. The matrix is really the only choice where the functional departments are large, strong and well established and have to handle a continuous stream of concurrent projects.

Other organization forms

HYBRID

It is quite common for the organization of a company to have a hybrid structure in which two or more of the project organization forms so far described exist together. Hybrid organizations can also be found in projects involving more than one company.

In one form of the single company hybrid structure, those individuals and groups whose work is totally utilized on a project are allocated full-time to the project as a dedicated project team. Those who cannot be allocated full-time to one project, or who possess rare skills, are retained within their functional departments and assigned to projects part-time on a matrix basis.

One example is that of a mining engineering company, which conducted a number of projects of various sizes in a fairly stable balanced matrix organization. Occasionally, a project would arise that involved only one of the functional departments. For instance, one client wished to reclaim some workings in a deep underground copper mine that, several years earlier, had been inundated when a surface tailings lake broke through with tragic consequences. A project of considerable size was authorized to reclaim the lost sections of the mine but, as this was almost all piping and pumping work, the project was set up as a team within the functional department that dealt with fluids and piping.

The project manager's relationships with each functional department may also differ. For example, in a chemical company all the work may be carried out internally. The project manager might be from the engineering department and have under his or her direct control the construction personnel involved. The design group might be from a different department, so that the project manager would have only a balanced matrix relationship with them. The operations department will be the client, and it is very likely that the project manager would have only a weak matrix relationship with them, with very limited authority or influence.

In a large project, involving several companies, it is very possible that the companies would have radically different organization structures. The managers responsible for project work inside these companies would therefore have different authority relationships with their people. The overall project manager might then have the difficult task of integrating all these diverse forces.

MODULAR AND NETWORK STRUCTURES

Some companies, whose business is primarily project-oriented, use modular and network structures to obtain maximum flexibility. In this arrangement, individuals, functional groups and complete, small mixed organizational units operate as discrete entities with loose, flexible networks of relationships within and between them.

These entities can operate on a modular basis. They are 'plugged in and out' of projects as required. They are combined and recombined in varying network structures for different tasks or projects. While in a project, they are full members of the project team. But they only remain in that team for as long as they are needed for the project. Consultants and computer software companies often operate on this basis and develop the flexible attitude of mind needed to operate this form of organization successfully.

Methods for clarifying organizational responsibilities

The methods outlined in this section are useful for defining the responsibilities of project managers and others engaged in a project. They can be used in any organization but are particularly helpful in removing some of the ambiguities and uncertainties that are especially prevalent in matrix organizations.

THE CONTRACTOR–CONSIGNEE PRINCIPLE

One method for overcoming potential conflict between the project manager and functional managers uses the contractor–consignee principle (Prigl and Stoldt, 1990).

A reality of project life is that the project manager often has less difficulty with managing contributors to the project from outside companies than with functional managers in his or her own company. The project manager usually has written contractual relationships with these outside companies, and they need to maintain goodwill and reputation to ensure future business. The project manager has a formal basis for authority with the personnel of these contractors through written contracts or purchase order agreements. There may not be complete superior–subordinate authority, but the authority is formal and both parties in each case know the extent and limitations of their contractual relationship.

Personnel working for these outside contractors can, for all intents and purposes, be integrated into one project organization and work together as a team. Conventional contracts have clearly defined deliverables and there is a legally binding path for the resolution of any dispute.

The project manager's position within his or her own company is usually one of getting the work done without specific line authority or written contract for controlling the in-house project work. In-house work may not be clearly defined or specified, with costs, schedules, resources and objectives loosely set and difficult to control. The project manager thus often has greater difficulty in bringing pressure to bear for improved performance with in-company groups than with external contractors.

On this basis, there are benefits for the project manager, the functional managers and for the project itself in setting up internal contracts (real or pseudo) between the project manager and the functional managers. This 'contractor–consignee' arrangement can eliminate many of the problems outlined for matrix organizations. The contracts may be based on work packages, cost accounts, products or other deliverables; the jargon is immaterial. The important point is to define each specific element of work and make that the subject of an informally or formally agreed contract between the project manager and the relevant functional manager. Each contract is self-contained, essentially a small sub-project with a simple management structure limited to the responsibility of one functional manager. An internal contract of this type has the following characteristics:

1 One person is responsible for fulfilling it.
2 There is a formal work specification.
3 It has its own schedule, with key events or milestones that interface with the overall project plan.
4 It has its own manpower/resources plan.
5 It has a time-phased budget.

6 It has a control and information system.
7 Its performance can be measured.

When this contractor–consignee arrangement is used in a matrix organization it can resolve some problems, particularly with functional or balanced matrices. It can provide a better basis for the project manager's authority, increase motivation of the staff involved and improve project performance.

THE RESPONSIBILITY MATRIX

A responsibility matrix is a graphical and very useful way of indicating who is expected to do what on a project. It can be used in any form of project organization. A simple example is shown in Figure 5.4. Key project personnel are listed along the top of the chart and various tasks or general functions are entered in the left-hand column. Symbols at relevant matrix intersections can be placed to show which person is primarily responsible for each function or task. Other symbols can be used to show those who have a secondary responsibility, or who must be kept informed.

Task type / **Responsibility**	The client	Project manager	Project engineer	Purchasing manager	Drawing office	Construction manager	Planning engineer	Cost engineer	Project accountant	and so on
Make designs		✚	●							
Approve designs	●	■	✚							
Purchase enquiries		■	✚	●						
Purchase orders	■	■	✚	●						
Planning	■	■	✚	✚	✚	✚	●	✚		
Cost control		●		✚		✚		✚		
Progress reports		●	✚	✚	✚	✚	✚			
Cost reports		●		✚		✚		✚	✚	
and so on										

● Principal responsibility (only one per task)
✚ Secondary responsibility
■ Must be consulted or informed

Figure 5.4   Matrix of responsibilities

Some writers make the error of stating that all project tasks need to be entered in the responsibility matrix. This could lead to a very bulky and inflexible document. It should be possible to limit entries either to work packages or to functions (as in Figure 5.4). On a large project, however, it may be necessary to compile a separate responsibility matrix for each major work package or for each sub-project within the main project.

The responsibility matrix permits individuals to check what their responsibilities are, so that nothing is overlooked and job overlapping is avoided. It will often form an important part of a manual of project procedures, drawn up and issued for any project of significant size.

6 Organizing the Larger Project

Basic forms of project organization structure were introduced in the previous two chapters, where the importance of integration was emphasized – not only to coordinate the project tasks but also to establish teamwork and minimize or manage conflict. These issues become even more important in larger projects, with their more complex organizations.

The importance of the 'internal' project organization structure

Larger project organizations have to encompass both the global multi-company organization (the external organization) and the more complex internal project organization. Here, the internal organization means the structure of the relationships between the individuals and groups working on the project, viewed as a separate organizational entity. It ignores the external relationships of the organizational elements with their parent departments or companies.

The concepts outlined in previous chapters must be expanded when considering larger projects. The global organization of a smaller project might involve only one or two companies, and one or two functional departments in each of those companies. Even with this small number of 'building blocks' there can be problems with the form of organization used and the definition and allocation of responsibilities for the individual manager and segments of the project. These problems are compounded exponentially with larger projects, where 10, 20, 100 or even more companies and organizational units might be involved.

A large project will almost always be a multi-company undertaking, but many of its personnel and groups can be allocated full-time to the project. Therefore most of its external relationships may be based on the dedicated project team or project matrix forms of organization.

Whilst the external relationships of organizational elements with their parent organizations or companies must be considered in almost all projects, in larger projects special consideration must be given to the design of the internal organization structure. Too often, this special consideration is not given. As a result, the people involved have a hard fight simply to overcome the impact of an unsatisfactory organization. This chapter will concentrate on these internal relationships and structures.

Most large projects can be organized internally in several different ways. Among the variable factors are:

- sizes of the organizational units
- degree of centralization or decentralization (whether the hierarchy or superstructure is 'tall' or 'wide')
- overall form of the organization structure.

The relatively simple structures of the functional matrix or dedicated project team have to be extended to include such concepts as:

- internal functionalization
- divisionalization
- the project headquarters assuming the role of a parent company
- the federal project organization
- complex permutations and combinations of organization structures (for example, matrices/ within matrices/within divisions).

To show the problems involved, we must consider the changes necessary to the project organization as the project size increases. We shall start, therefore, by briefly re-examining the organization of small and medium-sized projects. Although our examples show relatively simple structures, they do demonstrate the alternative organizational forms available and some of the problems associated with them.

Small and medium-sized project organizations

SMALL PROJECT ORGANIZATION

The upper section of Figure 6.1 shows a simple, single-group project organization comprising individuals from different functional backgrounds. For this simple example we have chosen

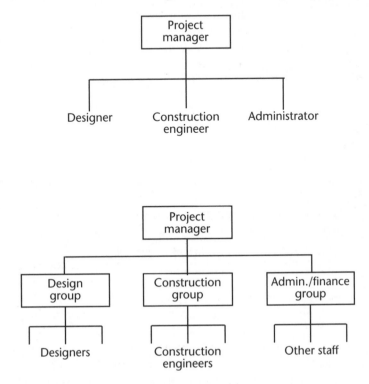

Figure 6.1   Small and medium-sized project organizations

design engineering, construction and administration/finance. These individuals are shown as members of a small mixed project group (or organizational unit) despite the fact that they may still belong to their function groups as already described. This, therefore, might actually be an external matrix organization. This is the internal project structure implicitly assumed when the basic organizational forms were described (in Chapter 5).

This embryonic project group is organic. The potential for teamwork and individual motivation is high with a low risk of conflict. Integration is good, because the project manager is very close to everyone involved. Such an organic group emphasizes informality, flexibility and adaptation between individuals, and is recognized as being appropriate to the management of change. Summing up, in this small, organic project group conflict tends to be minimal, motivation is high, teamwork should prevail, and there is a great feeling of vitality and enthusiasm.

MEDIUM-SIZED PROJECT ORGANIZATION

As a project grows in size, individuals from the different functions are replaced by functional groups. Each of these groups generally has its own supervisor or group manager, as shown in the lower section of Figure 6.1. Thus the medium-sized project organization is already developing functionalization within the internal project organization. This internal project structure is a functionally organized, hierarchical pyramid.

Despite internal functionalization, this medium-sized project organization form escapes many of the problems generally associated with the functional organization of projects. The integrating manager (the project manager) is fairly close to the action and the organization is small enough to allow mutual adjustment and effective horizontal groups. Nevertheless, there is now a two-tiered level of organization – namely, a functional organization operating within an external project organization of some form. The potential for teamwork and individual motivation is still fairly high, with relatively low potential for conflict. But the conditions are not quite as favourable as they were in the small, organic group project organization.

Larger project organizations

When a project grows larger there can be a tendency to extrapolate the conventional functionally organized pyramid structure used in the medium-sized project. The result can be that shown in Figure 6.2. This is a single large organizational unit where the only key integrationist superior is the project manager. Functional groups from the medium-sized project are replaced here by functionally organized large groups or departments. These large groups could belong to different companies in any of the conventional external project structures but, in the internal structure, they are part of the traditional pyramid hierarchy.

In this single organizational unit structure, the organization pattern of the larger project may have turned a complete circle, so that the internal organization of the project is totally functional, having all the problems previously described for the functional organization in projects. In particular, the project manager integrator is now very far away from the 'coal face' or day-to-day activity, with all that implies for the growth of conflict. Integration must depend largely on mutual adjustment and informal horizontal groups within the project organization.

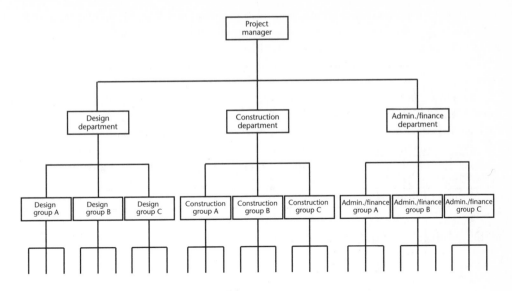

Figure 6.2   Functional organization of a large project

The problems of integration and other difficulties associated with the functional project organization mean that, as projects get bigger, it becomes impossible to continue with a single organizational unit. A large project organization structure must be divisionalized with dedicated internal project teams, or the functional structure has to be supplemented with a matrix. Thus a large project has to develop its own internal organization structure, with multiple organization units handling different segments of the project. Each unit may integrate one or more companies, and different companies may be involved in different organizational units. The project itself must now be considered as a parent organization or company. The organization units have become separate projects or sub-projects, and the 'project headquarters' now has to manage these multiple, interrelated sub-projects.

The basic 'building blocks' of any project organization can be assembled in different ways. Each structure will give a different shape and size to the management hierarchy and will influence human behaviour and the project performance in different ways. In particular, these can encourage or discourage teamwork, conflict and the motivation of individuals and groups.

The number of management levels in the hierarchy, and the complexity of the organization structure, will be influenced by the following factors:

1 The number and size of the organizational units
2 The organization structure form of these units
3 The extent of functionalization
4 The span of control at each level
5 The degree of centralization or decentralization.

These factors interact with themselves, with the number of levels of management and with the complexity of the structure, some as cause and some as effect.

This multi-project, large project organization can be organized in many different ways, based on the organizational forms previously described. It can maintain its own internal

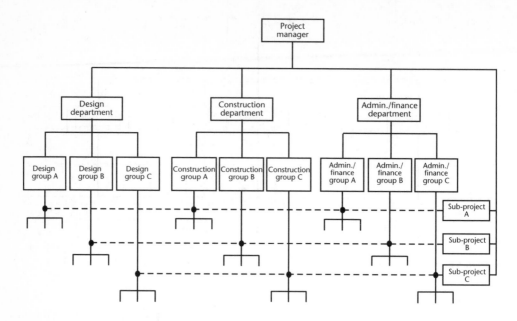

Figure 6.3   Matrix organization of a large project

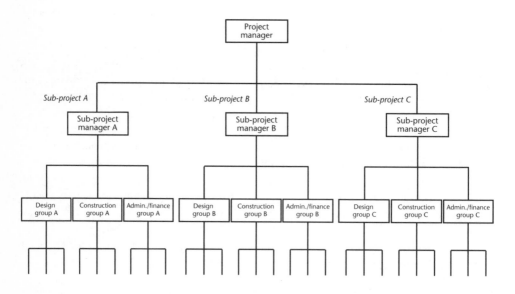

Figure 6.4   Divisional organization of a large project

functional departments or divisions intact and adopt any or all three forms of the matrix organization. Alternatively (particularly in the very big project) it may adopt the divisional form of organization and create a dedicated team for each organizational unit or sub-project. Then again, it could adopt a hybrid organization (part matrix, part divisional).

Some of the many ways in which the nine basic organizational groups shown in the single organizational unit structure of Figure 6.2 can be organized are shown in Figures 6.3, 6.4 and 6.5. Each of these is described in the following sections. The organigrams are

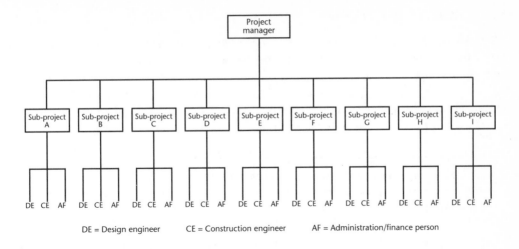

DE = Design engineer   CE = Construction engineer   AF = Administration/finance person

Figure 6.5   Federal organization of a large project

simplified and the basic variations that they demonstrate might be multiplied several times in a large project.

MATRIX ORGANIZATION

Figure 6.3 shows matrix relationships superimposed on the functional organization just described (and illustrated in Figure 6.2). The purpose here is to improve integration at the basic group level. In this example, three matrix organizational units are formed, and each project engineer or sub-project manager integrates those members of the various functional groups and departments who contribute to his or her segment of the project.

DIVISIONAL/DEDICATED PROJECT TEAM ORGANIZATION

In the organization structure shown in Figure 6.4, the project is divided into three separate organizational units or sub-projects, each of which is a mixed-function, dedicated project group. This creates some decentralization, but this effect is often reduced by retaining strong central administration, planning, control and financial functions at the centre.

SMALL UNIT OR FEDERAL ORGANIZATION

In Figure 6.5 each of the nine basic groups from our example forms a small, mixed-function unit so that the project is split into nine segments. This creates a decentralized, flat organization structure known as a federal organization. This federal organization can, however, be modified in the following ways:

- It can be made more centralized by retaining strong central staff groups.
- It can be made 'taller' by introducing another level of management between the nine units and the project centre. For example, three such managers might be introduced, each of whom could manage, coordinate and integrate three of the small dedicated project teams.

MORE COMPLEX STRUCTURES

All the variations just described can be used whilst retaining the same number of basic groups actually to carry out the work, and to form the foundation of the hierarchy. The complexity and height of the organizational hierarchy can obviously increase in the larger project, where all of the above might form only one of many divisions. In the very big project, there can be permutations and combinations of these basic organization structures, or multi-layering.

Thus, in the divisional form, separate project divisions could have:

- a functional medium-sized project structure
- functional departments and a matrix structure and
- dedicated project teams (that is, a further divisional breakdown of the organizational unit or sub-project).

Alternatively, within one matrix organization there may be another matrix structure, and within that yet another, and so on!

Practical aspects of the basic forms in larger projects

CENTRALIZATION VERSUS DECENTRALIZATION

There will typically be a management hierarchy in each functional department and in each organizational unit. In a large project, a senior management hierarchy or superstructure will exist to manage and integrate the many organizational units. Thus the organization structure of a large project will include several levels of management. In some projects, the number of these levels might be considerable, and projects with more than ten management levels have been known. These multiple management levels create very tall superstructures or management hierarchies. In addition to the general shape of the structure, two other factors in particular have significant influence on performance and human behaviour – namely, *centralization* and *bureaucratization*. An important decision that needs to be made in such organizations is the extent to which centralization or decentralization should be used. There are several conflicting needs:

1 Although it is possible to divide a big project into discrete segments that can be handled almost as independent or separate projects, there is also a need to integrate these segments. This need for integration will vary during a project's life cycle and from one project to another. Integration needs are usually highest at the beginning of a project (the initial design stages) and at the end (commissioning). Integration needs are typically lower during a project's construction, manufacturing or programming stages.
2 There is a need for control and performance measurement, formalization of procedures and standardization across the whole project.
3 There is a need for individual project units to be as autonomous as possible for maximum internal teamwork and motivation.

The relevance of centralization and control to performance and human behaviour means that attention to the above-listed needs must be appropriately balanced.

CENTRALLY CONTROLLED PROJECT ORGANIZATION

The conventional approach is that the project manager has to plan and control all project activities. This view is reflected in the power of much project management computer software. In order to plan and control a large project effectively, central staff functions that support the project manager have increased. This eventually leads to the formation of a project headquarters with strong staff groups at the centre. In other words, line and staff positions are created, with all that implies for engendering conflict and politics.

Tall hierarchical structures, with small spans of control, generally emphasize close control of subordinates at all levels. Strong, centralized departments occupying staff positions in the organization often assist in this control. Tall structures are normally combined with centralized decision-making, have a structured hierarchy of graded authority and control, together with formalization and standardization of procedures, organizational rules and regulations. Tall structures, therefore, tend to produce a disciplined and rigid organization. This enables senior management to 'be in control', and superiors are readily available to subordinates for consultation and support. However, the organization is mechanistic and very bureaucratic. Centralized authority tends to slow down decision-making, leading to 'organizational arthritis', reduction in individual initiative and little autonomy at lower (even middle) levels. Teamwork and motivation are thus reduced. Also, political manoeuvring and conflict are commonplace in the tall hierarchy, and information tends to be distorted, diluted or even censored as it flows up and down the hierarchy.

Overcentralized control can result in the creation of a tall, hierarchical, complex organization that will inevitably become overbureaucratic and lead to the following problems:

- Integration of the work and the people becomes more difficult as the project gets bigger.
- The complexity of large project organizations leads to uncertain authority and responsibility which, in turn, increases the risk of conflict and politics.
- Large project organizations tend to develop internal functionalization, which leads to functional orientation, culture clashes and groups with incompatible objectives.
- Centralization of large project organizations can lead to problems with the following:
  - information overload at the centre.
  - large central groups in staff positions, set up in attempts to deal with the information overload.
  - a tall management hierarchy, with too many levels of supervisory managers.
  - longer times needed for decisions.
- The organization tends to become formalized and bureaucratic.
- Motivation and teamwork are impaired.

Although divisionalization (leading to a measure of decentralization) can reduce these problems, there is a general tendency to implement only pseudo-decentralization. Many so-called decentralized organizations are decentralized in name only, because important factors, controlled by the centre, negate the effects of this decentralization. One way to overcome this is to make a more definite move towards a decentralized organization, the extreme example of which is the 'federal' project organization.

FEDERAL ORGANIZATION

The opposite extreme to the centrally controlled project organization is the flat, flexible, decentralized federal organization structure. Here the pyramid, functionally structured organization is replaced by a flat organization that generally promotes decentralized decision-making, much smaller central staff groups and an organic style of operation. Organizational units have more distinct objectives and can, indeed, be named as profit centres. Hierarchical interference and control from the centre are minimized, whilst horizontal communications and comparisons are encouraged.

In the project federal structure, the project organization is arranged into semi-independent organizational units, each of which deals with a distinct segment of the project. Each unit can therefore be given its own time, cost and performance objectives. The organizational units can be aligned with the work breakdown structure (WBS) and organization breakdown structure (OBS) described later in Chapter 8.

This federal form came about because of problems associated with the centralized structure described above, and also because of experience in larger projects and developments in project systems and organization theory. Today's project systems (and their associated computing systems and networking) are not restricted to the management of time, costs and resources but can be integrated with the WBS and/or the OBS. They can thus be used to support the decentralized management of projects and federal organization structures. These systems can help to motivate individuals and groups by giving them targets and subsequent feedback on their performance.

The federal project organization might seem similar to the divisional form but there is one essential difference. Accountability, as well as responsibility, is delegated to the units. So, the federal organization involves not just decentralization (where the centre delegates tasks to the units whilst retaining control) but gives considerable autonomy to the smaller organizational units. This distinction between accountability and responsibility is important, and it is the delegation of accountability to federal unit managers that distinguishes the federal organization from other project organization forms.

Accountability is the associated condition of being answerable for the satisfactory fulfilment of those tasks.

Responsibility is the obligation incurred by job-holders in the organization to perform tasks assigned to them effectively.

Delegation of accountability and responsibility

One of the most fashionable and effective steps that can be taken in any organizational restructuring is to eliminate one or more levels of the management hierarchy. Although the federal organization is an extreme solution, and may be too decentralized for integration purposes across the whole life cycle of a project, it is a pointer to the advantages of decentralization and the adoption of a flat organization structure. It can handle the control requirements, it increases motivation and teamwork, and it reduces the risk of conflict. However, many benefits of the federal organization can be achieved by delegating accountability and responsibility using the modern approach to project organization.

The modern approach to project organization emphasizes the delegation of personal accountability to every manager, right down the line to individual work element and group managers. There must be discrete responsibility for individual project tasks, not only for the efficient completion of these tasks but also for motivating individuals and encouraging teamwork. Each manager and group should know what is expected of them, and know what they must do to achieve high performance.

This concept should extend to the internal company contractor–consignee assignments and to the various cross-boundary groups that exist in a multi-company project. This includes the formal, matrix and informal horizontal groups of managers and others who must interact, are interdependent and share responsibility for discrete segments of the project. Consider, for example, a case where electrical design engineers from the client, from a consultant and from the contractor, possibly with a project engineer, together constitute a group that is responsible for the electrical design of a project. Every such group must be defined and recognized (particularly by those in the group) as a discrete organizational group having shared objectives and mutual self-interests. There must also be someone whose responsibilities are the leadership, management and integration of the group – that is, someone who can act as a key integrationist superior, no matter what his or her positional authority happens to be.

The individual manager, group, contractor–consignee and organizational unit responsibilities are then discrete. Each entity has its own deliverables, clear objectives, performance and output criteria and acts as a cost, performance and profit centre. Each has a high degree of autonomy, with both responsibility and accountability for results. This high degree of delegation enables the organization structure to have wider spans of control, which results in a flatter, less hierarchical structure with fewer management levels.

This approach has a very positive psychological impact. Consequences include the following:

- Individuals and groups can identify themselves with the smaller unit, which increases internal solidarity and unit loyalty.
- Team development and teamwork are facilitated.
- The approach creates shared values, common clear-cut objectives, and aligns self-interests.
- Individual, group and unit motivation are increased.
- Hierarchical steering and control are minimized, and replaced by self-control within the overall agreed budgets and plans.
- Dysfunctional conflict and politics are reduced.

Adopting this approach will need the following changes in many organizations:

- a significant change in attitudes and culture – for example:
  - delegation of accountability as well as responsibility
  - reduction of supervision and control from the centre
  - allowing junior managers to operate in a largely autonomous manner
  - sharing of power among the senior managers: the project is now being managed by a group of managers, in the manner of a federal organization.
- establishment of a management information and performance criteria system, which in turn will facilitate the loose/tight form of control consistent with delegation of accountability and responsibility

- implementation of a good reward system
- establishment of a career progression structure, which is usually less apparent and more difficult to define in the absence of a tall hierarchy.

In practice there has to be balance between formalization and central control, on the one hand, and decentralization and an organic style of management, on the other. Some factors must be centrally controlled, but as much as possible should be decentralized. The organizational units should be made as autonomous as is consistent with the requirements for integration and control. These guidelines are, of course, somewhat vague. 'As much as possible' or 'as soon as possible' can mean very different things to different people. However, the actual balance realized will be contingent on each unique case.

Organization and the project life cycle

Project organizations are not static, but change as the project progresses through its life cycle. Almost every project goes through a similar series of life cycle stages, beginning with the initial concept and ending when the project is commissioned and handed over. Strictly, of course, the whole life cycle extends until the product of the project has no further use to its owner and is scrapped but, for the purposes of managing the active project, the following stages are common and relevant:

1 conception
2 definition
3 design
4 procurement
5 execution
6 commissioning and handover.

These stages are not always clearly separated and usually overlap considerably.

Project authorization must usually wait until the project has been defined. Once authorized, the main project contractor can start issuing such contracts as are deemed necessary and the true project organization will be given life. The size of the organization will grow during design, be greatest during execution, with many more people, functions and companies involved than in the other phases.

Insufficient attention is often given to the commissioning phase, in spite of its extreme importance. In the oil industry, for example, commissioning amounts to an additional execution phase. In any project of significant size, whatever the industry, commissioning is a complex phase and includes a project interface involving handover to the owner or operating organization.

When the time available for the project is short and the completion date is critical (as it often is), all efforts must obviously be made to start and finish each critical task as soon as possible. This will usually generate considerable overlaps between the different life-cycle phases and between some individual tasks. For example, the project designers will be expected to alert the purchasing organization to any long-lead items as early as possible, without waiting for their designs to be completed. Project purchasing, therefore, and some execution tasks will be started as soon as sufficient design work has been done. Even in a less hurried approach, the life-cycle phases can be expected to overlap. During commissioning, for instance, execution work will continue – if only to deal with bugs and snags or make finishing touches.

In the design phase of a large project, the various companies carrying out the design may form one or more functional organization units, with a limited amount of consultancy input from the execution group. With the exception of this relationship, these organizational units will contain almost all the interactions and interdependencies, and design will be the lead function. This condition can continue for a considerable time on a big project. However, when the project enters its next phase (which will usually be construction, manufacture or some other form of project execution) these same organizational units will expand until they become mixed design, procurement and execution organizational units. Execution then takes over as the lead function.

Thus the organizational units and the organization structure of the project as a whole will change with each stage of the project life cycle. The organization will grow in size and complexity until the commissioning phase. So the project organization structure can never be considered as a static entity. It is dynamic, and can be expected to change considerably as the project progresses through its life cycle. A typical progression might be as follows:

- *Conception*. During the conception stage the organization is small, probably contained within one company. The organization structure is fairly simple, perhaps comprising a small dedicated project team.

- *Definition*. Several functional departments have become involved at the definition stage but external company participation is limited to consultants. Although the organization could become a balanced matrix, there will essentially be only one or a few organizational units.

- *Design*. When a large project enters the design stage it will probably start to become a multi-company project and enter the global realm. At this stage the organization structure is expanded considerably, with many more organizational units. The number of organizational units will increase still further as the project moves into its execution stage.

- *Execution*. When the execution stage is reached, the project structure could become divisional in form, with perhaps a matrix structure within the divisions. Whereas the organization might have been centralized in the concept and definition stages, once design and execution take place it could become decentralized.

- *Commissioning*. The organization is likely to revert to a more centralized form of operation during commissioning.

Management contracting

There are several common variations of the global project organization, some of which involve contracting out one or more management roles. In any project there are normally several discrete management roles that can involve the use of management contractors. These include the following:

1 an overall management role that manages and integrates all those involved, including the client, design and execution contractors;
2 client management roles (which may involve contractors or consultants acting as their agents):
  a) pre-contract management, organization, planning and control of:
    • conception
    • definition
    • the contracting process;
  b) post-contract:
    • decisions, approvals, liaison, direction
    • administration, supervision, technical monitoring and quality control of:
      – design and procurement
      – execution/construction;
3 design management role;
4 execution/construction management role.

Each of these roles requires different skills, cultures and experience. Each role player can have different objectives. The role players also need the resources – experienced people – to carry out their roles. The project owner or sponsor that has these skills, cultures and resources will be able to carry out all of these functions in-house, thus reducing organizational problems. However, in many industries this is the exception rather than the rule. For example, in the building and construction industries, consultants, architects and construction contractors are traditionally employed by the project owner or client and, increasingly, specialist management contractors are used.

Two, three or more principal players share these roles, involving the contracting and/or combining of these management roles in several ways as in the following examples:

• dual management of a project, often involving a mirror image form of organization structure
• tripartite management of a project, as in the traditional building and construction industries
• management contracting:
  – construction management
  – design, manage and construct (design and build)
  – project management contracting.

DUAL MANAGEMENT OF PROJECTS

In several industries, such as computing, oil, chemical and defence, there are often only two principal companies sharing the management role, namely the client (owner) and the contractor. Although other companies may be involved, their roles are secondary to the two principal players.

Both the client and the contractor are likely to have their own project managers, so that there tends to be dual management of the project. In very large projects there could be several principal contractors, each of whom forms a dual management team with the client. This concept of dual management is thus extended to cover the client and each principal contractor as if there were multiple projects.

Dual management can take several forms:

- The client's project manager and team lead in the project management role, with the contractor taking a secondary role.
- A main contractor takes the prime management role, whilst the client takes the secondary role. In a very large project, the main contactor may project manage the other principal contractors – that is to say, the main contractor has a project management services contract.
- Both project managers manage their respective company's roles, and they form an implicit partnership. This partnership might be effective or stormy.
- A principal contractor's project management team is combined with the client's team in an explicit partnership. Both teams will manage the project jointly.

These organization structures are implicit in many industries, but are developed most clearly in the oil and associated industries. Here, project owner companies usually have many of the required skills but do not possess all the resources needed for the typically large projects handled. Thus these project organizations tend to involve the owner's project management team working closely with the management team of the contractor (or contractors).

Relationships can take any of the above forms and often there is a mirror image organization. For example, the owner can carry out the overall project management (the management contracting itself) and the owner's team can be supplemented or mirrored by the contractors involved. Alternatively, a contractor can be employed to carry out the overall management role, and the owner's project management team will mirror the contractor's organization.

Thus there is a mirror-image organizational structure in which the owner and the management contractor (or principal contractors involved) have almost duplicate organizations. Often, the owner's project structure will merely be a skeleton image of the contractor's structure. These projects are usually large and divisionalized, with different contractors involved in the divisions or sub-projects.

Overall accountability and responsibility (and thus active project management and integration) may be vested in one of the following:

- the owner's project team, in which case the owner is said to be doing his own management contracting
- a specialist management contractor
- a shared arrangement between the principal contractor and the owner's project manager(s). Project management in this case is thus a dual responsibility, and teamwork between the two project managers is essential. Similarly, each party's functional groups, or groups working together in an organizational unit, must work together as a team if performance is not to suffer. Each party will have both common and different objectives, but at least they will probably have common cultures.

There has been a move away from the full mirror-image form of supervising contractors in these industries, owing to the large amount of resources needed, the inefficient use of these resources, their cost and the adverse human reactions of having someone constantly looking over one's shoulder. This has resulted in other forms of this type of global organization having one of the following characteristics:

- a greatly reduced owner's supervisory team, down to a skeleton mirror image employing only a few supervisory people or even to the almost complete replacement of supervision by reliance on the contractor
- a merger of the owner's and contractor's staff into one team or partnership, with the work being shared on an individual contract
- a longer-term owner–contractor partnership. This might last for many years and cover several projects.

These later organizational forms are based on trust and teamwork between owner and contractor. They are simply bigger examples of the practice followed previously by many smaller companies, when successful experience with a contractor on one project led to a mutual willingness to negotiate new contracts. Projects are discussed in the pre-contract stage, with the contractor assisting the client in the project conception, definition and design before actually carrying out the work. This is an example of a process sometimes called simultaneous engineering or concurrent engineering. These arrangements can work well, to the advantage of both parties in the so-called win–win situation, provided that there is trust, mutual support, respect and open communication.

Successful partnership arrangements can provide the contractor with a long-term workload and less interference by the client's personnel. Staff requirements in both the client and contractor organizations are reduced. Time is saved over the project life cycle, and the owner has access to a resource pool of skills and know-how on which to call.

There is also a move away from the 'adversary' roles which can intrude into contract work. Much effort in the adversary case is spent in the design and legalistic interpretations of contracts, rather than in the advancement of actual project work. Integration and cooperation between the parties can produce better results than the legalistic interpretations of contracts, continual bickering and concentration of exploiting the contract for the benefit of one party or the other.

A word must be inserted here on an aspect of European legislation that can affect long-term partnerships. The European Public Procurement Directives cover projects and some service agreements offered for contract by organizations in the public sector over specified contract value limits. They require the project opportunities to be advertised in the *European Journal* so that the contract opportunities are transparent and open to tender by all potential contractors within the EU.

TRIPARTITE MANAGEMENT OF PROJECTS

In the building and civil engineering industries the project owner or client does not usually have the skills, culture and resources needed to carry out all the management roles. Larger public and private sector clients might have some of the skills but are still unlikely to have the necessary resources for large projects. Thus, in these projects, the conventional approach is to engage consultants, architects and quantity surveyors, and to use specialist project and construction management contractors.

Traditionally the management roles in such projects are shared between three parties, each of whom might have their own project manager (even if the title 'project manager' is not always used). These three parties are:

- the client or owner
- a consultant or an architect
- a construction contractor.

In this arrangement the client's representative or project manager often performs a weak role in the overall project. This generally involves the client's project manager being the contact for the project in the owner's company, for the purposes of obtaining decisions when needed, monitoring progress, keeping the owner's senior management informed on progress and snags, and authorizing payments of the contractors' invoices on receipt of release certificates from the consultant or architect.

The consultant's or architect's traditional role is to advise and assist the client in carrying out the project definition and contracting process, as well as with the management and execution of design, plus administration, supervision and quality control of the construction contracts. In the building industry, administration of the construction contract is normally shared with a quantity surveyor. The consultant or architect carries out the lead role in the project but, traditionally, this falls somewhat short of overall project management and integration. They are not usually accountable and responsible for all aspects of the project, including the construction phase.

Construction and building projects have become more complex, involving a large number of specialist skills or trade disciplines (such as mechanical plant, heating and ventilating, electrical, electronic, and computer installation). Several different specialist contractors are often needed, therefore, as well as those carrying out basic building or construction activities. In addition to technical reasons, the client might believe that better prices can be obtained by seeking out specialist contractors, or there might be a wish to support local firms. Whatever the reasons for this proliferation of contractors and subcontractors, they all need to be managed and their work must be integrated. Thus an overall construction management role is needed.

Contract procurement method

The traditional tripartite management of projects is less popular because of the following factors:

- There is no single-point accountability and responsibility for the whole project.
- Overall integration between client, design and construction contractor is weak or missing. In particular, there is more need for integration:
  - between designer and construction contractor;
  - of multiple construction contractors.
- There is an adversary bias associated with this form of organization.

If the consultant or architect carries out this management role in addition to their other conventional, professional duties, role conflict becomes a possibility unless they can differentiate them. In past projects there have been problems where the traditional role of the consultant or architect has been more attuned to the initial consultancy, design and construction administration roles rather than to project and construction management roles. There is a significant difference in the skills, cultures and experience between these two groups of roles, and it is difficult to combine them. If one organization carries out more than one of these roles, it must differentiate them internally. There is thus a preference for moving away from the tripartite management of these projects towards other contract procurement methods, such as construction management, design and build, and management contracting. These combine several management roles.

CONSTRUCTION MANAGEMENT CONTRACTING

As an alternative to using a principal contractor, there is a preference towards using management contractors to manage and integrate the construction or building contractors through one of the following arrangements:

- a construction management agent for the client, in which case the contracts are let directly by the client, and the construction management contractor acts as the client's agent
- a construction management contract, or management contractor, in which case the contractor lets the construction contracts directly after approval by the client. The management contractor may also have widely varying responsibility for integrating both design and construction.

These arrangements each lead to the necessary improvement in integration and management of multiple contractor construction.

DESIGN, MANAGE AND CONSTRUCT – DESIGN AND BUILD

In the design, manage and construct form of organization, one contractor is employed to design, manage and construct the project. As in construction management contracting, the contractor's role may take a variety of forms, including the following:

- as principal contractor, who carries out all design and construction, with only minor subcontracts
- as the client's agent, managing the consultants and contractors who carry out the actual design and construction work
- as management contractor who is responsible for, and manages, these consultants and contractors
- a combination of principal contractor for design or construction, and management contractor for the other functions.

These forms of organization thus also improve the integration of design and construction.

An example of a contract matrix for a design, manage and build contract

Figure 6.6 shows an example of a project organization (a contract matrix) for a construction project in which a project owner has entrusted a complete design, manage and construct role to a managing contractor. Here, the managing contractor employs home office staff capable of the main project design tasks. The principal project manager and project management team are also part of the managing contractor's home office staff.

Some of the advance funding for this project is provided by a bank, which requires a guarantor to secure all or most of the loan and protect the sunk costs (a kind of insurance policy for the bank). The guarantor and (especially) the bank will need expert advice whenever the main contractor submits claims for payment to the client. In these

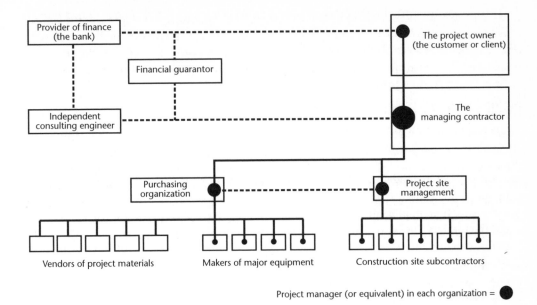

Figure 6.6   A contract matrix for a construction project of significant size

circumstances it is customary for an independent consulting engineer (often referred to simply as 'the engineer') to be appointed for this purpose. All premiums and fees are usually payable by the client.

The managing contractor has a purchasing department responsible for obtaining major equipments and bulk materials. The major equipments could include electrical installations, climate control equipment, security systems and the like for an office development. For a petrochemical or mining complex they would also include process plant items and heavy equipments such as cranes and locomotives. Major purchases are usually projects in their own right, so that each vendor would have its own project manager for their local design and execution tasks.

When work starts at the project site, a management team is established under the command of a site manager employed by the managing contractor. The site manager integrates the work of many subcontractors and is responsible to the managing contractor (and ultimately to the client) for all aspects of construction. On a large overseas petro-chemical or mining project, the site organization can be far bigger than that of the managing contractor's home office organization. The site organization for a very big project might have to provide an airstrip, roads, shops, school, banking, messing, hospital and many other facilities to sustain a large force of temporary workers in the first instance, and the client's operating staff and their families in the future.

Payment routes can vary, but each claim must be certified before the managing contractor can pass it to the client for payment. Certification must usually be independent, and the final arbiter here will be the engineer, whose expertise is especially important when certifying claims for 'soft' activities such as design tasks. A professional quantity surveyor will usually certify progress payments for site construction and the customary system of goods inwards inspections and receipts will trigger payments for purchases.

Not shown in the organigram in Figure 6.6 is the organization responsible for getting purchases to the project site. In international projects a freight forwarder, perhaps reporting on a day-by-day basis to the purchasing agent, would perform the coordinating role and either assist with or arrange shipping, transport and border documentation formalities.

PROJECT MANAGEMENT CONTRACTING

There is still a need for an overall project management and integration role with any of the above forms of organization, even with the design, management and construct form. All three principal parties (client, designer and constructor) need to be integrated in the management of the project as a whole. In addition, the client's pre-contract and post-contract responsibilities must be executed, managed and integrated with the other project stages. Thus the client still has responsibility for the following three management roles, either directly or through the client's consultants and project management contractors:

- pre-contract
- post-contract
- overall project management.

The client, as the project owner, is responsible for ensuring that the work and people of all the parties involved are managed and integrated. If lacking the necessary skills, experience and resources, the client can hire management contractors or consultants to carry out these roles in his name. However, their function is then not to advise or consult, but to perform an executive managerial role.

The project management role is critical in the pre-contract project stages. Too often, during the conception, definition and contracting stages, ineffective management of the project sets the stage for project failure, the responsibility for which lies solely with the client. If the client does need to appoint management contractors, this must be done as early as possible and certainly no later than towards the end of the concept stage. This need is, unfortunately, not always recognized until it becomes too late.

The client's role in the post-contract stage is also important and is often carried out by the other parties involved. This role thus needs to be managed, both in itself and as part of the overall project management. To achieve the best results the client must either carry out the overall project management role himself (if he employs suitable managers) or must employ a project management contractor to carry out the role, either alone or in conjunction with the client. This contractor must 'be on the side' of the client and be able to balance impartially the conflicting needs of all the parties involved in the project.

Part 2 Summary

Companies handling projects must either replace or augment the traditional functional company hierarchy with some form of project organization. All forms of project organization are a balance between the need for labour specialization and the need to integrate labour. Integration, with development of teamwork and management of conflict, is usually the prime function of the project manager.

The organization for a project of any significant size comprises individuals, groups, departments, companies, complete organizational units and an organizational super-structure or management hierarchy, tied together by a network of relationships. Designing a project organization involves the following:

1 dividing up the work
2 dividing up the people
3 determining the external relationships of the component parts to their parent organizations
4 determining the internal relationships
5 deciding how to group individuals
6 establishing integration methods
7 determining the degree of centralization and allocating authority.

A unique characteristic of project organization is that it has an internal structure (linking the component parts that work on the project) and an external structure (which links these component parts to their external parent organizations).

The internal structure for a small or medium-sized project often takes the form of a single mixed group or conventionally organized unit. The external structure is more complex and its basic forms can be one of the following:

- dedicated project team
- functional matrix
- balanced matrix
- project matrix
- contract matrix
- hybrid
- modular networks.

The dedicated project team is most effective for achieving the goals of a project but risks using resources and special skills inflexibly or inefficiently, especially when the company is handling several projects.

Matrix organizations retain functional departments intact, use resources more flexibly, and can integrate several, separate companies into one undertaking. The matrix can be set up with different 'strengths', with the functional matrix giving least power to the project manager and most to the functional managers. The balanced matrix attempts to balance power, whereas the project matrix gives the project manager the greatest degree of authority.

Whenever a functional or balanced matrix organization is chosen, the contractor–consignee principle should be implemented to reduce the risks of conflict and ambiguity associated with dual command.

Hybrid structures (in which some individuals are totally dedicated to the projects while others work in a matrix relationship with their external parents) can overcome the inefficient or inflexible use of resources normally associated with dedicated project teams.

The ultimate in organizational flexibility is seen in the modular network structure, where individuals can be 'plugged in and out' of the project as required and there is a network of relationships between them.

Larger project organizations are usually a mix of the basic forms, with each of several or many companies involved having its own external organization structure for its contributors to the project. A large project has to be organized with several organizational units, in the manner of a divisionally organized company. Each such organizational unit can be considered as a sub-project in its own right, taking any of the basic forms, complete with its own internal and external organization structures. The size of sub-projects, the span of control at each management level, the number of levels and degree of centralization or decentralization all strongly influence the amount of teamwork and conflict, individual motivation and overall performance.

Tall, centrally controlled organizations tend towards bureaucratic, arthritic organizations that reduce project performance but are good for integration. Flatter, decentralized organizations are often preferred and allow greater delegation of authority and accountability. These flatter organizations, of which the federal organization is the extreme case, give more flexibility and autonomy to organizational units.

The project organization must be contingent on all the above factors and a compromise might have to be adopted that is less than ideal for the project, but which takes account of other company needs. However, when projects are becoming more widely used and assume greater importance in the company's mission, this contingency approach should be applied with a conscious longer-term strategy of moving the organization structure to one that promotes higher project performance. In a dynamic, rapidly changing market this change has to be implemented quickly.

The chief executive or senior general managers have the responsibility for setting up the organization structure, and it is important that they specify it without ambiguity. The organization must emphasize the integration role of the project manager. There must be willingness to change the organization of a large project as it progresses through its life cycle.

In general, the organization structure should be kept as simple as possible and tall hierarchies should be avoided. The preferred trend is towards flat and flexible network structures, such as one, two or three level divisional or federal types having smaller organizational units and wider spans of control. Small is still beautiful (Schumaker, 1973). Provided that integration and control needs can be satisfied, 'small' can lead to higher motivation, teamwork and performance.

References and Further Reading for Part 2

Belbin, R.M. (1966), *Management Teams: Why They Succeed or Fail*, Oxford: Butterworth-Heinemann.

Graicunas, V.A. (1933), 'The Manager's Span of Control' in *The Bulletin of the International Management Institute*, March.

Huczynski, A and Buchanan, D. (2001), *Organizational Behaviour: An Introductory Text*, 4th edn, London: Financial Times/Prentice Hall. Don't be misled by the word 'introductory' in this title; this is a massive large-format paperback of over 900 pages.

Lawrence, P.R. and Lorsch, J.W. (1967), *Organization and Environment: Managing Differentiation and Integration*, Boston, MA: Addison-Wesley.

Moore, D. (2002), *Project Management: Designing Effective Organizational Structures in Construction*, Oxford: Blackwell. The discussion is this book is by no means restricted to construction projects.

Prigl, J. and Stoldt, S. (1990), 'Implementing Strategic Project Management at Mercedes-Benz AG, Car Division', *Managing by Projects*, 10th Internet World Congress.

Schumaker, E.G. (1973), *Small is Beautiful: Economics as if People Mattered*, London: Abacus, Sphere Books.

Thompson, J.D. (1967), *Organizations in Action*, New York: McGraw-Hill.

Wearne, S. (1993), *Principles of Engineering Organization*, 2nd edn, London: Thomas Telford.

PART 3

Planning and Scheduling

7 Introduction to Planning and Scheduling

Project management requires a logically structured sequence of processes. Structure is plainly the dominant feature when considering project organization. But nowhere is the structured approach more important than in the planning and control functions. Structure and logic should be keywords for any project manager. It is not by accident that critical path networks are also known as logic diagrams. Even in perfect conditions, with low risk, good management support and a clearly defined project, many variables must be solved along the path to effective planning and control. It is only through a systematic, structured approach that truly representative plans and budgets, the foundations for control, can be made.

Processes of planning and control

GENERAL REQUIREMENTS

The amount and quality of information available to project managers will vary according to the stage of the project life cycle but, in general, their role will be to create order out of uncertainty and chaos.

When a project is at its very beginning, information may be scant and unreliable. Among the project manager's first tasks will be to determine what the project is, to establish or crystallize its objectives, and to determine how the project is to be carried out (the project strategy). If contactors are to be employed, this will also include determining the contract strategy.

The work required to achieve the objectives will then have to be defined and quantified before the people needed to carry out the work can be assembled, both within and outside the parent organization. This might involve contracts being let to other companies, as well as expecting contributions from many different groups and departments of the parent company.

Responsibility for elements of the project work must be assigned and a project organization set up. These organizational elements will have to be coordinated, and relationships and communication links established – that is, all these people will have to be integrated. Particular care will be needed to achieve effective integration, coordination and communication if several companies are to be involved in the project.

Work will then have to be sequenced and scheduled so that it can be carried out in a logical and practical manner. The quantities and types of resource needed will have to be calculated, both as day-by-day forecasts and holistically over the complete time span of the project. Cost estimates must be made, and used to construct time-phased budgets, cash outflow schedules and (for higher management use) net cash flow schedules. All these estimates, plans and schedules must be treated as a single integrated entity, and must be related to the project organizational elements.

Many decisions will have to be taken and resources allocated to start up a project and carry it through successfully to fulfil its time, cost and technical objectives. The mechanism enabling the project manager to take these decisions, allocate resources and carry out the above actions is the project planning process. Planning should integrate the many diverse elements and companies involved. It must provide the communication links, so that all can be managed as one 'global' organization instead of several separate entities.

Every project has to be planned more or less uniquely, and effective project planning is critical to project success.

THE FRAGILITY OF PLANS

Rarely, if ever, does everything go to plan or budget. Just as in the military field, where a plan only lasts until the enemy is engaged, so, in the project field, deviations from plan and unexpected events can start to occur as soon as work begins. Productivity and performance will sometimes differ from planned assumptions. Errors and omissions in the original plan will become apparent. Many changes will be made before the project is finished, some possibly affecting even the scope of the project.

All this does not mean that the original plans were unnecessary or futile. Project plans are required not only for effective initial decisions and efficient resource allocations but also subsequently, throughout the life of the project, to enable the project manager to deal with changes in work and resource requirements as they happen.

Plans, therefore, are fragile and can easily be overtaken by unexpected events that render them inaccurate or actually misleading. If the plans are to be used as benchmarks for day-to-day control they must be kept up to date, so that they always reflect the true scope and condition of the project. To achieve this, the project manager must be able to determine quickly and with minimum effort how all parts of the project are progressing and how the people and organizations involved are performing. The manager then has to highlight problem areas and deviations from the plans and budgets, so that he or she knows when, where and how to take action to keep the project on track towards its objectives.

All this depends on the regular collection and analysis of progress and cost information to allow comparisons of actual progress and costs against the baselines of schedule, cost and resources established in the project plan. Schedule and cost variances identified in this process, whether these are fact or forecast, are an important factor for project control.

PROJECT PLANNING IN THE CONTEXT OF PROJECT CONTROL

Planning launches a project and is critical for project success but launch planning is, of course, the dominant factor of project management for only the early part of the typical project life cycle. Once the project starts, control becomes dominant. After the launch phase, planning and control merge for the remainder of the project life cycle into one integrated management function. Once a project is launched, control *is* project management. Without effective control the project manager has insufficient influence over the project. The project might eventually meander to completion, but it will inevitably take longer and cost more than it would have done with effective control.

Planning and control, therefore, are not separate functions. They interact with each other and are interdependent. Project planning and control could be termed as the 'management of cost, resources and time' but is often more simply called 'project control'. This control extends far beyond the planning and control of the project schedule. All the activities and organizational units involved are within its boundaries. Activities such as cost management, materials management, design information, quality, safety, and changes to the project are all included in the control process.

PROJECT PLANNING AND CONTROL IN THE CONTEXT OF PEOPLE

In addition to the technical or 'management science' aspects just described, there are many human relations aspects to project control. It interacts in many ways with the 'people side' of project management. Planning, if undertaken correctly, should always increase the involvement and participation of the key groups and managers contributing to a project. This is essential if their commitment to the project objectives and to the execution of the project plans is to be won.

Planning and control can help to overcome problems in establishing the project manager's authority and power, both with people in departments of the parent company and with people drawn from other companies involved. Commitments agreed to during the planning process effectively give power to the project manager to enforce them. Also, the project manager's central position in the project control information system, combined with the ability to make reports to senior management and the implied power to exercise control action, can enhance the project manager's power.

Planning can also help to develop cooperative working relationships and teamwork. It does this by making explicit the interrelationships and interdependencies of the people and groups involved, and the integration requirements. The planning process is an ideal 'team development problem-solving workshop', which is one of the most effective organizational development tools when building teamwork.

The control function influences motivation in several other ways. The traditional accounting view of control is that, without an effective system to monitor and measure performance, an organization and the people in it will inevitably become slack and inefficient. Therefore the time and cost to completion of a project will always be greater if there is no real objective measurement of performance and control. Thus it is assumed that the implied threat of control will motivate people to a higher level of performance.

This traditional view is only one of the motivational functions of control: there is another that can have a greater influence on performance. In project work, planning and control can be combined to become a strong motivator towards achieving higher performance. On the one hand, people are given personal targets or goals that they know must be achieved if they are to be seen as performing well whilst, on the other hand, they receive feedback from the control process on how they actually perform against those targets. Thus planning and control should be used to promote time- and cost-consciousness, so that everyone is motivated to achieve their personal targets within the framework of the overall project plan.

PROJECT CONTROL WHEN THE PROJECT ENDS

Project control even has a role to play at the end of the project life cycle, when all work is done and the results are history, and when control can have no further practical effect on the finished project. This role is in the post-project audit process, which some call the project post-mortem. Post-project audits have two important uses:

1 They can be used to resolve (if necessary, in the courts) the claims and counterclaims that can arise as the result of a project. Information available in the original plans and budgets, the control records relating to actual performance (particularly to changes made during the life of the project) can provide essential evidence both for the prosecution and for the defence. The absence of such information can be telling evidence in itself.
2 It is important to learn from the experience of past successes and failures. Too often, this experience is lost without a post-project audit and report to document the way in which the project was conducted and completed. The project planning and control records provide the basis for this.

Summary

Effective project planning and control are critical to project success and, in summary, provide a means for achieving the following tasks when used effectively:

1   Define and document the project's objectives.
2   Define and document the project strategy, including any intended contracting strategies.
3   Define the work that must be done to complete the project.
4   Organize the project by:
    • deciding who does what;
    • allocating and defining authority, accountability and responsibility.
5   Integrate the work and the people involved.
6   Establish channels of communication and coordination.
7   Establish a global organization, linking all the groups and companies involved in the project.
8   Set a logical sequence for carrying out the work efficiently.
9   Determine and allocate the resources required (for example, the manpower budget).
10   Determine and allocate the time-phased planned expenditure (budget of cash outflows).
11   Integrate costs, resources and schedule.
12   Following from (10), calculate the project's net cash flow forecasts.
13   Integrate the project management activities and systems.
14   Make the many initial decisions and resource allocations needed to launch the project.
15   Establish the baselines for project control.
16   Provide management information that enables the project manager to manage and be in control of the project (rather than simply act as an administrator).
17   Make the many decisions and resource reallocations needed throughout the life of the project.
18   Increase involvement, participation and commitment.
19   Enhance the power of the project manager.
20   Develop cooperative working relationships and teamwork.
21   Motivate people to achieve higher performance, through goal setting, measurement and feedback.

22 Create a sense of urgency and cost-consciousness.
23 Provide information to support:
   • a post-project audit;
   • resolution of legal disputes or arbitration issues.
24 Above all, improve work efficiency and achieve the project time, cost and technical objectives.

8 The Structured Approach to Planning and Control

The principal methodology for achieving integration is 'structuring', both of the project and of the organization. This structuring not only provides the framework for integration but also helps in the organization of the project, design of management systems, planning and control, and in managing people. All projects of any significant size depend largely on structuring. In project work this can involve structuring both the project organization and the project itself, and the merging of these two structures to provide a framework for integration.

Structuring of a project and its organization are not innovations. Organizations have always been structured to varying extents, and so has planning and control. The planning process has generally involved an instinctive, ad hoc structuring of a project, requiring the division of the larger project into smaller elements for planning. The evolution of project planning software packages since the late 1960s has encouraged some form of structured planning, even if only into sub-projects and phases.

For many years planners have also used sorted reports, often on an ad hoc basis, to produce plans for individual organizational element or specific resource categories. This is a first step towards planning that respects the organizational structure. Accounting systems have also structured the project, and sometimes its organization, using a code of accounts as the basis for the financial control.

Nevertheless, this structuring has tended to be ad hoc, unsystematic, and not applied to total integration. Yet there is a vital need for a formal, systematic method for structuring any project and for facilitating this integration. Structuring is both central and critical to the effective management of the project.

The functions of structuring

Structuring is required in the following areas:

- organization of the project
- design of the project management systems
- management of people.

STRUCTURING IN THE ORGANIZATION OF THE PROJECT

Structuring carries out two steps in the design of an individual project organization, as follows:

1 It defines how the work involved in the project is broken down into divisions and subdivisions that are of a suitable size for allocating to the individuals, groups, functional departments, organizational units and companies involved.
2 As the second step, structuring defines how the people involved (principally managers, professional people and technical staff) are grouped together at the lower, middle and higher levels. Some of these people might come from several external organizations and companies.

The merging or intersection of these two structures thus identifies or defines the following:

- the work required to complete the project and its component parts, as well as how these component parts fit together to make up the overall project
- the workload of all the contributing organizational elements, both at the level of the basic working group and for every larger organizational element up to the total company or companies.

Structuring thus helps to ensure that all the work needed to complete the project is identified, defined and integrated, and that no work or cost is missed out. The two structures and their intersection also identify the responsibilities of all the managers concerned (both project and functional), the organizational elements and the companies involved in the project. This clarifies and communicates to all participants (including clients and contractors) the accountability and responsibility of all the participating managers, organizations and companies.

In addition, this structuring provides a means of disaggregating the project's objectives, both for the main elements of the project itself and for the organizational elements. It thus identifies the individual objectives for everyone involved. The structure and its substructures not only communicate the authority and responsibility of the managers involved, but also provide a common basis, language and dictionary for information consolidation and communication. They establish a common language to describe the project, its component parts, and the organizational entities involved, which forms a basis for communication.

STRUCTURING AND THE DESIGN OF THE PROJECT MANAGEMENT SYSTEMS

The project structures provide the basis for coding each work assignment in both the project and organizational structures. Coding uniquely identifies all the work involved and how it is integrated. For example, the coding system will identify the work involved in major or minor elements of the project, and the groups, departments and companies responsible for this work. Conversely, it will also identify all the project elements with which each group, department or company is involved.

The coding system also gives a basis for designing and integrating the project's managing systems. All the systems can be related to each work element, work assignment and higher level of consolidation of work and assignments. Consider, for example, the planning and control systems. Each group work assignment in a project subdivision must be planned if it is to be carried out and controlled effectively. This planning includes work scheduling, manpower or resource planning and cost budgeting; in other words, an integrated set of three plans. These plans must be consolidated or integrated into higher level sets of plans for the following:

1 the total project, and each division and subdivision of the project (that is, a hierarchy of plans)
2 plans for the total commitment of each basic group on each subdivision of the project, and for each department, division and company involved
3 in the case of a multi-project matrix, where these groups, departments and companies are working on several projects simultaneously using common resource pools, the plans for these organizational entities and their commitments on all the projects.

The project structure and coding system identifies what plans are required and provides the basis for their integration in both the project and organizational dimensions.

Project structuring also identifies what has to be controlled and is a basis for the design of the project management information and reporting system. It identifies the basic group work assignments for which information must be collected, analysed and reported. It further identifies the elements of the project and the managers of those elements for which information must be consolidated, analysed and reported in order to ensure effective management of the project. Again, the coding system is used for this consolidation. In a similar manner, all the other project systems, such as work definition, estimating, materials, quality, drawings and other documentation will use the structures and their coding to give a common framework for integration.

STRUCTURING AND THE MANAGEMENT OF PEOPLE

The project structures identify work assignments for groups, departments, organizational units and companies, which can be established as pseudo- or real contracts to enable use of the contractor/consignee principle. The managers of each of these organizational entities can have their own 'contracts'. Everyone involved has his or her individual accountability and responsibility defined.

Project structuring and the establishment of these pseudo-contracts contribute greatly to the motivation of those involved. All managers and organizational elements have their own unique goals, objectives, and plan baselines of schedule, resources and costs, the setting of which they have contributed to or participated in. Everyone thus knows that their performance is being monitored and that, if it is unsatisfactory, it will be brought to the attention of senior management, to the possible detriment of their careers.

A far more positive and effective motivational influence is the fact that people have participated in setting their own goals. They know what is expected of them for high performance and they get feedback on their success or otherwise in meeting their individual targets. In addition, clear-cut peer performance comparisons can be made and this further motivates management and group performance. Systematic and effective structuring enables individual achievement to become a reality for every manager and group, and so contributes to higher project performance. However structuring, because it defines interrelationships and group identities, can also be used to encourage teamwork.

SUMMARY

Structuring the project and its organization in an integrated and systematic manner has the following functions:

1 It is an aid to the organization of the project because it:
   • carries out the basic steps of creating a project organization
   • identifies the work to be done
   • identifies the responsibilities for this work
   • disaggregates the project's objectives and
   • facilitates communication.
2 It is the basis for designing the project management systems because:
   • it provides a framework for total integration;
   • the structure and its related coding system integrate:
     – the work to be done
     – the project organization and
     – the project management systems;
   • it establishes the hierarchy or plans and control reports in two dimensions (the project and its organization) and provides the foundation blocks of these systems, which is to say that:
     – the intersection of the project structure and the organization structure identifies these basic foundation blocks for planning and control at the level of the work of one organizational element on one subdivision of the project;
     – thereafter the project and the organization structures identify the hierarchy: the levels of planning, control and reporting for the project and for its organizational elements.
3 It is an aid to managing the people in the project:
   • The project manager, and every manager of an organizational element or group, have their own unique objectives and planned baselines for schedule, costs and resources.
   • They have participated in setting the goals and baseline plans.
   • They know precisely what they have to do to achieve good performance and they get directly related feedback in control information and reports.
   • They also get benchmarking feedback on the performance of their colleagues.
   • Thus structuring facilitates the motivation of project people and groups and can be used to encourage teamwork.

All this enables even the largest and most complex projects to be planned and controlled effectively and can contribute to higher project performance in many ways. Thus structuring should be applied to all projects from the earliest possible stages of their life cycles.

Work breakdown structure (WBS)

The term 'work breakdown structure' is a name for an end-item-oriented family-tree-like subdivision of the project, products, deliverables, or items to be built, work tasks and services required to complete the project. It defines the project, the work to be done and can display them on a chart. It is very similar to a bill of materials used in production planning for a manufacturing project. Essentially, it is a methodology for project organization, planning and control based on 'deliverables' rather than simply on individual tasks or activities.

Large projects can be daunting challenges for any project manager but, without some form of WBS, they are impossible to design, organize, manage and build. All but the very tiniest project must be broken down logically into parts that are manageable. How this breakdown is to be achieved is not always obvious.

TASK LISTS

An important part of any WBS is to list all the tasks that comprise the project workload (both hardware and software tasks). Task lists are necessary, for example, if a full cost estimate is to be made. Omission of significant tasks from the list can lead to inadequate budgets and underpriced project proposals. In the context of planning and control, tasks forgotten at the beginning of a project will certainly make themselves felt when their absence is discovered later on.

A task list can be regarded as a two-level WBS. The project is at level 1, and all the tasks are fitted into level 2. This degree of breakdown will be totally inadequate for most projects but can be a starting point for producing a multi-layered WBS.

Methods for assembling task lists depend on many factors, not least of which is the personal preference of the project manager. Some people like to start by writing down a summary of all the tasks that can be foreseen, and rearrange them later under various parts of a formal WBS. Others will start from the WBS and enter the tasks into a prestructured format. Another method is to identify all the tasks by drawing a critical path network for the project, in as much detail as possible, with key managers present to contribute to the process (possibly involving brainstorming). Checklists embodying the experience of previous projects are invaluable and can help to prevent serious omissions. The preferred sequence of compilation is not important as long as it results in all the significant tasks being identified and arranged in a logical, hierarchical WBS before actual work on the project starts.

A suggested format for a task list, as it might be needed early in the project life cycle, is shown in Figure 8.1. Each task is given an identifying code for subsequent use in project management software for processing a critical path network. These ID codes are not usually the same as the codes used in the hierarchical WBS, although some planners endowed with greater than average intelligence and competent software do manage to attain that ideal.

Task ID code	Task name or description	Estimated cost €	Estimated duration (days)	ID codes of immediate predecessors

Figure 8.1   Format for a simple project task list

Task lists can be an appropriate place for listing cost estimates, at least for provisional purposes. This saves work and space by combining the task list and initial cost estimate into a single document.

An estimate of each task's duration can either be included in the initial task list or it can be added later, having been considered during construction of the network diagram. The time units used must always be stated.

The final column is optional. Its purpose is to show the ID codes of tasks that must immediately precede each task if the work sequence is to be practical, achievable and logical. It can be a precursor to the construction of a logical network diagram. Tutors have been known to criticize their students for not including this information when they compile task lists for their coursework assignments, but that is an approach that owes more to academia than to the real world. Experienced project managers prefer to determine the task sequence later, when the critical path network is drawn. To list all the predecessor tasks for a large project when the list is first compiled, with no network diagram, would be an impossible mental feat. The list of predecessors is, however, of great use when reported by the computer after it has processed the project network diagram because it facilitates checking to ensure that the data have been entered correctly, with no link or task omitted.

WORK BREAKDOWNS BASED ON THE PHYSICAL COMPOSITION OF A PROJECT

A very common form of WBS is the 'family tree' or 'goes into chart', used by manufacturing engineers and product designers for many years. In this form, the WBS has a fairly obvious and logical pattern suggested by the physical nature of the final product.

A single manufactured product can usually be considered as a mix of components and raw materials that, during various stages of production, are transformed into minor sub-assemblies, larger sub-assemblies and, last, the final project assembly. A prototype automobile, for instance, might have a WBS as illustrated in Figure 8.2. This will suggest how the project might be organized into design groups, and will have a great influence on manufacturing sequences when the time comes to build the prototype.

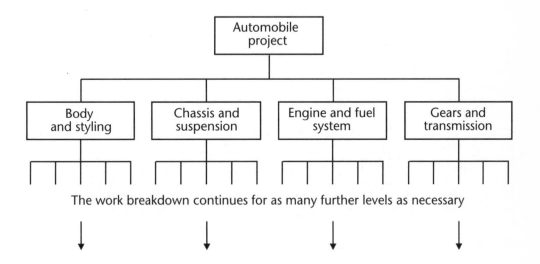

Figure 8.2   Outline work breakdown structure for an automobile project

The breakdown should be hierarchically coded, so that each component and every task can be referred to by a unique identifier that can be used not only during manufacture, but also for planning, work control and costing (coding is described later in this chapter). If the automobile should subsequently go into production in any quantities, then the same WBS will become the framework not only for manufacture, but also for parts listing and the provision of spares.

In the case of a typical engineering project, the WBS is seen to have a clear and essential role, and it will be based principally on the physical structure of the finished project.

WORK BREAKDOWN BASED ON NON-PHYSICAL CHARACTERISTICS

In recent years it has become recognized that the project management approach can be applied to many ventures that, at one time, would not have been considered as projects. The relocation of a company, a corporate organizational change, the launch of a new brand name, the staging of a spectacular public event, a national fund-raising drive by a charity are all undertakings that can be treated and managed as projects. If the project is of significant size it will need a WBS so that the project can be divided into parts that can be allocated for action and organization. However, without physical project characteristics, the form of the WBS might not be so obvious as in the case of an engineering project.

Suppose that a society wedding is to be planned and executed as a project. Hundreds of guests are to be invited from inland and overseas, large crowds are expected to gaze upon the celebrities, and much planning and organization will be needed if the ceremony and subsequent reception and entertainments are to end happily and safely. Various options suggest themselves for the work breakdown pattern, some of which are shown in Figure 8.3. Note that only parts of the work breakdowns can be shown on a small page so that each option would extend in practice to include more work packages than those illustrated here.

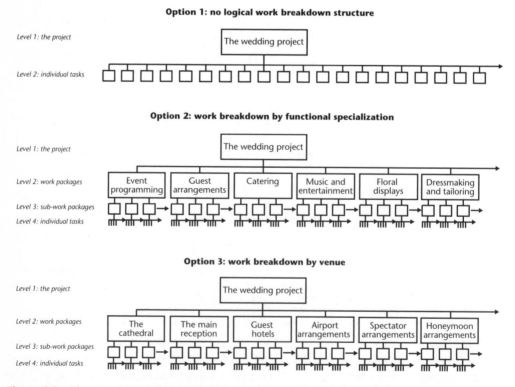

Figure 8.3   Three work breakdown structure options for a large wedding project

In Figure 8.3, option 1 is hardly a WBS at all, but is a simple task list. Level 1, the top level, is the entire project, whilst level 2 of this breakdown contains all the identified tasks with no further attempt at a hierarchical breakdown structure. Very small projects can be conducted adequately with just such a task list, but this wedding is not a small project. Many managers and organizations must take part and be integrated. So, except possibly as a first step in planning, option 1 can be discounted and a work breakdown must be found that will be of more practical use in managing this project.

At option 2, the project manager has decided to allocate all the tasks across a WBS that is defined principally according to specialist functions. The diagram shows some of the resulting work packages at level 2. Taking 'floral displays' as an example, this work package would contain all tasks having anything to do with floral displays, wherever they will be needed. At level 3, the breakdown might then have a sub-work package for every location, with one for the cathedral flowers, another for the reception, another for flower displays along the procession route, and so on. Level 4 contains all the day-to-day tasks needed to complete each sub-work package. Arranging the WBS in this way immediately suggests a corresponding organizational breakdown, with either a manager or a contracting organization in charge of each work package, and with supervisors or other managers being made responsible for the sub-work packages and the allocation of tasks within them.

Option 2, therefore, is a case where giving thought and time to compiling a logical work breakdown assists greatly in the allocation of responsibilities, organization, and subsequent planning and control of the project.

For many projects, especially in those without a physical product as the end result, the project manager might have some difficulty in deciding how to structure the work breakdown because more than one logical pattern can be foreseen. This is the case in the wedding project, and another work breakdown possibility is shown in Figure 8.3 as option 3. Here the project manager has decided to divide the main project into level 2 work packages that group the various tasks according to their geographical location. Taking the floral displays again as an example, we find that there is now no main work package for the flowers as at option 2. Instead, there will be several level 3 sub-work packages for the flowers, with one for the cathedral, another for the main reception, and more at several other locations.

Using option 3 instead of option 2 will cause considerable differences in the way in which the project is organized and in how the tasks and people are integrated into the whole project. In the case of option 3, a manager would probably be appointed to look after each location, so that one person would be in sole charge of all the cathedral arrangements, another manager looking after the main reception, and so on.

Thus the choice of WBS can have a profound effect on project strategy, organization, planning and control. In the wedding example, option 2 offers possible economies of scale because it groups the various trades and disciplines conveniently. This would allow, for example, a single florist contractor to be appointed to supply all the floral displays, wherever they might be needed. Option 3, on the other hand, suggests advantages in logical planning and day-to-day control, with the project moving from one manager to another as it proceeds through all the events on the wedding day. The one certain point that emerges from this discussion is that some form of logical breakdown is essential, with option 1 being no option at all.

MORE EXAMPLES OF WORK BREAKDOWN STRUCTURES

Figure 8.4 shows part of a WBS for a fairly large construction project. The scope of this project is so large that there are many levels to the work breakdown, only seven of which have been shown in the limited space at our disposal. The construction industry has long been a successful user and developer of project management methods, and construction projects generally lend themselves to obvious and logical WBS. The project is at the top of the pyramid, at level 1, but had this been part of a programme of projects, the whole programme would be level 1 and all the individual projects in the programme would be placed at level 2.

We shall develop the argument for rational WBSs using a simple project, which we have called project X. The network diagram for this project is shown in outline in Figure 8.5. Critical path network analysis is explained in the following chapter but, for breakdown purposes, this simple example can be regarded as a work flow chart that progresses from left

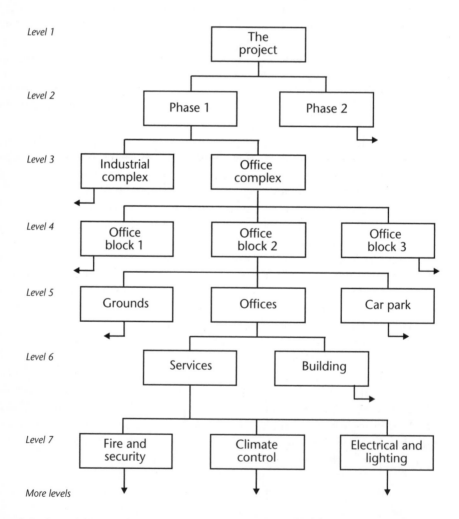

Figure 8.4   Part of the work breakdown structure for a construction project

to right. The WBS for this project is shown in Figure 8.6 where, for clarity, only a few of the work breakdown elements are shown. The project is at level 1, major elements are at level 2, and each element breaks down further into level 3 sub-elements packages and then (not shown) into a fourth level of individual tasks. Further levels may be needed for some small components.

In a larger project, much of level 2 can be occupied by non-physical elements that are commercial or other non-physical elements of the project that are not part of the project's tangible 'deliverables'. However, project X is hardly a big project and all the major work packages can be contained in level 2 in this instance. Thus, for project X, the project manager has identified six major work packages for level 2. Taking just one of these as an example, the electrical sub-assembly breaks down into three smaller elements at level 3 – namely electrical

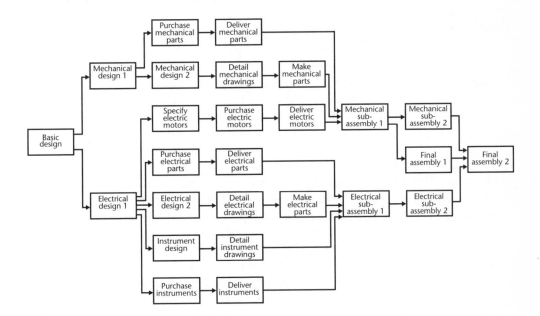

Figure 8.5   Outline network diagram for project X

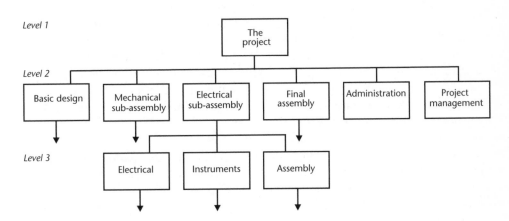

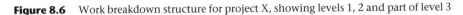

Figure 8.6   Work breakdown structure for project X, showing levels 1, 2 and part of level 3

tasks, instrumentation tasks and assembly tasks. There might be lower levels in the work breakdown for small components.

GENERAL GUIDELINES FOR COMPILING A WORK BREAKDOWN STRUCTURE

The general guidelines for applying the WBS are as follows:

1 Each WBS element or work package at level 2 is a subdivision of the project for which management believes it to be worth integrating management, planning and control. It is thus a discrete part of the project, with its own definable deliverables and for which it is of benefit to have plans, control information and analysis that integrate all the contributors. This allows progress and performance in terms of cost, resources and schedule to be measured.

2 The project is further broken down through several levels of division until the lowest level considered necessary is obtained. Each lowest-level WBS element can then be divided into meaningful work assignments for individual groups or people and each assignment can be planned and controlled as a separate entity.

3 There is no need to break down each level 2 element to the same number of lower levels. Breakdown in each case should only be taken to a level that serves some useful purpose. However, the lowest level in each case is divided into a series of work assignments, as described in (2) above.

4 Each higher level WBS element is similarly an identifiable part of the project that must be planned and controlled as an integrated whole. This involves consolidating the planning and control of lower-level 'children' elements into their 'parent' higher-level elements.

5 In breaking down the project in a hierarchical manner, each level of the WBS is a logical and desirable level of planning. Each element in these levels is justified in having its set of integrated plans. Similarly, each level in the structure is a level at which the managers of the project desire to have control information collected and analysed, and each element in these levels is justified in having its own performance analysis and reports.

6 In practice the project should not be divided and subdivided over and over again to create a large number of levels simply for the sake of structuring. Each level of breakdown should be significant, logical and necessary for the management, planning and control of the project. Each level provides for the integrated management, planning and control of smaller and smaller parts of the project, and there are limits to how far this breakdown is useful to the management of the project. Each level provides information on an integrated part of the project, possibly to different people on different levels of the management hierarchy, and this information should be considered necessary for the effective management of the project. Each additional level of breakdown considerably increases the amount of information collection and reporting required and reduces the size of the work assignments to functional groups.

7 Four to six levels are usually adequate for most projects.

8 In the simple example of project X two levels of breakdown would be sufficient, and there would only be a further breakdown to a level 3, as shown in Figure 8.6, if this served some useful purpose. This could occur on a large project, where each element at level 3 was of such a significant size or importance that the project management believed it necessary or desirable to have integrated planning and control for these lower level project elements.

9 On large projects involving separate contractors for major project elements, and/or divisional or organizational unit type organizations, there may be two sets or tiers of WBSs – one for the project as a whole and one or more for the individual contracts (contract breakdown structure), divisions or organizational units.

10 Integrative work which is common to more than one WBS element at any one level of breakdown is shown as a separate WBS element. Similarly, this applies to any item which it is pointless to try to allocate accurately, for instance with a crane whose use is spread among several WBS elements. In the case of project X (Figure 8.6), basic design and final assembly are common integrative elements to the two sub-assemblies and are thus shown as separate WBS elements at level 2. However, integrative work which is unique to one element is included within that element. For example the assembly of the electrical sub-assembly is included with that level 2 element.

11 All cost-generating items should be included in the structure, either within the individual elements (where this can be identified and sensibly allocated) or as separate WBS elements. In project X, project management and administration are included as separate WBS level 2 elements, each with its own budget.

The two-dimensional approach to project structuring

The classic two-dimensional method of project structuring involves the following components:

* work breakdown structure (WBS)
* organization breakdown structure (OBS)
* cost accounts
* work packages/activities
* a coding system based on the above
* cost breakdown structure (CBS)
* a WBS dictionary that defines the elements and cost accounts.

The first of these components, the WBS, has already been described. This chapter will continue with descriptions of the remaining components.

ORGANIZATION BREAKDOWN STRUCTURE (OBS)

The OBS of a project is concerned with its internal organization and not the relationships of the organization elements with their parent organizations, matrix or otherwise. It is the 'internal' organization chart of the project and is constructed in a similar way to the WBS.

In the OBS, level 1 represents the total organization of the project as one element. Level 2 then represents the first division, or breakdown of the project into its main organizational elements. This process is repeated until the lowest-level OBS elements are identified. These lowest levels are usually the basic working groups, disciplines or (on small projects) even individuals who are carrying out the work. These groups may be mixed, but are more often single functional groups.

The work of these lowest-level organizational elements can then be divided into meaningful work assignments on individual lowest-level WBS elements, each of which can be planned and controlled as a separate entity.

The same general rules for structuring the WBS apply to the structuring of the OBS. However, the number of levels used depends on the size of the project, its organization and the number of people involved. For example, in a multiple company project, the level 2 elements would represent the individual companies involved. Figure 8.7 shows how the various levels of breakdown might change for different project sizes.

Level	Smaller organization	Medium organization	Larger organization	Multi-project organization
1	Total organization	Total organization	Total organization	Multi-project organization
2	Departments	Divisions	Companies	Individual project organization
3	Groups	Departments	Divisions	Companies
4		Groups	Departments	Divisions
5			Groups	Departments
6				Groups

Figure 8.7   Levels of organization breakdown

In the project X example, level 1 is the overall projects organization (or company) and the level 2 elements are the main departments or discipline involved in carrying out the work, namely:

- design
- procurement
- works.

This level of breakdown might be sufficient for some small projects. However, in a larger project, or if any of the functional groups have resource limitations or work on other projects at the same time, then it will be necessary to have a further level of breakdown to the individual functional groups, as shown in Figure 8.8. This enables the work of these groups to be integrated, planned and controlled, with progress and performance reports produced for each group, department and the organization as a whole.

The lower-level OBS elements will thus be the functional groups carrying out the work. The integrative plans produced for these elements, and the information, analysis and reporting, will represent the integration of all the work carried out by each group on all of the lowest level of WBS elements in which it is involved. Similarly, the integrative plans and control information for each higher-level OBS element will consolidate the lower-level OBS elements for which it is responsible and which it manages. All the managers in this hierarchy has their own set of plans and control reports for all their areas of responsibility. The OBS thus represents one axis or dimension of the project control and information system for the

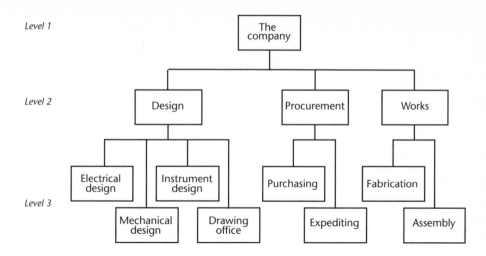

Figure 8.8   Three-level OBS for project X

functional managers concerned in the project. In the same way, the WBS represents the other dimension of these systems for the project management structure of the matrix.

COST ACCOUNTS

The WBS breaks the project down until its lowest elements are identified, and they in turn are divided into work assignments for individual groups.

The OBS breaks the organization of the project down until the individual function or other groups are identified.

The contribution of each of these groups to the project is then made up of work assignments on the individual lowest-level WBS elements. Thus the work assignments of individual groups on the lowest-level WBS elements are common to both the work and organization breakdown structures and are the foundation blocks of both structures.

Thus if the WBS of the project is viewed conceptually as being the vertical axis and the OBS as being the horizontal axis, the integration of the WBS and OBS identifies the work assignments and organizational responsibilities for groups on the lowest-level WBS elements, as shown in Figure 8.9. Terminology varies from one country to another and with time but, especially in US government projects, each work assignment is termed a 'cost account'. This term is not universally used or accepted and often other names are used for this intersection of the WBS and OBS. One of the commonest is 'work package'. Although this does provide the gist of the meaning better than cost account, formal US government systems use work package to define something akin to a project activity or task, as used in planning techniques.

In practice, the term 'work package' is commonly used very loosely to describe any self-contained 'package of work', and it is often applied to the work involved in a WBS or OBS element. The actual name used is immaterial. The important point is that what is referred to is a complete and discrete project task or work assignment of a single organizational entity on a single WBS element. It is of manageable size, relatively independent of other work assignments (at least internally) and is the responsibility of one manager who can be called a cost account manager.

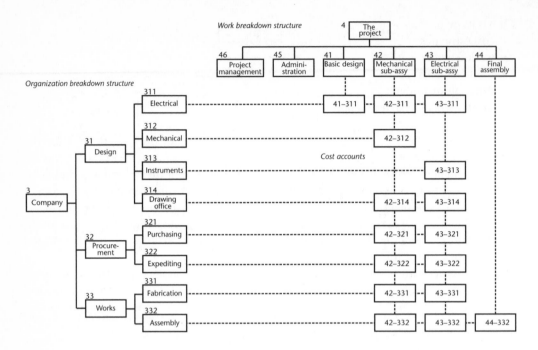

Figure 8.9   Cost accounts: the WBS and OBS come together and are coded (project X)

The WBS, the OBS and the cost accounts together establish the common framework of the project management systems. This integrates the work to be performed, the organization structure and individual responsibility for work at all levels with the subsystems for planning, control, work definition, estimating, change control, resources, expenditure, quality, materials, information analysis and reporting. The cost account is a natural and logical management centre on which to integrate all these factors. The assignment of work on these lowest-level WBS elements to individual group managers provides a key automatic integration point for these systems and for the management, organization, planning and control of the project.

The work involved in each cost account has to be specified, planned, resourced and budgeted, and these sets of plans are the foundation blocks, or lowest level, of complete plans in the hierarchical, two-dimensional planning and control system. This permits distributed (but integrated) planning and control of the project. Each of these plans will include one or more work packages or activities, describing how the cost account manager intends to carry out the work on the cost account. These in turn have resources and budgets assigned to them, and they may have simple variance analysis carried out on them as work progresses. However, the cost account is the principal centre where information is collected and analysed, where performance is measured and from which reports are produced. These, then, are the basic foundation blocks of the total project information and reporting systems for progress and performance.

Each cost account has the following characteristics:

1 A single person is responsible for it.
2 There is a single specification of the work involved.

3 It has its own:
- cost estimates
- work schedule
- resource plans
- expenditure budget.

4 It has its own analysis and reports.

Just as these factors are defined for the project as a whole, so they are defined for the individual cost accounts. The work, resources and expenditure required to complete a lowest-level WBS element are identified by the sum of its cost account in the vertical axis. Similarly, all the work, resources and expenditure of one functional group are identified by the sum of its cost accounts in the horizontal axis. In turn, each of these factors is defined for each of the 'parent' higher-level work and organizational elements at all levels by the sum of their lower-level 'children' elements. Thus each WBS and OBS element has all of the above-listed characteristics, just as for an individual cost account.

Each cost account is therefore a 'plug-in module' or mini-project in both the planning and control functions. Each is common to all the structures used. These structures consolidate and integrate these modules in different ways to produce higher level plans and control reports. Each of the project work and organizational elements, and each individual costs account is identified as the accountability and responsibility of one manager. Thus accountability and responsibility are clearly defined, as are the work to be done, the objectives and performance requirements in terms of schedule, resources and cost. Thus planning and control is personalized.

WORK PACKAGES ACTIVITIES

Each discrete activity, task, job or material item is, in most cases, represented by the activity or task customarily used in planning (as described in the following chapter). It typically has a start and finish, an end product of some form, is of relatively short duration, and is the responsibility of a single organizational entity. It will also have estimated cost and resource requirements. Cost accounts are typically made up of several activities, and the resource and cost budgets of each cost account are the sum of those in its activities.

THE CODING SYSTEM

The key to integration through structuring of the project, its organization and the project management systems is the use of a systematic and 'significant' coding system. Although it is useful to describe the cost account as the integration of the vertical WBS and the horizontal OBS, this gives only a diagrammatic or conceptual picture of the structures. In practical use, it is the coding system that is used to structure the project, identify the cost accounts, WBS and OBS elements and establish their relationships.

Although a code of accounts has long been used by accountants, in a structured approach to project management the project coding system is used for all the project systems to identify and integrate everything. Thus the organization, the work definition, the planning and control of work, resources and money, the project accounts, the estimating, the materials, the reporting, the change control and so on will all use the same coding system as a common framework to represent the structures used and to aid integration. All data and information input and output will use this coding system. In many organizations this may cause problems because there will almost certainly be an established accounting system that would be difficult to change, for either practical or political reasons. Ideally, the project coding system and the accounting coding system should be the same. If they are not, and the accounting system cannot be changed, then it is essential that there should be a transformation or 'translation' process that changes data and information held in the accounting codes into the project codes. Fortunately, easy-to-use, widely available database software packages can usually make this translation relatively simple.

A logical coding system is central to a structured approach to integration and is a vital component of project management information systems. Coding involves using a multidigit or alphanumeric assembly of characters, in which each character or grouping of characters has a particular meaning or significance. Each code uniquely identifies a cost account, WBS or OBS level and element, and their parent–child relationships in both the WBS and OBS dimensions (and in other structures, if required). Each level of structure is represented by a part of the code. One code, or part of the code, represents the WBS. Another represents the OBS. The combination of these identifies cost accounts common to both structures. This can be demonstrated using our simple project X example. Figure 8.9 is the diagrammatic representation.

Coding the work breakdown structure
Refer to the top group in Figure 8.9 (p. 114), which shows the coded WBS for project X.

1 *Level 1 WBS code*
The project itself can be represented by the first part of the WBS code. One or more characters can be used, bearing in mind that if a company has several projects to include in the total database, then a sufficient number of character fields must be reserved. This must allow not only for current projects, but also for projects expected over the reasonable life of the whole system, and that includes archived data for completed projects. Project X is coded 4 for simplicity. In practice a longer code would probably be needed. At least one company, for instance, runs its project codes in a sequence that starts with the last two numbers of the project start year and continues with a two- or three-digit number in a series that is refreshed each year. If project X happened to be the fourth project authorized in 2007, for instance, it might conveniently be coded 07-004.

2 *Level 2 WBS code*
The next character or group of characters identify level 2 WBS elements. Bear in mind, of course, that if numeric codes are used, a single digit will limit the number of elements to nine, two digits 99, and so on. There was a time, in the early days of data processing, when numeric codes were preferred because they used less scarce memory and processor time. Alphanumeric codes have greater capacity, so that a single character can accommodate up to 35 WBS elements. Another consideration when designing a coding system is that mixed numeric and alphabetic characters can be easier to use, with less chance of transcription or keying errors. However, project X is simple and needs only a single numeric field for its level 2 WBS codes. The code for the level 2 elements, complete with the project prefix 4, are as follows:

41 Basic design
42 Mechanical sub-assembly
43 Electrical sub-assembly
44 Final assembly
45 General administration
46 Project management.

All plans, budgets, costs, reports, estimates, materials and so on for these WBS elements are identified by this coding. For example, every data item for project X containing the WBS code 43 must pertain to, or be used on, the electrical sub-assembly.

Designers of coding systems often reserve 9, or 99, or 999 (according to the number of characters used in the field) for non-classifiable items.

3 *Level 3 WBS code*
When the WBS is extended to a further level, an additional character or characters will be needed. We have not shown this third level in Figure 8.9 to retain clarity but, as an example, the level 3 codes making up the level 2 electrical sub-assembly for project X would be as follows:

431 Electrical
432 Instrumentation
433 Assembly.

Coding the organization breakdown structure
The organization structure is coded in similar fashion to the WBS coding, as follows:

1 *Level 1 OBS code*
The company or overall organization may or may not be given a code. In project X the company is coded as '3'.

2 *Level 2 OBS code*
The next one or two digits represent the organizational elements (which might be company departments). In many cases these will actually be called department codes. Figure 8.9 shows that, for project X, the following level 2 OBS codes have been allocated:

31 Design department
32 Procurement or materials management department
33 Works or factory.

3 *Level 3 OBS code*
The next field in the OBS code represents the level 3 OBS elements, or the groups. Taking the design department for the company handling project 'X' as an example, the following codes have been allocated to represent the various design groups:

311 Electrical design group
312 Mechanical design group
313 Instrument design group
314 Drawing office.

Thus each character in the OBS code is significant and identifies an element of the project organization. The codes also denote the 'parent–child' relationships. For example, all groups with an OBS code having the same second field character or characters will belong to the same department. In project X we know that every OBS code where the second digit is '1' refers to the design department.

Cost account coding

When the WBS and OBS codes are combined, each cost account is uniquely identified and its relationships and position in both the WBS and OBS structures are established. For example, in project X the cost account code 43-311 provides the following information:

1 It identifies the cost account to be the electrical design of the electrical sub-assembly.
2 The first two digits, 43, identify this cost account as being part of the work needed to complete WBS element 43, the electrical sub-assembly. All other cost accounts beginning with 43 also belong to this WBS element.
3 The OBS code 311 identifies this cost account as the work and responsibility of OBS element 311 (the electric design group).

Thus each cost account code uniquely identifies the work, the major project element of which it is a part, and who is responsible for it.

Activity coding

Generally if an activity identification number (ID code) is used in planning, then it is also used in this coding system. If project X has an activity 912, for example, it would be coded 43-311-912 in the overall system, and all other activities belonging to the lowest-level WBS element would be identified in this manner.

COST BREAKDOWN STRUCTURE (CBS)

The CBS follows a hierarchical structure of elements in the same way as the WBS and the OBS. This can be demonstrated using a construction project, as shown in Figure 8.10.

Level 1 is the total cost of the project. Level 2 contains the major cost breakdown elements, or primary code of accounts which, for this example, comprise:

- bulk material
- equipment
- direct labour
- indirect labour
- subcontracts
- other costs.

Level 3 is the further breakdown of these primary cost elements into their secondary code of accounts. For clarity only one level 2 element, equipment, is shown broken down in Figure 8.10. This demonstrates that level 3 components or secondary code of accounts for equipment are as follows:

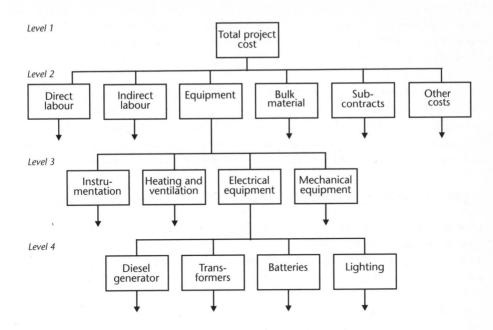

Figure 8.10   Part of the cost breakdown structure for a construction project

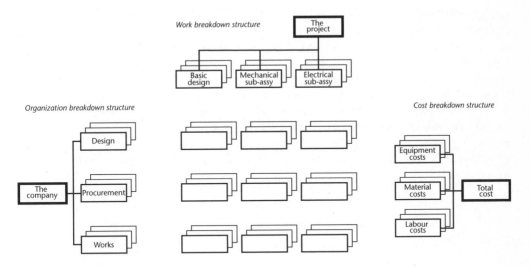

Figure 8.11   The three-dimensional WBS–OBS–CBS structure (for project X)

- electrical equipment
- instrumentation
- heating and ventilation
- mechanical equipment.

Level 4 is the further breakdown into the tertiary code of accounts. Again, for clarity, only one level 3 element has broken down in Figure 8.10. This is the electrical equipment, the level 4 components of which are:

- diesel generator
- transformers
- batteries
- lighting.

The CBS enables costs to be collected, analysed and reported for any cost-generating item and consolidated in a similar manner to the other structures. The allocation of codes is similar to the arrangements for the OBS and the WBS. It would identify, for example, the equipment cost for a cost account, for a WBS element or for the total project. This concept is illustrated in outline in Figure 8.11, which depicts the three-dimensional structure for project X.

WBS DICTIONARY AND CATALOGUE OF COST, RESOURCES AND TIME

In conjunction with the WBS/OBS structuring and coding, a dictionary that defines the elements and cost accounts should be compiled and issued. This ensures that everyone involved in the project understands the meaning and content of each of these elements. The dictionary can be extended to include the scope of work, and the cost, resources and time requirements. This dictionary could form part of the comprehensive project manual that is commonly produced by companies whenever they set up the systems for large new projects. This systematizes and consolidates work that must always be done at some stage in the planning of a project because, for each project activity, the estimated time, resources required and estimated cost must be identified. This is simply the necessary project planning and control database.

The sum of the cost and resources of all the work packages or activities belonging to a particular cost account must equate to the cost and resources assigned in total to that cost account. This is sometimes termed the 'rolling up' of costs and resources. In turn, the sum of the costs and resources of all the cost accounts belonging to each lowest-level WBS or OBS element must roll up to the total cost and resource requirement for that element. This rolling up has to be repeated through both the WBS and OBS structures until the cost and resources for the whole project are obtained. This process ensures that all costs and resources are identified at the lowest levels, yet can be reliably and systematically consolidated or rolled up into the larger project and organization elements.

9 Structured Project Planning – With the Dimension of Time Included

So far, three dimensions have been identified in the project structure (symbolized in the WBS, OBS and CBS). There is another, very special and important dimension that happens also to be a precious resource. That dimension is time. This chapter extends the discussion about project planning structures to include time.

Introduction to planning with critical path networks

Project planning in the first half of the last century was invariably done with the now very familiar bar charts, either set out on paper or constructed on wall-mounted boards. Today there is a widespread fashion for calling these bar charts 'Gantt charts', after their progenitor, the American industrial engineer Henry Gantt (1861–1919). Bar charts are visually effective and easy to interpret without special training so they remain (deservedly) popular. Anyone who can construct an office holiday chart should be able to draw a project bar chart. The principle is illustrated in Figure 9.1 (a). Many managers and supervisors still prefer bar charts to the more sophisticated network diagrams for day-to-day use and, even when the root planning has been carried out with critical path network analysis, modern project management software is used to convert networks to bar charts for use at the workplace or project site.

However, bar charts have their deficiencies, notably their inability to show the interdependencies between different tasks clearly. From the 1950s onwards, various critical path network methods emerged from European and American sources and today we must assume that any competent project manager (and most readers) will have at least some working knowledge of one or more of these techniques. However, for those completely new to the subject, we start this chapter with a brief account of the critical path method.

TWO DIFFERENT FAMILIES OF CRITICAL PATH NETWORKS

Because critical path network concepts were developed from several separate sources in America, the UK and continental Europe, different strains emerged. All of these share a few basic characteristics, as follows:

- Unlike bar charts, network diagrams do not need to be drawn to a timescale.
- All network diagram methods show activities or tasks graphically in their logical sequence.

(a) Bar chart or Gantt chart

Activity description	Date						
Activity 1	▬						
Activity 2	▬▬						
Activity 3		▬▬					
Activity 4			▬▬				
Activity 5					▬▬		
Activity 6						▬▬▬	

(b) Activity-on-arrow network diagram

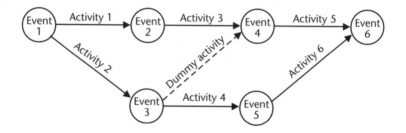

(c) Activity-on-node nework diagram

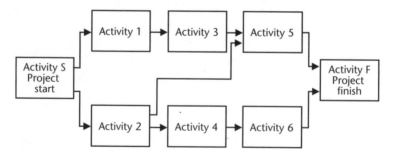

Figure 9.1   Three planning chart methods

- All action flows from left to right through the network diagram.
- The diagrams display clearly how tasks are interdependent upon each other, especially with respect to their starts and finishes.
- The earliest possible completion time for the project can be calculated.
- The earliest possible starting and finishing times for each activity can be calculated.
- The latest permissible starting and finishing times for each activity can be calculated, which means the latest times permissible if the project is to be completed at its earliest possible time.

- Activity priorities can be quantified, which is important when allocating scarce shared resources or focusing management attention.

Each method has its own strengths and weaknesses but all critical path network techniques fall into one of two families, which can be labelled as activity-on-arrow and activity-on-node. Reference to Figure 9.1 will make this distinction clear.

Activity-on-arrow networks

Figure 9.1(b) shows a small activity-on-arrow network diagram that contains all the notation needed to draw a large project network diagram using the arrow method. Activity-on-arrow networks are often called simply 'arrow diagrams', sometimes abbreviated to ADM.

Each circle represents an event in project work and time. It has no duration in itself but occupies only an instant in time. An event usually marks the start or finish of an activity or group of activities. It might be the start or finish of the project. Events act as nodes that link activities.

Each arrow represents a project activity or task (the terms 'activity' and 'task' are usually synonymous). Arrow length has no significance but arrows must always be drawn in the left-to-right direction. No activity can start until the event at the tail of its arrow has happened. The description for each activity and its estimated duration are written along the relevant arrow.

ID codes can be allocated to events and these will also provide ID codes for the linking activities. Thus, in Figure 9.1(b) the arrow that is described as activity 4, because it links events 3 and 5, would have the ID code 3-5.

The dotted arrow 3-4 is a dummy activity. This has no work content but is used solely as a linking constraint. In this case it means that activity 4-6 cannot begin until both activities 2-4 and 1-3 have been finished.

ID codes for arrow networks were essential for computer processing. Once, almost all networks were arrow diagrams but nowadays project management software is based on activity-on-node networks and there is no easily available program that can still accept arrow networks. This does not mean that arrow network diagrams are extinct. They are particularly useful during brainstorming or group planning sessions at the beginning of a project because they are far easier to sketch freehand than other methods.

The allocation of time estimates and subsequent time analysis calculations are generally similar for all types of network. However, arrow networks must be converted to activity-on-node format for computer processing. Therefore all our following examples are given as activity-on-node diagrams but, for those who are interested, there is a wealth of literature describing arrow networks: see, for example, Lock (2003) or Lockyer and Gordon (1996).

Activity-on-node networks

Figure 9.1(c) shows a small activity-on-node network diagram, drawn in the most common format of a precedence diagram (often abbreviated to PDM). This is the same plan as that shown in Figure 9.1(b).

Each box in a precedence diagram represents a project activity or task. The project action flows from left to right through the diagram, with the arrows denoting interdependencies between the various activities. Thus activity 5 cannot begin until both activities 2 and 3 have been completed.

The links in precedence networks do not denote any activity and, in that sense, they are similar to the dummy activities used in arrow networks. They usually have zero time and run from the finish of one activity to the start of the next. This is the default condition assumed by most computer software, but other less common, more complex links are possible in precedence networks. These are described in Chapter 11.

Precedence networks do not customarily show events but, if desired, activity boxes can be inserted to act as events, in which case the estimated duration for each of those activities will usually be zero. It is always good practice to ensure that every network begins and ends at a single node. This, in some cases, might mean creating zero duration activities labelled 'project start' or 'project finish' as appropriate. Such start and finish activities are effectively project events or 'milestones'. Conversely, it is bad practice to have more than one start and finish node, because this will complicate subsequent time analysis. Also, computer software will report all start and finish nodes and more than one of each should indicate errors or omissions in the input data – that is, a failure to insert a network link that leaves one activity with no successor (an apparent finish node called an end dangle) and the other with no preceding activity (a start dangle).

Although the ID code for the start activity could be simply 'START', it is best practice to give the start activity the lowest possible value ID code (such as A001). Similarly, the finish activity should have the highest value ID code (such as Z999). This practice will help to ensure that the start and finish activities appear first and last when the data are sorted by the computer for reports.

Figure 9.2 shows an activity box in greater detail. Although this is the preferred way to show an activity for a precedence network, screen space limitations and less-than-perfect plotting capabilities mean that most computer programs must omit some of the data shown here when they plot and print a project network.

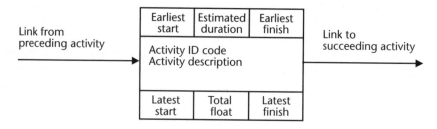

Figure 9.2   Representation of an activity in precedence notation

A precedence network example

The simple network for project X shown in Figure 9.3 (p. 126) can be used to illustrate critical path analysis using the precedence diagram method. An outline version of this network appeared as Figure 8.5 (p. 109), but activity time estimates have now been added, allowing time analysis to be carried out.

NETWORK LOGIC

The pattern and sequence of activities, with their links, must be drawn to represent the work process considered most efficient and practical by the project manager or planning group. All network planning is most effective when the initial logic and time estimates are produced at a group meeting, where senior project participants (managers and functional specialists) can suggest work patterns and help with time estimates. When these key people are asked to take part in setting up the project plan, the resulting plan is more likely to be practicable and achievable. Later, when the work is actually done, those who have contributed to the plan should feel committed to it and can be held accountable for performance.

All significant work activities should be on the network, but this does not mean including every possible small work step. Each activity should be a discrete piece of work or time-consuming process within the responsibility of one manager. A useful rule is always to split activities up so that the network links include all occasions when managerial responsibility shifts from one person to another. Such break points in the plan will be found invaluable later when it comes to assessing and controlling progress. The network must include all significant purchases, but a single activity can often be used to group all the purchases needed to perform a task (such as a mechanical sub-assembly). Any expected delays, such as waiting for clients to approve drawings or waiting for materials to be delivered, must be included as network activities even if no actual work or cost is involved: elapsed time is the important factor.

A well-conducted planning session, perhaps run on brainstorming lines, allows all those present to arrive at the most logical and practicable work sequence or process, with no tasks forgotten and nothing seriously out of place or unnecessarily repeated. Critical path networks provide the notation that allows the planner to express the intentions clearly on paper. Even without duration estimates and time analysis, following the work pattern embodied in a good network diagram can contribute significantly to efficient working and save project time and money.

ESTIMATING ACTIVITY DURATIONS

An estimate must be made for the duration of each activity in the network. Any time units can be used but, once chosen, it is best to use the same units throughout the network. Some software can accept mixed units (such as hours and days) but the resulting reports are very messy.

The default calendars in most computer software will assume that Monday to Friday (the weekdays of the Western world) are working days with no work possible on Saturday or Sunday. This means that an activity estimated to take five days should take one calendar week, unless it is allocated to a specially created calendar. The use of special calendars is discussed in Chapter 10 but many project plans need only the default calendar, provided that it has been modified to remove non-working dates such as public holidays.

Each duration estimate should be the best judgement of the total time expected to elapse between starting the activity and its completion.

If the activity is one on which several people could work together, its duration will naturally depend on how many people can be allocated when the time comes to do the work. An apparent planning problem arises if the planner has to be concerned with how many people will actually be available when the time comes to do the work, bearing in mind that other activities across the organization might need the same resources at the same time. Project planning and scheduling is, however, a logical process that can be conducted in a series of relatively simple steps. The solution here is to ignore, for the moment, the demands of other activities and make each duration estimate based on the optimum number of people

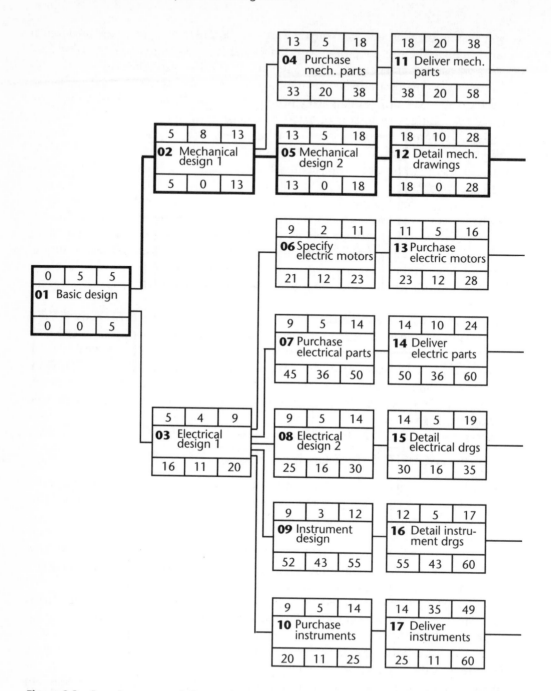

Figure 9.3   Precedence network diagram for project X

for the job – provided always, of course, that the organization actually employs that number of people in total. The allocation of people (or any other resources) to the plan is a separate process called resource scheduling, which the computer can carry out after time analysis and the determination of job priorities (as defined by their float or slack). Resource scheduling is discussed in more detail in Chapter 10.

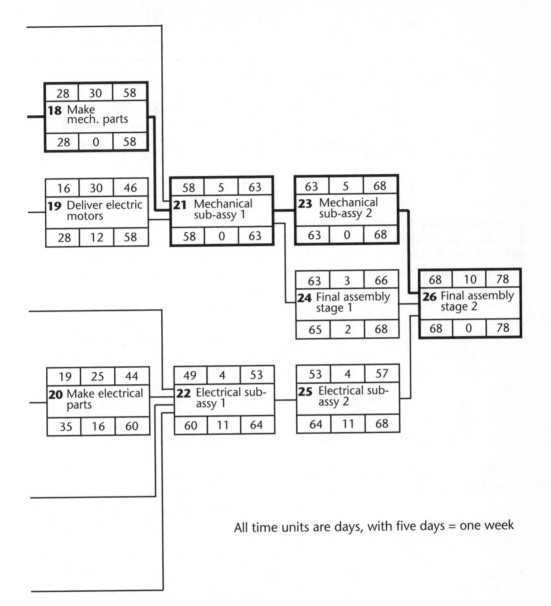

All time units are days, with five days = one week

TIME ANALYSIS

Time analysis is the process of using the estimated times for all network activities in calculations to determine the start and finish times of individual activities, and the expected duration of the whole project. These calculations have the valuable additional feature of assigning activity priorities in a quantitative fashion. The task will usually be carried out by a computer, but many people like to carry out a preliminary time analysis mentally as soon as the network has been drawn, just to check that the total project duration is within the desired completion time. If the indicated time is not acceptable, then the network logic must be reviewed to try to shorten the overall duration. Time can sometimes be saved by changing the intended work pattern or by planning for increased resources. Chapter 11 deals with some of these time-saving measures.

When time analysis is first carried out manually, the results emerge as numbers of days or weeks rather than calendar dates. This is for two reasons:

1 Time analysis is an arithmetical process that is far easier to carry out mentally using simple numbers instead of calendar dates. The computer will eventually convert the numbers into dates, based on the default or other specified calendar.
2 When the plan is first made, the starting date for the project might be uncertain or simply not known.

Calculating the earliest possible times

The earliest possible start and finish times for all activities can be found by adding the activity duration estimates from left to right through the network, along every path, until the final activity is reached. This is known as the forward pass. The earliest possible start time for any activity is the sum of the duration estimates along the path of its preceding activities. If there is more than one such path, the longest path must be the decider.

This process is demonstrated in Figure 9.3, using the numbers entered along the tops of the activity boxes. Look, for instance, at activity 21 (mechanical sub-assembly 1). This has an estimated duration of 5 days, which is written in the central space. The earliest possible start for this activity is day 58, determined by the path through activities 01, 02, 05, 12 and 18.

The figure in the top right-hand section of each activity box is the activity's earliest possible finish date, calculated, of course, from the activity's earliest possible start date and its estimated duration. Thus the earliest possible finish date for activity 21 is day 63.

The earliest possible finish date for the whole project is seen at the end of activity 26. This is 78 days, which conversion to calendar dates will show to be just under 16 weeks.

Calculating the latest permissible times

Consider activity 26 in Figure 9.3. This is the concluding activity for project X, and its earliest completion time is also the earliest possible completion time for the project. The question must now be asked, 'What is the latest permissible finish time for this project?'. Usually, project completion is wanted as soon as possible, so here the latest permissible finish time for activity 26 is day 78. This result is written in the bottom right-hand section of the activity box.

Once the latest permissible finish time for an activity is known, its latest permissible starting time can be found simply by subtracting its estimated duration from the finish time. In the case of activity 26 this is 78 minus 10, and the resulting latest permissible start time is written in the bottom left-hand corner of the activity box.

In the same way as earliest possible times were found by a forward pass through the network, so all the latest permissible times can be found by a backward pass, working from right to left through all the possible paths. The start of activity 25, for instance, can be delayed until day 64 without affecting completion time for the project. The latest permissible finish for any activity is the latest permissible start time of the succeeding activity minus the activity duration. Where an activity has more than one immediate successor, its latest permissible completion time is the earliest of the latest permissible successor start times.

Float, or slack

Float is the amount of time by which an activity can be delayed without delaying the whole project. Slack, nowadays, is just another term meaning the same as float. Notice that all the activities along one path in Figure 9.3 (shown in bold) have the same earliest possible and latest permissible dates. This means that every activity along this path is critical to the earliest possible completion of the project and a delay in any activity would result in a corresponding delay to the project finish. None of the activities on this 'critical path' has any float or slack because none may be delayed if the project is to finish on time.

Critical activities demand priority for management attention when controlling progress or allocating scarce resources. Computer-based resource scheduling programs will assign resources first to those activities with least float and may, if required to work within total resource limits, delay the starts of activities that possess float to obtain smooth resource loading.

Float is usually a shared commodity along any path through a network. There are several categories of float but only two are commonly used.

Total float is the amount by which an activity may be delayed without affecting the start times of any following activities, provided that its preceding activities have finished at their earliest possible times. Thus total float is defined as follows:

> Total float = the latest permissible completion time for the activity
> *minus*   the earliest possible start time
> *minus*   the estimated activity duration.

Negative total float will result if the planner or project manager attempts to impose a target date on the project (or any activity in the network) that is earlier than the earliest possible date determined by the forward pass.

Free float is the amount by which an activity may be delayed without affecting the start times of any following activities even when the activity's preceding activities have been delayed to their latest permissible times. Free float is comparatively rare. It cannot be a negative quantity. Calculation differs slightly between arrow and precedence networks. For a precedence network the free float of any activity can be defined as follows:

> Free float = earliest possible start time for the next activity in the path
> *minus*   earliest possible start time for the subject activity
> *minus*   estimated duration of the subject activity.

Time analysis tabulation

Most project management computer software comes with a range of standard reports that should include a time analysis table. The Gantt chart view in Microsoft Project, for instance, has a basic table at the left-hand side of the screen that can be expanded and customized by inserting columns to produce a full time analysis table, along with many other items of data, such as costs.

The time analysis tabulation for project X, given in day numbers rather than calendar dates, is shown in Figure 9.4.

Activity ID	Activity description	Estimated duration (days)	Earliest start	Latest start	Earliest finish	Latest finish	Free float	Total float
01	Basic design	5	0	0	5	5	0	0
02	Mechanical design, stage 1	8	5	5	13	13	0	0
03	Electrical design, stage 1	4	5	16	9	20	0	11
04	Purchase mechanical parts	5	13	33	18	38	0	20
05	Mechanical design, stage 2	5	13	13	18	18	0	0
06	Specify electric motors	2	9	21	11	23	0	12
07	Purchase electrical parts	5	9	45	14	50	0	36
08	Electrical design, stage 2	5	9	25	14	30	0	16
09	Instrument design	3	9	52	12	55	0	43
10	Purchase instruments	5	9	20	14	25	0	11
11	Deliver mechanical parts	20	18	38	38	58	20	20
12	Detail mechanical drawings	10	18	18	28	28	0	0
13	Purchase electric motors	5	11	23	16	28	0	12
14	Deliver electrical parts	10	14	50	24	60	25	36
15	Detail electrical drawings	5	14	30	19	35	0	16
16	Detail instrument drawings	5	12	55	17	60	32	43
17	Deliver instruments	35	14	25	49	60	0	11
18	Make mechanical parts	30	28	28	58	58	0	0
19	Deliver electric motors	30	16	28	46	58	12	12
20	Make electrical parts	25	19	35	44	60	5	16
21	Mechanical sub-assembly, stage 1	5	58	58	63	63	0	0
22	Electrical sub-assembly, stage 1	4	49	60	53	64	0	11
23	Mechanical sub-assembly, stage 2	5	63	63	68	68	0	0
24	Final assembly, stage 1	3	63	65	66	68	2	2
25	Electrical sub-assembly, stage 2	4	53	64	57	68	11	11
26	Final assembly, stage 2	10	68	68	78	78	0	0

Figure 9.4   Time analysis tabulation for project X

Hierarchical, multi-level planning

Planning and control of projects using the structural approach is hierarchical, multi-level, rolling wave, increasingly two-dimensional and distributed, but integrated. This is a tongue-twisting description of how project planning should logically be carried out.

A large project may need thousands, or even tens of thousands of activities to be listed and scheduled if it is to be controlled effectively. At one time this could result in project plans covering the walls of a large room. There is even a story of an early American project network diagram that was drawn in chalk on the floor of an aircraft hangar, and photographed by a camera mounted on a roof gantry. Very large network diagrams or bar charts are unwieldy, prone to errors, and difficult to keep up to date to accommodate changes. Although networks containing over 1000 activities have often been used successfully, large networks do not suit today's project management software and hardware technology, where we are dependent on computers to display them on small screens or print them with software that can never produce the compactness possible by a person drawing with pencil and paper.

One problem with attempting a large, all-encompassing plan is that different people in the project organization need different levels of detail. Senior managers need a coarse level of detail or summary plan. Firstline supervisors require more day-to-day detail. Those at middle management level need an intermediate amount of detail. Simple single-level plans can be fine for small or medium-sized projects, but larger projects require hierarchical, multi-level planning to overcome the problems of dimensionality and detail. Modern project management software provides several possible solutions to these problems. Two different basic approaches can be taken:

1 Draw one large network for the project and code the activities and/or resources with a view to filtering and sorting data so that each manager gets his or her report content on a specific 'need to know' basis.
2 Draw a hierarchy of the networks, each purpose-drawn for the level of detail needed.

Both these methods will now be described, but they are not mutually exclusive and best results can be obtained by combining both approaches.

CODES FOR FILTERING AND SORTING

The use of codes will depend on the capabilities of the software being used but most systems allow the allocation of departmental codes to activities, by which activities can be filtered so that each departmental manager gets work schedules and other reports containing only activities for which he or she is directly responsible.

Activities can be designated as milestones. A milestone is any significant activity or event in a project that marks a stage of progress or achievement. Computers can produce schedules and progress reports containing only milestones, and these make good summary reports for higher management.

If resource scheduling is included in the planning process, each type of resource must be given a code. Such codes are useful not only for the actual data processing but they can be used after resource scheduling to produce schedules, loading forecasts and progress reports that pertain only to a specified resource type. Thus, the computer can filter and sort not only by department but also by the different group resource skills.

There are systems (including later versions of Microsoft Project) that allow WBS codes to be entered in a separate field, which gives obvious advantages for sorting all output reports.

Specific filter codes are available in some systems that correspond loosely to OBS levels, sometimes in a simple series of 1 to 9. These codes allow reports to be filtered for different management levels.

There are, also, codes that define security levels, so that unauthorized people cannot access certain levels of data or change (and possibly corrupt) the system parameters.

Some software can be customized (provided someone with adequate software skills is available) to allow sorting on part of the activity description field. If such a facility exists and is to be exploited, great care must then be given to how activity descriptions are written. This adds the dimension of sorting by product code or part number.

HIERARCHICAL NETWORK FAMILIES

Figure 9.5 shows how several networks can be drawn at different levels, the number of levels used depending on preference and the size of project. Four levels are sometimes used, as follows:

- Level 1 – a summary plan
- Level 2 – a series of intermediate level plans
- Level 3 – detailed plans
- Level 4 – short-term detailed work plans.

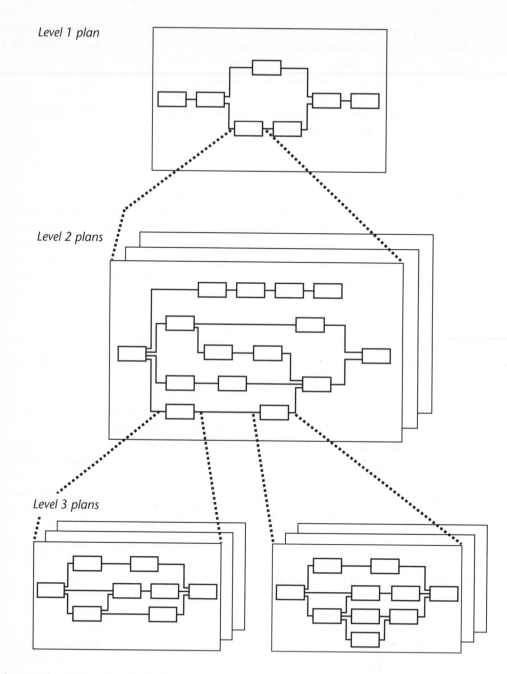

Figure 9.5   A hierarchy of critical path networks

These levels of plans are used formally and systematically to expand the project into its component activities, usually based on the WBS. Each single activity or group of activities in a higher-level plan is expanded into a greater number of more detailed activities in the lower-level plan. The different levels of plans are linked together using interface activities or milestones.

All modern project management software of any repute can convert network diagrams into bar charts, which means that a hierarchy of bar charts can also be produced, corresponding exactly to the pattern of network breakdown chosen. This could be represented graphically by substituting bar chart equivalents of the networks in Figure 9.5. Bar charts are preferred to network diagrams by those untrained in critical path network techniques. However, for control purposes there is nothing better than tabular schedules, derived from the networks, in which the computer has filtered activities to suit each manager and sorted their sequence to assist in allocating jobs to people and following up progress. Such tables, especially after the computer has carried out resource scheduling, are often aptly known as 'work-to' lists.

The question now arises, 'Who should produce all these different plans?'. This is a matter for delegation and careful coordination. The project manager should certainly be directly involved at level 1, but will probably have to delegate responsibility for planning at the lower levels to various departmental and group managers, some of whom might be employed in external companies. The computer model can easily be corrupted with so many people contributing to the plan and entering data, and a project support office is an invaluable facility for integrating all this planning and maintaining the integrity of the overall schedule. The role of the project support office is discussed in Chapter 19.

Level 1 plan

A level 1 plan is a summary plan which outlines the project in skeleton form. It is used throughout the project as a top management reporting and review document, but it is usually the only plan possible in the early project evolution or conception stages. A level 1 plan is thus also the initial project plan, lacking in detail and with all its activities being large increments of work, such as high-level WBS elements or cost accounts.

A level 1 plan, therefore, shows only highly consolidated activities and project milestones. It is a broad-scale plan embracing design, procurement, manufacturing and/or construction, and commissioning. It contains the first approximate estimates of the timing for each of the stages, rough estimates of the resources required and the costs. It allows certain key points in the schedule and important interrelationships to be estimated approximately. It should highlight those parts of the project that deserve to be emphasized.

At this level, the plan gives the first indications of requirements for material and equipment dates. In the initial stages it acts as a strategic planning tool to establish the project strategies and objectives. It can quickly be constructed and modified to show different ways of carrying out the project, yet allows key points to be located and relationships to be determined.

Using appropriate software, a level 1 plan can be used as input to a wider multi-project computer model in 'what-if?' calculations to test the effect of the proposed new project on overall resource usage and possible risk to the timings of other projects that are already in progress.

Nevertheless, a level 1 plan will be very coarsely detailed and timescaled. It might comprise only 15 or 20 activities for an average project. Even on a North Sea oil project costing more than a billion pounds, the level 1 plan contained only 70 activities. On most projects, therefore, a level 1 plan is clearly unsuitable for the complete integration and management of all the project stages and must be expanded into at least a level 2 plan or series of plans.

Level 2 plans

A level 2 plan can show the broad sweep of activities with all milestones included. It collects under one description sizeable elements of the project involving several or many detailed activities. It permits detailed examination of the project's structure and allows relationships between the various parts of the project to be seen and studied. It defines the limits between which individual activities, or groups of activities, can move without affecting the project completion time. There may be a separate level 2 plan to elaborate every activity in the level 1 plan.

Thus each level 2 plan expands one or two activities from the level 1 plan, allowing far more detail to be considered. Each level 2 plan is a middle management decision-making and control tool. It identifies responsibilities in the project and organizational structures. The relatively large amount of data included means that formalized, computer-based planning techniques should be used if the results are to be as accurate as possible, reportable and flexible to change. But on all except small projects, the size of the activities in level 2 plans will be too great to allow day-to-day (or even week-to-week) scheduling and control of work, so that further breakdown into level 3 plans is necessary.

Level 3 plans

Level 3 plans are made in sufficiently fine detail to determine and allocate the work to be done. They are likely to be structured in several ways, particularly on the basis of specialist disciplines involved. Level 3 plans thus tend to be modular plans, with each plan or module covering an element of the project or the work of a particular group. Often this is the lowest level of integrated planning and scheduling needed for the complete project.

Level 4 plans

The day-to-day, week-to-week work of individual people and small groups must be planned and controlled within the overall framework of the higher levels of planning. But, whereas the higher level planning must, to a large extent, be supervised centrally (perhaps by a project support office), planning at the workface is usually the task of individual group managers and supervisors. The higher-level plans will establish the critical path, schedule resources globally and produce work-to lists that should lie within the resource capacities of the various groups and departments. When level 4 is reached (it might be level 3 in smaller projects) planning is removed from the computer model and entrusted to the methods more appropriate to and preferred by the lower-level managers and supervisors. This leaves these managers and supervisors with a degree of discretion, because it is they who best know the individual capabilities of their staff and can allocate tasks accordingly.

Level 4 plans can be made with simple bar charts. Job cards can be used to define each small task if required. Standardization with other systems is less important at this level, and managers can be allowed to use their own preferred methods, provided that these are adequate for subsequent progress monitoring and reporting back to the higher levels. In manufacturing projects for example, an activity in a higher-level plan might cover a small sub-assembly, leaving the local group manager responsible for design to break the activity down into its constituent drawings and components and allocate the tasks. When the time comes to manufacture the individual parts and assemble them, production engineers and production controllers take over planning for the actual manufacture and assembly, outside (but within time limits given by) the project planning hierarchy.

ROLLING WAVE PLANNING

Rolling wave planning is a commonsense approach to the planning of projects that have very long durations. The concept is illustrated in Figure 9.6, which also indicates graphically how the method acquired its name. The dilemma of a planner faced with producing plans for a project that is expected to last for several years is that, whilst the activities and small tasks expected to take place during the first few months might be clearly envisaged and drawn in a critical path network diagram, it is not always possible at the start of the project to forecast work in such depth of detail further ahead. Yet, if a critical path is to be calculated in any plan, all the paths through the network must be specified from the beginning of a project to its end. Often the information needed to plan the later stages of the project in detail is generated as the project proceeds through its earlier stages. In such projects the rolling wave concept can be applied to overcome this difficulty.

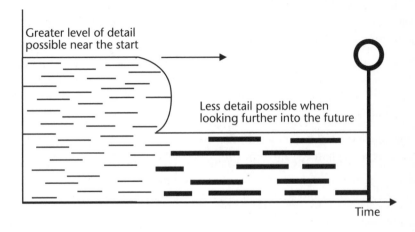

Figure 9.6   The rolling wave principle in project planning

At or just before the start of a project it is generally possible to create a level 1 summary plan for the project but with level 2 or 3 plans only for the early stages. A little later in the project, as more information is generated by the initial stage, it might be possible to make level 2 plans for the entire project, plus level 3 plans looking as far ahead as the middle stages. Later, as the middle stages in their turn generate more information, the final level 3 plans can be created.

This can be likened to a rolling wave, moving from left to right through the plans, from the start of the project towards its finish. The work in front of the rolling wave is only planned in coarse detail to level 1, or possibly to level 2, with the crest of the wave signalling the development of the level 3 and 4 plans. The same concept can be used within cost accounts or larger work packages. The earlier activities are fully defined work packages, even including day-to-day instructions. The later activities are larger planning packages in which the work cannot be fully defined and detailed. The level 1 plan, and later the level 2 plans, integrate the lower-level plans and provide a framework for this rolling wave planning. A full critical path for the project thus exists, from its beginning to its end, allowing float to be calculated and work and resources to be allocated in line with true priorities.

Examples of hierarchical planning in practice

Different companies use the hierarchical approach to planning in different ways, either to suit their preferences or because of the different natures of their projects. We can conclude this chapter by describing aspects of three of the many possible cases, as follows:

- an individual project for a module or link-up in a North Sea oil platform
- a general hierarchical multi-level planning methodology for structured projects
- very large project applications.

Another case, multiple simultaneous projects, is discussed in Chapter 10.

A NORTH SEA OIL PROJECT

Level 1
The top tier, or level 1 network plan will often be a simple bar chart containing only milestones but constructed in logical sequence with links between activities considered and shown. This plan is used for reporting to the project client or to the main contractor's steering committee. It will usually equate to a similar level 1 budget dataset within the cost control framework.

Level 2
The level 2 network is the overall master schedule. This is used to record intermediate milestones by stage and main system interfaces. Line management will use this schedule to identify problem areas and adverse trends that demand their urgent attention.

Level 3
Level 3 plans determine the activities of participating companies and internal departments, and must be prepared by the relevant managers, within the contraints set by the level 2 summary plan. These are the detailed plans that generate work-to-do lists and might need resource levelling.

Level 4
The level 4 planning is represented by detailed work instructions at individual or group level (perhaps using job cards) organized into an appropriate sequence within the parent activity's scheduled start and finish dates.

General
The method of linking these levels allows consistent planning and progress data to be summarized upwards (rolled up) from the lowest level 4 instructions into condensed reports that are suitable for use at the higher management levels.

In the reverse, downward direction, scheduled early start and finish dates are passed to the dependent reports and thence to the material registers. This allows 'look ahead' reports to be produced for, say, 14- and 56-day time spans. These will feature detailed work instructions (for example, on job cards) and lists of materials to be expedited.

A GENERAL HIERARCHICAL MULTI-LEVEL PLANNING METHODOLOGY FOR STRUCTURED PROJECTS

Traditionally, projects have been planned along the project axis or 'dimension'. The plans were implicitly structured to outline what was required to complete the project deliverable and its component parts. In the simple example of project X, the engineering project introduced in the previous chapter, this would involve planning the work required to complete the basic design, mechanical sub-assembly, electrical sub-assembly and the final assembly. Planning and control in this project dimension is necessary to integrate the work of all the organizational groups that contribute to the project and to its individual elements, as defined in the WBS.

Sometimes, somewhat as an afterthought, responsibilities for the work or specialist disciplines involved are assigned, and the output data are filtered and sorted to produce plans for the principal organizational elements or functional disciplines involved. In project X this would be:

- design
- procurement
- works.

Examples of lower levels for this project would be:

- electrical design
- drawing office

and so on.

This results in plans that are structured in an organizational dimension, as well as in the traditional project dimension, but more or less on an ad hoc basis. Yet this organizational dimension is the one in which people and groups are arranged and managed. It is critical that not only is the work of these people and groups planned and controlled, but also that their performances are measured and reported.

Planning, after all, is concerned with who does what and when. Planning on an ad hoc sorted resource data output is inadequate, by itself, to manage all the groups, departments and companies involved in any project of significant size. Although there may be managers in charge of project elements, the resources (especially the skilled people employed) are more likely to be managed on a functional discipline or trade basis. Thus the work of these people must be planned and controlled on that basis, as well as on a project element basis.

Thus planning and control in this organizational dimension is also necessary to integrate the work carried out by each organizational element on all of the project elements to which it contributes. In addition, the move towards emphasizing personal accountability and responsibility of group managers at all levels, and the use of the contractor–consignee concept, necessitates planning and control oriented to this organizational dimension.

The principal advantages of planning based on the OBS compared with more traditional ad hoc planning are that it is systematic and produces a consolidated hierarchy of plans. Thus the plans for individual functional groups or disciplines are consolidated into department or company plans and these plans, in turn, are consolidated into higher-level organizational element plans.

Therefore, in addition to dealing with the time dimension, planning and control should be carried out in both the WBS and the OBS dimensions if it is to be fully effective. Although hierarchical, multi-level planning and control can be applied independently of a structured approach, it finds its full expression when that approach is used. The planning levels used are then the levels in both of the structures, and the individual plans used at each level are those for each of the elements at that level. This is a complex idea to explain, but it can be demonstrated using a simple case, based on project X.

Hierarchical planning structures in project X

The common foundation block, or planning module, in project X is the cost account. The plans (the schedule, resource budget and expenditure budget) of each individual cost account are integrated and consolidated in the vertical dimension to give the plans for the lowest-level WBS element. Similarly, the plans of the individual cost accounts are also integrated and consolidated in the horizontal direction to give the plans for the lowest level OBS elements. Thereafter, the plans for these lowest-level elements in both dimensions are integrated and consolidated (rolled up) to give the plans for the higher-level WBS and OBS elements. This rolling up process is continued until the complete project and organization plans are reached.

Figure 9.7 shows (in Gantt chart form) the hierarchy of plans for project X structured in the project (WBS) dimension. The foundation blocks of these plans are the individual cost account plans. This is illustrated in Figure 9.7 where, for clarity, just one cost account has been detailed, which is for the work of the electrical design group on the electrical sub-assembly. This is coded as cost account 311-43 (according to the coding system already explained in the previous chapter, in Figure 8.9, p. 114) but we have chosen here to express each code in a different sequence, beginning with its organizational component instead of the WBS component (311-43 instead of 43-311). Each of these cost account plans is a discrete planning and reporting module for the work carried out by one organizational group on one element of the WBS. Every cost account module would be accompanied by its associated resource and expenditure budgets.

Plans for the parent of the lowest-level WBS element – the electrical sub-assembly 43 – integrate and consolidate the plans of all the organizational groups contributing to its completion. This includes the cost account plan shown in Figure 9.7 (311-43, electrical design) plus the plans for the following cost accounts:

- 313-43 Instrument design
- 314-43 Drawing office
- 321-43 Purchasing
- 322-43 Expediting
- 331-43 Fabrication
- 332-43 Assembly.

The process is repeated at the next level for the WBS, which for this simple case is the complete project, by integrating and consolidating the plans, resource and expenditure budgets of all WBS level 2 elements. This creates a hierarchy of plans on the project dimension, as shown in Figure 9.7:

- Level 1 is the summary plan for the project.
- Each level 2 WBS element will have its own level 2 plan, as shown in Figure 9.7 for the electrical sub-assembly 43.
- The individual level 3 plans will be the plans for each cost account, as shown in Figure 9.7 for the work of the electrical design group on the electrical sub-assembly.

Figure 9.8 shows another hierarchy of plans for project X, but this time structured in the organizational dimension. The foundation block modules are the same cost account plans as those used in the hierarchy of plans structured in the work or project dimension, although they and their parent elements are arranged differently. For example, the work of the electrical design group on the electrical sub-assembly, which is coded 311-43, is the same planning module as that shown in the WBS arrangement of Figure 9.7, and is a foundation block of both the WBS and OBS hierarchies.

Staying with the example of the electrical design group in project X, the schedule, resources and expenditure budgets for its parent level 3 OBS element (the total work of this group on the project) are obtained by consolidating (rolling up) the cost account plan for which it is responsible as shown below:

- 311-41 Basic design
- 311-42 Mechanical sub-assembly
- 311-43 Electrical sub-assembly.

Similarly the plans for the design department, at level 2, consolidate the plans of the level 3 OBS elements – that is, the plans of the various design groups which make up the design department:

- 311 Electrical design
- 312 Mechanical design
- 313 Instrument design
- 314 Drawing office.

This process is repeated for each level of breakdown until the consolidated plan, structured on an organizational basis, is obtained. At each level these consolidated plans can be exploded in greater detail when required.

All this is somewhat elaborate for the simple case of project X, but it demonstrates the application of two-dimensional hierarchical planning. The hierarchy of plans for this project in the organizational dimension, as shown in Figure 9.8, is thus as follows:

- Level 1 is the summary plan for the total organization.
- Level 2 plans are the consolidated plans for the level 2 OBS elements (in this case the departments, with only the design department shown in detail here).
- Level 3 plans are those for the level 3 OBS elements, which are the groups that comprise each department. The project X plan for the electrical design group, part of the design department, is detailed in Figure 9.8.
- Level 4 plans are the plans for each cost account, as shown in Figure 9.8 for the electrical design work on the electrical sub-assembly of project X. These cost account plans are, of

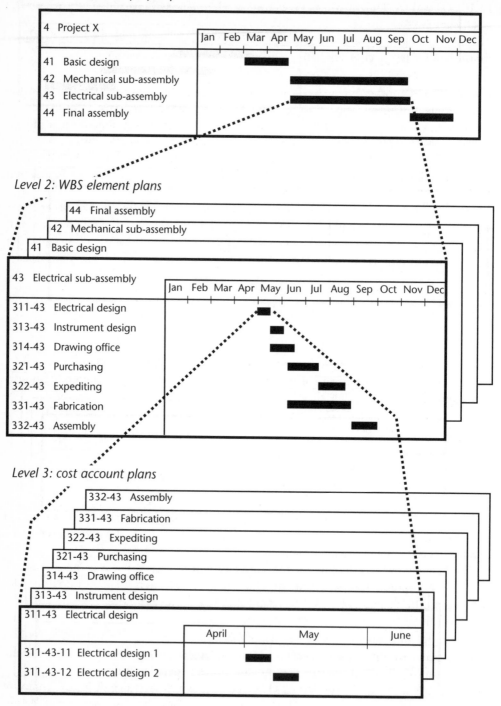

Figure 9.7   Plans for project X based on work breakdown structure

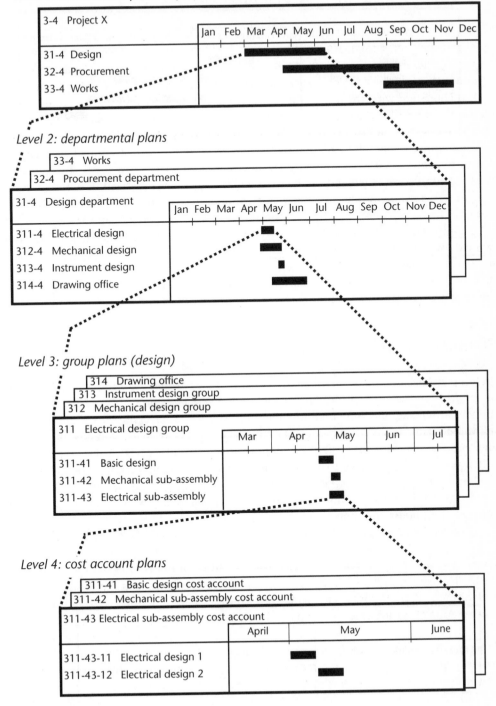

Level 1: consolidated plan for project X (coded as project 4) at company level (3)

Level 2: departmental plans

Level 3: group plans (design)

Level 4: cost account plans

Figure 9.8   Plans for project X based on organization breakdown structure

course, identical to the cost account plans shown at level 3 in the WBS dimension (Figure 9.7) because the cost account plans are the basic building blocks.

This permits consolidation and summarization for each level, yet also allows a full expansion of all plans when required. The mechanism for carrying this out is the coding system based on these structures. A logically designed coding system automatically consolidates the cost account plans and the control analysis and reporting on both the WBS and OBS, such that each is consistent with the other and they are totally integrated. All that is required is the creation of the basic project plans – schedules, resource and cost budgets – using a modular approach based on the cost account plans within the project WBS and OBS.

Combining a suitable coding system coupled with the use of competent computer software enables the user to produce plans and reports which are structured, integrated and consolidated, coordinated, and can be exploded to a great level of detail. A summary report plan or report can be produced for any element and, if there should be problems, it can be exploded into greater detail for the whole element, or any component part of it.

Thus the cost accounts, each WBS and OBS element and their managers have the factors defined for them in the same manner as the cost account and the overall project with, in particular, one person totally accountable and responsible for each. Each group, department, division or company, and each project WBS element and organizational unit, can have its own real or pseudo contract on the contractor–consignee principle.

Planning the very large project

Project planning and organization are always important but they are critical to the success of big projects (in the giant or mega-project league). A very large project is usually viewed as a number of separate medium-sized to large projects and it then represents a special case of multi-project management or programme management. Although the terms 'programme' and 'projects' are sometimes used in conjunction to describe a very large project and its constituents, we have chosen to use the terms 'project' and 'sub-projects' in this context. We shall use 'programme management' more specifically for the management of multiple projects that are connected only because they occur simultaneously in the same organization and, perhaps, share a common resource pool.

There are two principal variations in how a very large project might be planned:

1 Resources are shared between the sub-projects and planning is integrated in whole or in part. This case is similar to the multi-project planning described later in the next chapter.
2 Planning is decentralized, with parts of the project being planned separately and with integration occurring at level 1, or possibly level 2, plans.

Typically the owner company or its project management contractor will carry out overall project planning and control, integrating the work of all companies involved in the project. Then the more detailed task of planning all the sub-projects will be carried out by (and shared between) a number of construction or manufacturing companies, each of whom will have a contract for one or more of the constituent sub-projects. Each of these companies will have its own project management staff, and will be supervised by either or both the owner's and the management contractor's staff. To each of these companies the sub-project entrusted to them will appear, to a great extent, as a separate project but there will be overall supervision from the owner and/or management contractor, both to ensure success of the individual sub-projects and to ensure that they are interlinked with the overall project. An analogy here might compare the project owner or management contractor with an art designer who is commissioned to create a giant mural, and who employs many individual artists to paint separate areas of the whole picture.

It is in the planning of these very large projects that the hierarchical and rolling wave principles of project planning are essential. The number of levels needed might be more than the three or four shown in our simple examples, but not all would have to be fully integrated. Interrelationships required between the various sub-project plans are generally limited to key decision points or milestones, and the overall project plan need only include these to achieve full project integration. The number of planning levels and their integration will vary from one large project to another, but here is a typical case example:

- *Level 1 project plan*: a skeleton plan of the entire project, compiled by the project owner or management contractor, showing only the key project decision points or milestones, with most of the activities being individual sub-projects, contracts or sub-project phases.
- *Level 2 sub-project plans*: a series of individual sub-project plans, each made by the company responsible for the work or sub-projects, that integrate, by their interlinked milestones, into the complete project plan.

It might be necessary in some cases, where sub-projects are heavily interrelated, to introduce an intermediate level plan, placed between levels 1 and 2, that shows all the major and minor sub-project interfaces or milestones.

INDIVIDUAL SUB-PROJECT PLANS

Below the level 1 project summary plan, separate plans will be needed for every sub-project. Each of these can be constructed using the hierarchical principles described earlier in this chapter. Sub-project plans must show the relevant major and minor milestones of the main project. Progress information between milestones can be transferred from the individual sub-project plans to the higher-level project plan when the time comes to monitor and control sub-project and main project performance. This system can work effectively when each sub-project is handled by a separate company, with its own self-contained human resources.

Integration of the manpower plans for the individual sub-projects into one project manpower plan is required only when resources or facilities are shared between different sub-projects. That topic is considered in the following chapter.

10 *Resources and Calendars*

Resource scheduling is not new. Planners and managers have used charts – even blackboards – for well over 100 years in attempts to match the work within their groups or departments to the resources available. The older systems had several weaknesses, including inflexibility to change, inability to handle complex cases and the sheer eye- and mind-straining effort needed to set up and read all but the simplest schedule. The allocation of priorities to different jobs was often subjective and prone to interference or undue influence from the project owners or senior managers able to shout the loudest or intimidate with the most menace.

Throughout this book it is assumed that heavy reliance will be placed on computer systems, loaded with one or more of the many available project management software packages. All projects use resources and many can benefit from the resource scheduling capabilities of competent project management software. This chapter outlines the modern resource scheduling process for both single projects and programmes of projects (multi-projects) within one company or a small group of companies. It concludes with suggestions for the use of multiple calendars to overcome some of the difficulties that arise in planning and scheduling generally.

The need for resource scheduling

Consider a project owner who engages a managing contractor to fulfil a construction project, and imagine further that the managing contractor is a small company that gets results by hiring specialists and subcontractors to carry out all the design and actual project work. The owner should expect the managing contractor to recommend the overall project strategy and make at least the level 1 summary plan for the project. However, because neither the owner nor the managing contractor employs any direct labour or other significant resource, they have no need to carry out resource scheduling. That process is delegated to the many subcontractors.

If the managing contractor is one of the larger organizations that employs people directly to carry out design and some other project tasks, then the situation is completely different. The contractor will usually be handling several projects at the same time, all of which depend on the full- or part-time use of people from within the organization. Although much of the planning and scheduling at lower levels might be delegated to the subcontractors engaged for the work on site, resource scheduling within the contractor's own offices becomes important.

A manufacturing company that customarily has several projects in progress will use established production control methods for scheduling the day-to-day (or even hour-to-hour) work of its factory manufacturing facilities. But a succession of manufacturing projects cannot usually be conducted without the existence of a busy engineering design office. So the design and drawing resources needed for activities in the level 1 and 2 plans will have to be scheduled, for which suitable project management software can usually provide the solution. Those level 1 and 2 plans should summarize the manufacturing activities (perhaps down to sub-sub-assembly level), and the resulting time analysis will give key dates and priorities within which the production controllers can do their fine-detail manufacturing planning. This method can, and if possible should, be refined by including summary or coarse resource scheduling for the factory activities in the level 1 or level 2 plans to ensure that work is fed to the factory at a rate in line with its overall capacity.

In one heavy engineering company, total resource scheduling for all manufacturing projects was handled successfully simply by designating and scheduling the factory resources for all projects as either 'light machining' or 'heavy machining' on the level 2 networks. No manufacturing activity on these networks was broken down below sub-assembly level, so the networks contained relatively few activities (usually no more than 1000 for the whole level 2 planning set for a single project). Resource scheduling, even at this coarse level, was adequate for ensuring that the factory production controllers received their drawings and broad production target dates within a timeframe that did not conflict with the company's production capacity.

It is now possible to state a simple rule. Any organization, carrying out any kind of project that directly uses people or other scarce resources for its project work, must have some process in place for scheduling the provision and allocation of those resources. Setting aside manufacturing operations (for which specialized production control software exists), all other project resource scheduling can usually be performed using one of the many project management software packages that are available commercially 'off the shelf'.

Managers of very small groups might prefer to use simple charts, and these can be cheap and effective. Holiday charts have long fulfilled a similar purpose successfully. For medium-sized groups many advantages can be gained from using a computer system and, when the numbers of projects and people are too great for mental calculation, a computer becomes an essential tool. Without effective resource scheduling there will be too many occasions when people are idle through lack of work whilst others are overloaded, leading to schedule slippages, missed targets and disgruntled staff.

Principles of resource scheduling

RESOURCE CATEGORIES

There are several ways in which resources can be categorized but, for our purposes, it is useful to identify just two groups, namely those resources which can be scheduled successfully using project management software and those that cannot. This can be determined by a simple rule. We have only to answer the question: 'Can the named resource be quantified by simple one-dimensional units?' If it can, it can be scheduled. If not, it probably cannot.

Here are some examples of resources that can be scheduled easily with project management software:

• people with special skills or trades (the basic scheduling unit is one person of the designated skill type)

- manufacturing machines in a group where all the machines are either identical or sufficiently similar to carry out the same project manufacturing activities (the basic scheduling unit is one machine)
- any specified bulk materials of the same specification, such as facing bricks, rebar, coal, fuel oil, raw stock manufacturing material (the basic unit is the unit of quantity such as weight, volume or length)
- money of a particular currency (the basic unit is the unit of currency).

One resource that is impossible to schedule with project management software is accommodation space if the height, length, width and shape all have to be specified. This problem can be solved using models (either physical scale models or virtual models using suitable design software).

THE PROCESS

Resource calculations can take one of three forms: aggregation, scheduling (basic levelling) and optimization (true workload smoothing). These are illustrated in Figure 10.1. All the processes described here assume the existence of a critical path network diagram in which the duration and resource usage have been estimated for each activity.

For simplicity and clarity, we have illustrated the schedules for only one resource type. In practice, of course, more than one resource type would usually need to be scheduled and the project would more probably last for months or years rather than the few weeks of our example. Each chart in Figure 10.1 shows a different way of approaching resource scheduling. The resource quantity (say, the number of electricians available) is four, indicated on all the charts in Figure 10.1 as a heavier horizontal line. The shortest possible time in which the project can be completed (the duration of the critical path) is 20 days, marked by the winning post.

Resource aggregation

Resource aggregation is of limited value. After time analysis, the computer produces a work plan in which every activity is expected to take place at its earliest possible time, ignoring any float that an activity might possess and making no effort to reduce peaks or troughs in the resource workload. Then, for each day (or other specified period) the computer adds up the numbers of each resource type needed to fulfil the work. No attempt is made to deal with idle periods or resource overloads and the resulting schedules are, not surprisingly, impracticable to achieve.

Early software was capable only of resource aggregation. As Figure 10.1(a) shows, the results do not lead a practicable schedule and predict a very uneven workload, with resources idle on some days but seriously overloaded on others. Although the process can sometimes give a rough indication of the total resources likely to be needed for a project, modern software can easily perform more sophisticated resource scheduling, which must be preferred to simple aggregation.

Resource scheduling

The process described here, and illustrated in Figure 10.1(b) and (c), is the method commonly used by resource-scheduling software. The computer first carries out time analysis and calculates the amount of float possessed by every activity in the network. Process details vary

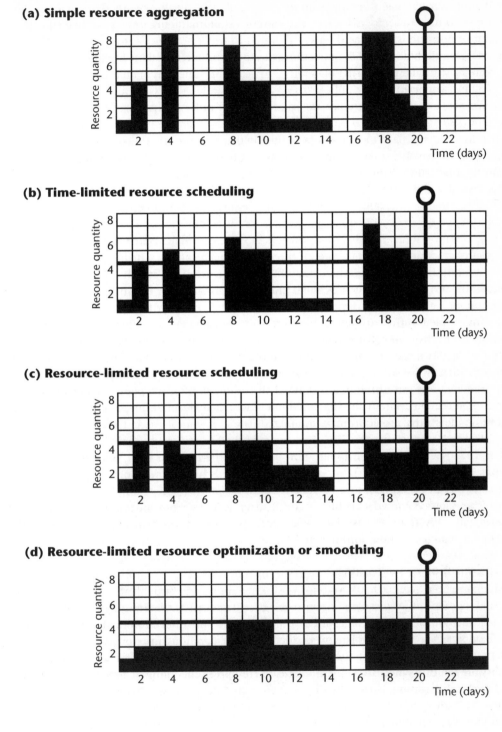

(a) Simple resource aggregation

(b) Time-limited resource scheduling

(c) Resource-limited resource scheduling

(d) Resource-limited resource optimization or smoothing

Figure 10.1   Different ways of scheduling a project resource

but, in a typical case, the computer will attempt to schedule every activity at its earliest possible time, but only if there are sufficient unallocated resources available. If all the relevant resources have already been allocated to other activities taking place at the same time, the computer will try to avoid overloading the resource by delaying the scheduled start and finish dates for the activity.

The planner is usually able to specify priority rules for assigning scarce resources to activities. Float is an important determinant of priorities. A popular and recommended method is to give priority to the activities that have least remaining float. If some of the total float in a network path has already been used in delaying the scheduled starts and finishes of earlier activities due to lack of resources, then the float in the activities that follow in the same path is reduced and is then known as the remaining float.

Provided that there are adequate resources to carry out the project within its shortest possible time, a workable schedule should result. The computer will not produce the smoothest pattern of resource usage possible, but it will make a schedule that shows project completion on time and with no day where more resources are called for than the numbers that are actually available.

But things are rarely so satisfactory. Often, there will be insufficient resources available to finish the project at its earliest possible time, making scheduling to satisfy both project time and resource constraints impossible. So a second priority rule must be made and communicated to the computer. Should the schedule be calculated to finish the project on time, at the expense of exceeding the resources available (a time-limited schedule)? Or should, instead, the computer be instructed always to observe resource constraints, even though that will delay the starts of some critical activities and extend the planned project finish date (a resource-limited schedule)? This is a decision for the project manager to make. If completion on time is vital, the time-limited schedule must be chosen, which will indicate a willingness to engage additional resources.

Figure 10.1(b) shows that the time-limited schedule will cause some resource overloads but the usage pattern, although not perfect, is better that that obtained by simple aggregation. Generally speaking, the computer will achieve far smoother patterns when a greater number of activities are being scheduled.

The resource-limited schedule (Figure 10.1(c)) is better from the resource usage point of view, but this smoother workload has been planned at the expense of increasing the scheduled project duration from 20 to 24 days.

Optimization or smoothing

The computer, having made one forward scheduling pass through the network, will not usually produce the smoothest resource usage pattern that is theoretically possible. In most cases this will not matter because projects generally have far more activities than those shown in Figure 10.1 and tolerably smooth workload patterns can be expected. Perfection in scheduling is an unattainable goal for several reasons. There will usually simply be no possible solution where there are no peaks or troughs in the planned resource usage. In any case, all calculations are based on duration estimates that can prove to be wildly inaccurate in practice. However, there are a few programs that will attempt to produce perfectly smooth resource usage patterns. They do this by making more than one scheduling pass through the network, so that the predicted usage patterns are improved at each pass.

Splittable and non-splittable activity scheduling

The computer will usually give the planner the option of making activities 'splittable' or 'non-splittable'. The computer is allowed to interrupt a splittable activity to divert scarce resources temporarily to enable a critical activity to be completed on time. The objective of activity splitting is to achieve smoother resource usage patterns, especially in time-limited schedules, but the interruption of activities in this way can lead to errors and inefficiencies and might not be to everyone's taste. Most people working on a task will probably be demoralized to some extent if they are taken off the task for a few days to work elsewhere on the project and then be expected to pick up the pieces and carry on as if nothing had happened. Performance is certain to suffer. The software default condition will usually assume that activities are non-splittable, and that option is always to be preferred.

Specifying the amount of a particular resource needed for an activity

Each resource type must be given a description and a short code for use in input data and output reports. The report codes will also be found useful for filtering output reports.

Suppose that an activity with an estimated duration of 24 days is expected to need four electricians, a resource that might be coded 'EL'. This would usually be shown on the network diagram and input to the computer as 24d 4EL. Note that prudent planners will never make the mistake of assigning four electricians to an activity when they draw a network diagram if they know that fewer than four electricians exist (and will continue to exist) in the organization. However, the planner does not need to consider that any or all of those four electricians might be needed more urgently elsewhere at the time when the activity comes to be scheduled. That decision can safely be left to the resource scheduling software.

Rate-constant, non-rate-constant and more complex resource patterns for an activity

The default condition of most software will assume rate-constant usage of a specified resource during the duration of an activity. This means that if (say) two units of a resource are specified for an activity, then two units of the resource will be employed on the task throughout its duration. This is the case for the four electricians indicated in Figure 10.2(a).

There are exceptions, for example, when using Microsoft Project – where the default condition might schedule on the basis of total activity work content rather than the estimated duration, resulting in some very peculiar (and undesirable) schedules. For instance, our example activity might be scheduled by the computer to use only three electricians, and the computer will itself make the decision to extend the duration from 24 to 32 days in order to accommodate the total workload of 96 man-days. Even more undesirable results can happen when the recalculated duration is not an integer, with the computer printing out schedules that include hours and even minutes. So, the planner must take care that the customization tools in such software are set for rate-constant resource usage within fixed activity durations if, as is usually the case, that is the planner's intention.

There are occasions when the planner knows that resource usage will not be rate-constant, but will follow some predetermined pattern, as suggested in Figure 10.2(b). Good software will allow the planner to depart from the default rate-constant condition and enter the expected pattern of use. The pattern might even be cyclical, with a small usage pattern being repeated two or more times regularly throughout the duration of the activity.

(a) Rate-constant: 4 people for 24 days = 96 man-days total work content

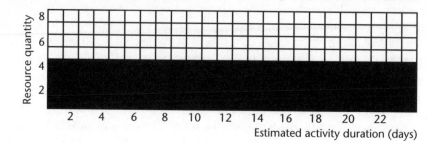

(b) Non rate-constant: still 96 man-days work content but with a different work pattern

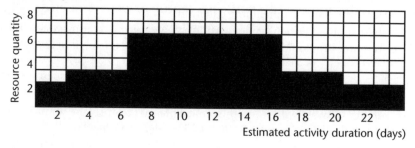

Figure 10.2   Different ways of planning resource usage patterns for an activity

Most software contains facilities that will never be taken up by the user. Think, for instance, of Microsoft Word, where the average user of this popular and capable word processing package exploits only a fraction of the total features available. All successful software undergoes continual development, during which feedback from users includes requests for additional features that the software company might view as worth including, thus leading to greater versatility and more facilities. Project management software is no exception. So the better project management programs have, over the years, become extremely versatile. The ability to deal with non-rate-constant resources in an activity is just one example of the features usually offered.

There are usually several different ways in which a particular scheduling problem can be solved. For instance, should the software be unable to cope with non-rate-constant resources there is a simple solution – that is, to break the complex activity down into a number of sequential simple activities, each of which does use resources at a constant rate. The case shown in Figure 10.2(b) would need five such separate consecutive activities – one for each change of resource level.

However, the really good news is that all of this attention to detail is usually unnecessary and overcomplicated. In practice, resource usage for any activity is rarely constant throughout its duration, but this factor can be ignored provided that the activity is one of many in the project that uses the same resources. Whilst the resource usage for an individual activity may be anything but rate-constant, resource usage spread over a larger number of activities will iron out the peaks and troughs in the overall schedule. So, for most purposes, the default rate-constant condition will be adequate and lead to practicable schedules.

Setting up the resource-scheduling parameters

CHOOSING RESOURCES FOR SCHEDULING

A project organization might contain specialist groups ranging in size from one person to several hundred people. Each skill type can, if required, be given a resource description and code, and then be entered into the resource-scheduling process. But it is rarely necessary to schedule every skill type. Consider, for example, a small engineering design group that designs the hydraulic and lubrication systems for machines designed by a much larger group of mechanical design engineers. If the mechanical design engineers are resource-scheduled, it will usually be found that the supporting demands made by them on the hydraulic and lubrication group are fairly constant so that the work of that group does not need to be entered into the resource-scheduling equation.

The best approach when implementing a new project planning system is to choose just a few key resources and schedule those. Others can be added later, if necessary.

SPECIFYING RESOURCE AVAILABILITIES FOR THE PROJECT

The computer software will expect the project planner to enter the number of people or units of each resource skill or type that are available for allocation to project work. This information must be entered in a resource file, often from a screen similar to that shown in Figure 10.3. This form will allow entries on several rows, with each row covering a given period.

If the organization is a matrix dealing with several projects simultaneously, the scheduling process must be multi-project, described later in this chapter. However, for the moment, assume for simplicity that only one project is being conducted. So, suppose we

Resource code: EL   Alternative resource code:

Resource name: Electrician

Resource type: Labour ✓   Materials ☐

Availability

Units	From	To	Unit cost	Threshold	Threshold cost
5.00	01 Jan 2007	30 Jun 2007	$45.00	2.00	$55.00
7.00	01 Jul 2007	31 Dec 2007	$45.00		
7.00	01 Jan 2008	31 Dec 2008	$48.00		

Figure 10.3   Example of data to be entered for a resource file

have a department of 100 qualified professional mechanical engineers, any one of whom could carry out a typical mechanical design task on the project in hand. How many of those 100 engineers should be declared as being always available for project work? Certainly not the entire 100 people, because at any given time some will not be available for project work. There will be those who are:

- away on staff annual leave
- attending a training course
- absent through illness
- working on unexpected tasks, such as answering customer queries, or fulfilling urgent small orders from customers
- working on internal projects, such as writing engineering standards
- carrying out rework, modifications or debugging arising from earlier, supposedly completed projects.

All these miscellaneous tasks and absences deplete the number of people who can be assigned to active projects. They can, together, be regarded as a kind of sludge factor, impossible to predict accurately or schedule. But we can make a general allowance to cover this sludge. If in doubt, start by allowing 15 per cent and declare the availability of mechanical engineers for project work not as 100 souls, but as 85.

The example in Figure 10.3 shows the input data for a group of electricians. It can be seen that the availability has been declared as 5 electricians for the period beginning 1 January 2007, rising to 7 from 1 July 2007. Thus one can plan for increases or decreases in the numbers of resources available in line with recruitment or redundancy planning.

A unit cost rate has been entered for the electricians in Figure 10.3. The computer will apply this rate when making cash outflow forecasts or when recording the actual costs of an activity against recorded progress. In this example, the company is planning for a pay award at the end of 2007, and the example shows how this can be allowed for in advance by entering the changed data on the next row, for 2008.

Threshold resources

The input screen depicted in Figure 10.3 allows for the declaration of threshold resource levels (under 'Threshold'). Some programs allow this facility. Threshold resources represent an additional level of resource, above the normally available limit, to be allocated by the computer only when these are absolutely necessary to prevent project critical dates being exceeded. These can sometimes be provided by hiring additional labour from an external agency or by accepting a degree of overtime working (although overtime working should really never be accepted as normal in scheduling, but should instead be held in reserve for use only in emergencies). Any form of threshold resource will usually attract a higher unit cost rate, and this can be entered in the resource file.

In the example of Figure 10.3, threshold resources have only been allowed for the first six months of 2007, taking the total availability of electricians to seven. From 1 July 2007 onwards, the company plans to take on two more permanent electricians. With seven electricians on the permanent staff the planner has predicted that threshold additions will not be needed after 30 June 2007.

Alternative resources

Another feature of some project management software is to allow the planner to specify an alternative resource skill for some tasks. This means that the alternative resource can be called in at times of overload instead of, or in addition to, the threshold resources. In the case of the electricians in Figure 10.3 the project manager has decided that only qualified electricians may perform the electrical installation activities and no substitution is possible. If it had been possible to nominate an alternative resource for emergency substitutions, the ID code for that alternative resource would be entered in the appropriate box on the input form (at the top right in our example).

Multi-project resource scheduling

Most companies undertake more than one project at a time, so resource scheduling cannot sensibly be confined to a single project. Some people seem to be overawed by the thought of scheduling more than one project at a time, but (thanks to project management software) the process is actually easier than single project scheduling for several reasons, including the following:

- Assessing the availability of resources is simpler – one only has to consider the entire groups of different skills and leave the computer to allocate them to the various projects.
- There is no need to be concerned about different project priorities. The computer will drive all scheduling from the float possessed by the individual projects and their activities.
- The system is flexible to change, so that the introduction or removal of projects is easily accommodated.

A planner or project manager who has mastered the art of resource scheduling on a single project should have no difficulty at all in progressing to full multi-project working.

PRINCIPLES OF MULTI-PROJECT RESOURCE SCHEDULING

Multi-project scheduling operates on exactly the same basis as single-project scheduling, except that the total sum of all projects in the company or wider organization becomes the project to be scheduled and all the individual projects can be regarded as sub-projects.

Priority rules for individual projects within the programme of projects

Sub-projects are not usually connected in any way by interfaces between their separate networks. So a multi-project model, unlike the single-project model, will have multiple starts and finishes in the overall network, as seen by the computer.

All these starts and finishes must be fixed in time by allocating scheduled (target) dates to them. Then when the entire model is scheduled (or rescheduled), the computer can carry out time analysis with respect to these dates, identify the critical paths and allocate float to every activity. It is this float that must drive priority for claiming scarce resources, so the model should be successful in scheduling the entire programme of work in line with all the individual project target finish dates.

There will be occasions when senior managers in the organization attempt to request higher priority for a particular project. Too many managers at higher levels, without the benefit of project management training, simply do not understand the concept of multi-project scheduling and cannot foresee the advantages that must accrue from using this elegant solution. This failure of higher managers to appreciate the benefits of scheduling and project management is well recorded in some of the case studies reported by Kerzner (2000).

BENEFITS BEYOND PROJECT MANAGEMENT

Once a viable multi-project resource schedule has been established, it can be regarded as a virtual model of the organization for manpower planning. Any competent form of scheduling and control will help the project manager to achieve project goals but, with multi-project schedules, senior management, strategists and corporate planners have a valuable forecasting tool that is likely to be far more accurate than that available from any other method.

The multi-project model is a good testing ground for assessing the effect of changes in the work programme caused by the introduction of proposed new projects, the cancellation of existing projects or changes in the scope or timings of individual projects. This process, known as 'what-if?' testing, is supported by competent project management software.

MAINTAINING THE INTEGRITY OF THE MULTI-PROJECT MODEL

A typical multi-project model will cover several projects comprising perhaps thousands of different activities. All must be supported with a framework of calendar and resource files. If too many people are allowed access to the model at system level, there is a risk that the model will be corrupted and become useless, needing many hours of work to restore it to viability. For that reason, whilst access to reports and (perhaps) the input of progress and timesheet information should be widely allowed, there must be a restriction on access to the system parameters. The project support office (Chapter 19) can play a vital role as guardian of the model.

Calendars in project management software

USING A SINGLE CALENDAR

When activity data are input to the computer for each activity record, the project management software will usually allow space for the file code of a particular calendar to be entered. If nothing is entered, the computer will assume that the default calendar is valid for the activity. This means that work can only be scheduled to start, finish or proceed during days that are classified as working days in the default calendar. Most default calendars assume a working week beginning on Monday morning and ending on Friday evening, with no work possible on Saturdays or Sundays.

The default calendar can (and should) be changed by specifying public holidays as non-working days. Some companies close down for a week or more during the summer months, and these dates should also be defined as non-working days in the default calendar.

Use of a single calendar is sufficient in many cases, but the software will allow a number of different calendars to be set up if required. This is discussed later in this chapter under the heading 'Multiple calendars'.

CUSTOMIZATION OF DATES IN REPORTS

Confusion can arise because of the different national conventions in expressing calendar dates. For example, 01/06/05 would mean 1 June 2005 to the average Briton but 6 January 2005 to a resident in the US. These differences could give rise to some fairly disastrous errors in international projects. However, project management software does allow the presentation of calendar dates to be customized. The safest option is to use the format 01Jun2006 or 01Jun06. This presentation will avoid confusion whilst taking up little space in report columns and network or bar chart plots.

TREATMENT OF HOLIDAYS

As mentioned earlier, public holidays and factory shut-down periods should be specified as non-working days in the default calendar and any other relevant calendar in use. Then no work will be scheduled to take place or start and finish during those days.

Holidays taken by individual people cannot usually be considered by project management software, and these are allowed for in resource scheduling simply by reducing the declared group availability of the particular resource skill. This also covers unforeseeable absences through illness, visits to the doctor or dentist, and attendances at short training courses. Averaging in this way has proved adequate in practice. There is, however, at least one programme that allows staff records to be entered and matched with day-to-day resource availability, and that system would allow individual staff holidays and other preplanned staff absences to be accounted for accurately – but that case is a rare exception and its facility is not essential.

A SCHEDULING PARADOX

A typical default calendar will assume that work can only take place during a weekday beginning at 08.00 hrs and finishing at 17.00 hrs. The time span between the close of work on one day and the beginning of work on the next is not available for scheduling. Putting this into a calendar context, if 1 June happens to be a Monday, then 17.00 hrs on 1 June is 'seen' by the computer as virtually the same instant in time as 08.00 hrs on Tuesday 2 June, because the intervening hours simply do not exist in the computer's calendar. Further, because Saturday and Sunday are non-working days in the default calendar, 17.00 hrs on Friday 5 June is virtually the same instant in time as 08.00 hrs on Monday 8 June. This can give rise to some interesting anomalies when the computer reports schedule start and finish dates for some activities.

An activity with a duration estimated at one day might be scheduled to start on 8 June, which means 08.00 hrs on that day. Its finish will also be scheduled for 8 June, but that means 17.00 hrs. So, the computer reports will print 8 June as the scheduled start date and 8 June as the scheduled finish date. However, suppose that an activity has been given a zero duration estimate (perhaps because it is a start or finish milestone). If the activity is scheduled to start on Monday 8 June, that means 08.00 hrs on that day. But the activity finish will be scheduled for 17.00 hrs on Friday 5 June. This is logically justifiable because, to the computer, these two times are the same instant. But some software will report the activity as starting on 8 June and finishing, apparently three days earlier, on 5 June.

MULTIPLE CALENDARS

Whilst the default calendar is usually sufficient for most activities in a plan, there are occasions when an activity should take place at times outside those available in the default condition. The software will allow a considerable number of different calendars to be set up, each of which can be identified by a simple code. Then, when an activity should be assigned to a special calendar, the appropriate calendar code must be entered when the activity record is entered during project data input.

Seven-day calendars

If an activity for concrete pouring is scheduled, that should be followed in the precedence network diagram either by a link with a specified delay or (preferably) by an activity labelled something like 'Cure concrete'. Concrete can cure at any time. It, and many other activities such as paint drying, are continuous and do not stop for weekends or public holidays. So these activities need all seven days of every week to be available for scheduling. This can be managed by setting up a suitable seven-day calendar. Perhaps this seven-day calendar would be given the file code '7'. Then, whenever a concrete-curing or paint-drying task is entered into the computer as an activity record, it is only necessary to enter also the calendar number 7 in the appropriate input field and the resulting schedules should be valid.

Different group working patterns

Quite often there will be groups in the same company that work different hours or even two or three shifts in a 24-hour period. The difficulty of scheduling these activities can be overcome by generating a special calendar for each different pattern of working times.

International differences

Summary schedules (level 1 or level 2 plans) for projects that include work in different areas of the world often have to cater for different working patterns in the various countries involved. Each country will have its own religious and national festival dates, and even the routine patterns of weekday working will differ. This is another difficulty that can be overcome by setting up the requisite number of different special calendars.

11 *Planning within Fixed Project Time Constraints*

The objectives for a new project will usually include a date by which the project must be finished and handed over to its owner. In the simple case of a project conducted by one company (the contractor) for another (the client or customer) there should be no ambiguity about the time requirement. But when the network diagram has been drawn and processed it is probable that the results will disappoint, dismay or shock all concerned by predicting a completion date well beyond that which is required. If the overlong schedule has resulted after resource scheduling by the computer, a remedy can often be found by increasing the available resources, perhaps through temporary hirings. But when the initial schedules disappoint, the cause will most often be a critical path that is too long to fit between the intended project start and finish dates, so that there appears to be no logical way in which the project can be completed on time.

This chapter will start by considering two methods (fast-tracking and crashing) for squeezing the critical path into the available timeframe. The discussion will concentrate initially on the timeframe for the one-contractor–one client project, using examples based on project X, the simple project that was introduced in Chapter 8 and whose network was presented and analysed in Chapter 9. The chapter concludes by glimpsing a more complex timeframe, when projects fall within wider structures, set not by simple one-to-one contractor–customer contracts but by the demands of multiple projects or even multiple programmes of projects.

Fast-tracking

All network diagram methods, when used in their simplest form, regard the network nodes as fixed barriers. The general assumption (and the assumption that will be made by computer software in the default condition) is that no activity can start before all activities on preceding paths have been finished. There is also a complementary assumption that any activity can start immediately following the completion of all activities on preceding paths. In practice, however, these assumptions are not always valid. Examples are easy to imagine. Purchasing of long-lead items can usually begin, on advance advice from engineers, some time before the design task is finished and certainly before the issue of a parts list or bill of materials. Delays between activities must occur, for example, when a concrete base has to be given time to cure before any load can be imposed.

Considerable time can be saved in a project schedule when the finishes and starts of activities along the critical path are allowed to overlap. The precedence diagram system allows for flexibility in the treatment of nodes by providing notation that can show complex

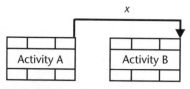

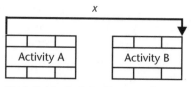

(a) Finish–start. Activity B cannot start until x network time units after the finish of Activity A. Most constraints are of this type, but x is usually zero.

(b) Start–start. Activity B cannot start until x network time units after the start of Activity A.

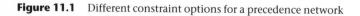

(c) Finish–finish. Activity B cannot be finished until x network time units after the finish of Activity A.

(d) Start–finish. Activity B cannot be finished until x network time units after the start of Activity A.

Figure 11.1   Different constraint options for a precedence network

constraints (links) between consecutive activities. There are four possibilities, including the usual default finish–start link, and these are illustrated in Figure 11.1.

COMPLEX PRECEDENCE CONSTRAINTS (LINKS) AND THEIR RELEVANCE TO FAST-TRACKED PROJECTS

Finish–start constraints

Finish–start constraints are the usual kind of link between activities in any network method, implying that no activity can start until all its predecessors have been finished. This is the kind of link that computer software will assume as the default condition unless the planner has given different instructions. Finish–start links usually have zero duration, but an estimated duration can be assigned to impose a minimum period of delay between two consecutive activities. In many ways it is preferable to represent such delays by inserting special activities (such as 'wait for paint to dry') because the logic is then more apparent in network plots.

Most activity relationships are not only shown as finish–start but *must* be specified as finish–start. Project X provides many examples, illustrated in the network diagram of Figure 9.3 (p. 126). Taking two consecutive activities at random, consider activities 10 and 17 in that diagram. The network logic, as it stands, tells us that the delivery period for the instruments cannot begin until the purchase order for the instruments has been placed. No sensible person would argue with that logic.

Start–start constraints

A start–start constraint means that the second in a pair of consecutive activities may be allowed to start after a specified time following the start of its predecessor. The notation is illustrated, as for all these complex constraints, in Figure 11.1.

Returning to the network diagram for project X (Figure 9.3), there are some pairs of consecutive activities whose finishes and starts might be allowed to overlap. Taking just one example, the planner might discover that activity 04 (purchase mechanical parts) can begin 3 days after the beginning of activity 02 because the engineers could warn the purchasing department in advance of known long-lead items such as bearings, weldments and castings. Allowing this overlap would save 3 days for the time needed for these two activities but, as they do not lie on the critical path and have float in excess of 3 days, there would be no advantage in changing the existing network logic.

Staying with Figure 9.3, the relationship between activities 12 and 18 should command the fast-tracker's attention because they do lie on the critical path and these tasks can, with advantage, be overlapped. Some drawings for manufactured parts will be available for use before the full 10 days of activity 12 have elapsed. It is quite likely that enough drawings could be released to allow manufacture to start just 5 days after the beginning of detailing. So activities 12 and 18 can be overlapped, as illustrated in Figure 11.2.

Fast-tracking is a technique that exploits the start–start constraints in precedence networks in particular. The process should shorten the critical path, and will often do so to the extent that alternative paths become critical instead, to become candidates in their turn for fast-tracking.

Finish–finish constraints

A finish–finish constraint means that the second of a consecutive pair of activities cannot possibly be finished before a specified time after the finish of its predecessor.

A particular application for this kind of constraint is created when finish–start constraints have been used in a fast-tracked network. Again referring to activities 12 and 18 in Figure 11.2, if the start of activity 18 has been shown to be dependent only on the start of activity 12, there is now no logical constraint at all on the finish of activity 18. Unless it is linked to the finish of 12, the network would mistakenly show the possibility that all parts manufacturing could be completed before mechanical detailing had been finished. So, finish–finish constraints are often used as the complements of start–start constraints.

Start–finish constraints

Start–finish constraints are rare and do not feature prominently in fast-tracking. There are no advantageous examples in project X and they will not be discussed further here. However, a very practical book by Devaux (1999) cites some uses for this kind of constraint – for example, in just-in-time production systems.

OTHER POSSIBLE FAST-TRACKING MEASURES

Another aspect of fast-tracking is that it requires a general review of project strategy in an effort to find ways of short-cutting the programme, possibly by making some fairly radical changes to the work content and sequence. Whilst the project scope will almost certainly be defined in a legally binding contract, it is sometimes possible to identify activities in the schedule that can either be omitted or delayed until after handover of the main project. Lateral thinking and brainstorming can sometimes uncover such time-saving remedies.

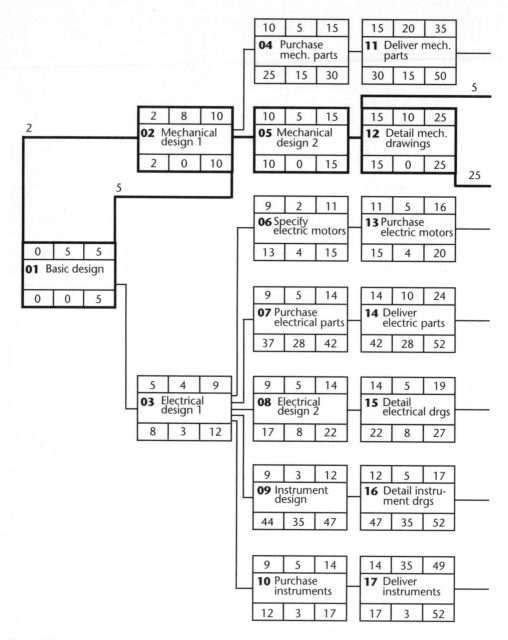

Figure 11.2 Network diagram for project X after some fast-tracking

FAST-TRACKING OF PROJECT X

Figure 11.2 shows the network diagram for project X after a modest degree of fast-tracking. In addition to saving 5 days by overlapping activities 12 and 18 as already described, a further 3 days can be saved at the intersection of activities 01 and 02. Remember that the duration of this project (the length of the critical path) was originally 78 days, as reported in Chapter 9. Fast-tracking at just two activity boundaries along the critical path has reduced this forecast to 70 days, a reduction of about 10 per cent. No extra costs should be incurred but, as in most

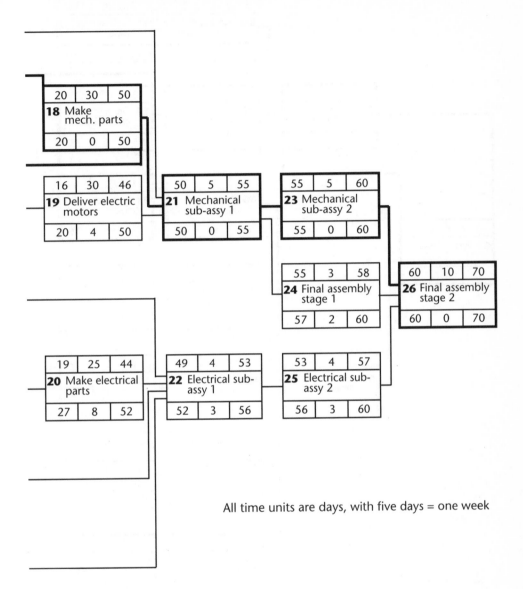

20	30	50
18 Make mech. parts		
20	0	50

16	30	46
19 Deliver electric motors		
20	4	50

50	5	55
21 Mechanical sub-assy 1		
50	0	55

55	5	60
23 Mechanical sub-assy 2		
55	0	60

55	3	58
24 Final assembly stage 1		
57	2	60

60	10	70
26 Final assembly stage 2		
60	0	70

19	25	44
20 Make electrical parts		
27	8	52

49	4	53
22 Electrical sub-assy 1		
52	3	56

53	4	57
25 Electrical sub-assy 2		
56	3	60

All time units are days, with five days = one week

cases of fast-tracking, this result has been achieved at the expense of increased risk. Shortening the critical path has had the effect of reducing the amount of float in other parts of the network, so there is now less 'fat' in the whole plan to accommodate slips and errors. The fast-tracked plan is more sensitive to the delaying effects of possible errors needing rework, so the designers and everyone else taking part in the project are under a greater obligation to 'get it right first time'.

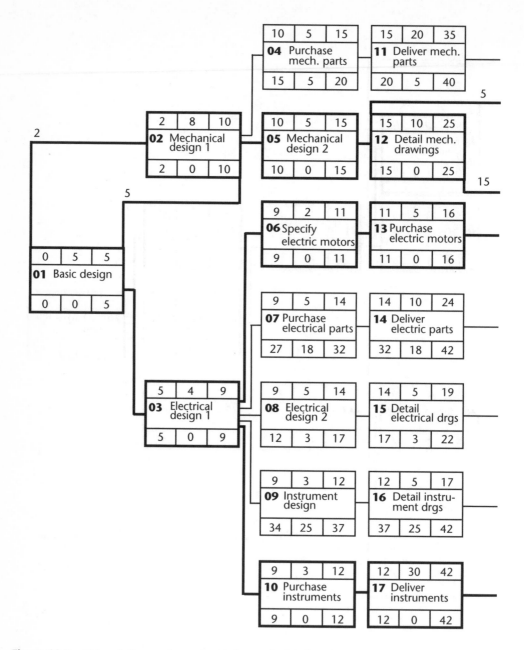

Figure 11.3   Network diagram for project X, fast-tracked and crashed

Saving project time by crashing the network

When the planner is placed under pressure to compress a schedule there is always a temptation to review the plan and reduce some duration estimates arbitrarily, perhaps with the implied exhortation, 'They will just have to do better and work faster'. Without a

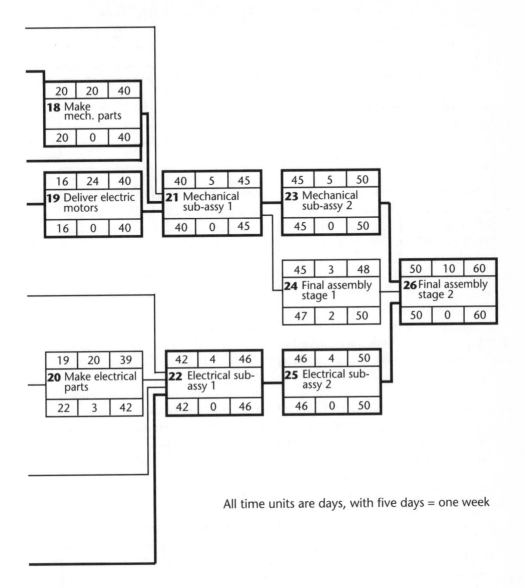

20	20	40
18 Make mech. parts		
20	0	40

16	24	40
19 Deliver electric motors		
16	0	40

40	5	45
21 Mechanical sub-assy 1		
40	0	45

45	5	50
23 Mechanical sub-assy 2		
45	0	50

45	3	48
24 Final assembly stage 1		
47	2	50

50	10	60
26 Final assembly stage 2		
50	0	60

19	20	39
20 Make electrical parts		
22	3	42

42	4	46
22 Electrical sub-assy 1		
42	0	46

46	4	50
25 Electrical sub-assy 2		
46	0	50

All time units are days, with five days = one week

considered strategy and the agreement of the relevant participating managers, this approach is wishful thinking. Disaster is the inevitable outcome. It is, however, sometimes possible to find practicable ways for achieving one or more activities in a shorter time than originally intended. This usually involves committing additional expenditure in one form or another. Here are a few examples:

• Provide floodlights at a project construction site to allow work to continue at night.
• Use machinery or plant with a larger capacity or faster working rate than that originally planned.

- Plan for the use of overtime. However, this is not generally a good strategy because overtime should, wherever possible, be regarded as a valuable reserve resource.
- Use alternative paints or concrete mixes to shorten drying or curing times.
- Subcontract work, even if the external contractor is relatively expensive.
- Double or treble the resources allocated to a task, even if this means working at slightly reduced efficiency (four people will not always halve the time of a job planned for two).
- Cut out competitive purchasing and simply opt for the supplier who can promise the earliest delivery, paying less or no attention to price.
- Use airfreight where surface transport would be the norm.

CRASHING PROJECT X

The original duration for project X was 78 working days (see Figure 9.3). The fast-tracking already described in this chapter has reduced this time to a planned 70 days (Figure 11.2). Now it is time to explain how a strategy for crashing the network can gain still more time. Once again, attention must be focused initially along the critical path.

Activity 18, with a duration of 30 days lying on the critical path, is an obvious candidate for crashing. It has been decided that the use of an external subcontractor, who has spare capacity and superior manufacturing facilities, can reduce manufacturing time to 20 days. This is expected to add $500 to the project costs.

When time analysis is repeated after crashing activity 18, it is found that other paths through the network are now longer, so that the critical path has moved. This highlights other activities for possible crash action. As each practicable crash action is planned, so the critical path will continue to change. This process of crashing, review and then further crashing must continue until the planner believes it would be impracticable or unwise to continue further. It might be possible, in theory at least, to continue the process of crashing to the point where all the activities are made critical. Any crashing, whether taken to extremes or not, will be at the expense of decreased tolerance to errors, higher risk of failure and more costs.

The resulting crashed network for project X is shown in Figure 11.3, where it is seen that:

- Activities 10, 14, 17, 18, 19 and 20 have been crashed.
- The planned project duration has been reduced to 60 days.
- There is now more than one critical path through the network.

Figure 11.4 tabulates relevant data for the six activities that have been crashed for project X. Note that a strategy has been recorded to support the crashing of each of these activities.

COST–TIME OPTIMIZATION

In Figure 11.4 the column 'cost per day saved' shows that it is cheaper to shorten the durations of some activities by crashing than it would be for others. For example, activity 10 can be shortened by two days for no additional cost, because the purchasing department has promised to place the purchase order for the instruments within three days instead of the customary five. The greatest cost per day saved is seen for activity 18, where each day gained has been at the predicted expense of $50.

When activities along the same critical path are considered for crashing, if there are two or more activities along the path that could be crashed and if, further, it is not necessary to

Activity ID	Original duration	Crashed duration	Days saved	Extra cost	Cost per day saved	Crash strategy
10	5d	3d	2d	—	—	Purchasing dept to give priority
14	10d	3d	7d	$ 35	$ 5	Send our van to collect ex-works
17	35d	30d	5d	$200	$40	Alternative but more expensive supplier
18	30d	20d	10d	$500	$50	Subcontract manufacture
19	30d	24d	6d	$120	$20	Pay premium incentive to supplier
20	25d	20d	5d	$300	$50	Subcontract manufacture

Figure 11.4   Analysis of the crashed activities in project X

crash all of them, the planner should choose to crash those activities where the cost per day saved is least.

A method is sometimes described, but rarely if ever practised, where an in-depth examination of crashing possibilities is undertaken with the objective of arriving at a solution where the project can be crashed as far as possible for the minimum possible cost. This approach relies upon first tabulating all possible crash actions in a format similar to that shown in Figure 11.4. The erroneous assumption is then sometimes made that the cost–time relationship for crashing any activity is linear, which might mean, for example, that in the case of project X if ten days can be shaved off the duration of activity 18 for $500, then five days could be saved for $250. So, this argument continues, there is a theoretical solution in which activities are crashed only as far as is necessary, giving preference to the cheapest crash actions, to arrive at a plan that has been crashed as far as possible for minimum cost. Although that ideal might never be possible, there is an underlying logic to this method that should be followed within sensible limits.

Timescale structures for sub-projects in a multi-project programme

One of the most common reasons for promoting fast-tracking and crashing is seen in consumer project development projects, where the goal is to achieve the shortest possible 'time to market'. There are, of course, many other occasions when a company must take measures to plan project completion as quickly as possible.

In a large project involving many different companies, we should assume that a master summary network exists at level 1, managed by a main contractor or chief project manager, from which all other activity times, at all lower levels of planning, are driven. So a subcontractor might be given target dates generated from a higher-level plan that, at first sight, appear impossible to meet. So here is a picture of a multi-layered hierarchy of companies and plans, where some companies might use fast-tracking and/or crashing to advantage when trying to plan to meet their own particular commitments within the whole scheme of things. One such framework is illustrated in Figure 11.5.

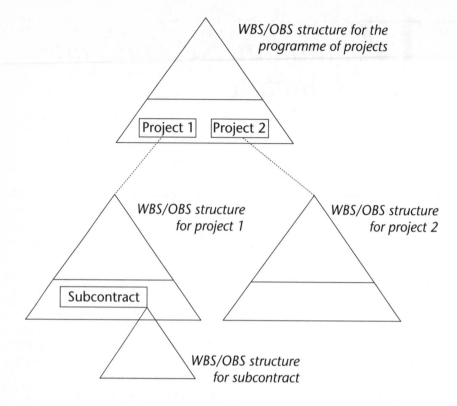

Figure 11.5   Multi-tiered WBS/OBS and planning structures

CHAPTER **12** *Standard Networks and Templates*

Many companies, in widely different sectors of commerce and industry, carry out projects that have some common characteristics, even though they are for different customers and different purposes. This chapter describes a few processes that can exploit similarities between successive past projects, particularly when planning and scheduling new projects. The use of critical path networks is assumed in every case.

Introduction to standard networks

Checklists are valuable aids in many areas of management. Critical path networks have, for many years, been recognized as an essential part of every project manager's toolkit. So, are there any circumstances in which both of these methods might be used together?

The principal function of a checklist is to reduce errors of omission. The best checklists, although they might originate in brainstorming sessions, are edited, developed and improved through experience so that they list all the factors that should be considered when dealing with a particular aspect of management. Thus each checklist should survive and be of practical use for many years. Project management checklists are not specific to one project but can be used again and again, improving with time.

Network diagrams have a different purpose. They are usually drawn for a specific project, with the intention of achieving the best possible work processes for that project. Unlike checklists, a completed network plan will place items in their best sequence, assign priorities to activities and, if required, provide the basis for resource scheduling. However, although a good WBS or task list might list all the essential elements of the project, there remains a risk of omission errors in the network plan that a relevant checklist might prevent. Unlike checklists, the usefulness of a typical project network diagram begins and ends with the project for which it was compiled.

Planning methods that combine the principles of checklists and project network diagrams result in the development of standard networks that, unlike typical networks, can be used repeatedly for successive projects. Standard networks combine the attributes of checklists and individual project networks. They have long life and improve with age. They can also save time and money. They enable working schedules to be produced soon after the start of a project with very little planning effort, yet are less prone to errors of omission than plans produced from scratch for a project. Standardization and repeated use means that the work processes for each project are based on retained experience in the organization.

A simple network-based checklist

One engineering company saw the benefits of combining the traditional checklist with a network technique for managing the opening stage of each new project. Although every project carried out by this company was unique, each had to undergo a standard sequence of formative processes before actual work on the project could start. The company developed a network diagram similar to that shown in Figure 12.1, which became known as a standard start-up network. Some of the activities were carried out in collaboration with the client, such as determining which drawing numbering method should be used, frequency of reporting, design standards, confirming the objectives, naming people as key contacts in the organization and so on. Other tasks in the plan were purely internal, many relating to project administration and records.

The illustration in Figure 12.1 has been simplified and adapted slightly from the original version for clarity but it shows enough to demonstrate the general concept. The network was printed on to A4 sheets and held in files as hard copy, so that one could be issued immediately (at practically no cost) every time a new project was authorized.

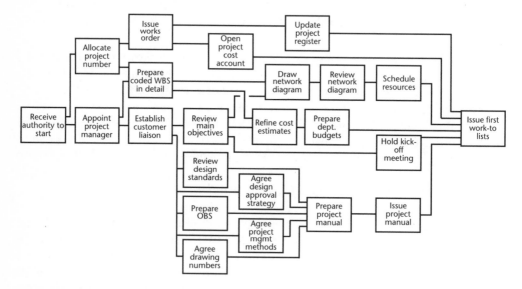

Figure 12.1   Checklist for opening a new engineering project, set out as a standard network diagram

Duration estimates were not made for activity durations on these networks, so time analysis was neither possible nor considered necessary. Unusually, therefore, here was a case of critical path network planning without a critical path. The network was used instead as a combination of checklist and work flow chart. It ensured an orderly, properly sequenced start to every new project, covering just the first few weeks of a project set to last for two, three or more years.

There were two tangible outputs from the use of this particular standard network-cum-checklist:

1 the issue of departmental or group work-to lists from a network-based project resource schedule

2 a project manual (sometimes known as a project handbook) that defines engineering standards, project management procedures and organizational features of the new project, as discussed and agreed where necessary with the project client.

Construction industry examples of standard networks

The methods outlined in this section are illustrated by examples from the construction industry, but similar applications can be envisaged across a wide range of industries.

SINGLE HOUSE PROJECTS

Consider a construction company that offers a catalogue range of houses from which private buyers can choose. Houses of similar design might be offered on a number of sites in different areas, and the company will be able to use the same design drawings for more than one house. Further, with only slight modification or 'customization', the same drawings can be used on a number of different houses in a particular design range. While this might be bad news for architects seeking new work, it has several advantages for both the construction company and the house buyers. These include:

- savings on design costs
- savings on design time, allowing productive work to start earlier on each project
- savings in operations planning
- savings in time wasted through snagging and rework because the designs are proven and debugged
- savings in construction time and materials, using designs that reflect best practice and experience
- increased confidence in project cost estimates with less risk of financial loss.

A common word here is 'savings'. And, if all this can be true for project design, why should it not be true also for project planning? So a network plan produced to show the logical sequence of activities in constructing one house (but with new start and finish target dates) could, with benefit, be used for a subsequent house of the same design. This principle can be applied not only to identical houses, but also to houses that are of broadly similar design and style. There might, for instance, be a range of houses contained in a brochure, all with similar construction but offering slightly different accommodation space. Perhaps some have a double garage and others only a single garage. A typical project might include a combination of these styles at one site. The standard network can be used as the planning and control basis for any house, once the project manager has reviewed it and struck out all the activities that are not relevant to the particular style.

Project manager's review and approval

The project manager's review and approval of the standard network is always important for any kind of project in any industry. For instance, the project manager will know which standard estimates should be changed according to the expected difficulties or complications of the particular job in hand. Where a composite standard network allows for all possible project options, the project manager will know which activities to strike out and eliminate from the subsequent planning and scheduling process. He or she can also amend the logic to suit any special project circumstances. However, when starting with the advantage of a well-designed standard network, this input from the project manager need take only minutes or an hour, as opposed to the many hours that would otherwise be necessary to plan the project from scratch.

STANDARD NETWORKS FOR MULTIPLE HOUSE CONSTRUCTION PROJECTS

Imagine a project to build a row of identical, or at least very similar houses. This might, for instance, be a local authority housing scheme. The contractor will start work at one end of the street, and the various trades will move from house to house in a sequence that should be orderly and planned. The planning method illustrated in Figure 12.2 might be considered.

A network diagram is produced for the first house. This network is complete with all time and resource estimates. The planner must find the point in the network diagram where the

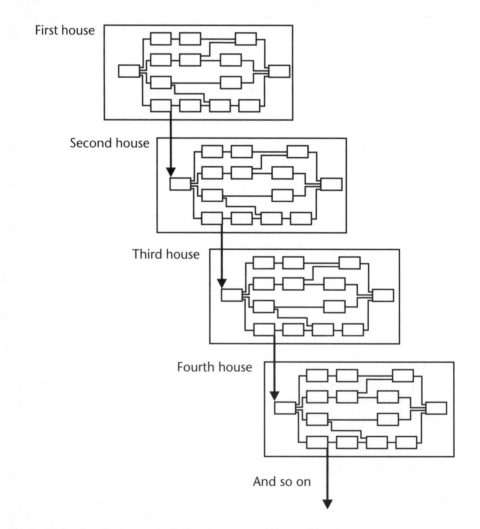

Figure 12.2   Standard networks for building a row of identical houses

first trades can move on to start work on the next house. This standard network is then entered in the computer as a sub-project, to be copied and pasted as many times into a project network in the computer as there are to be houses in the street. Each house is therefore treated as a sub-project in a multi-project schedule. The planner decides the start date for the first house in the project, but the computer will determine the recommended start date for each subsequent house, after it has performed time analysis and resource scheduling.

Some special skills might be needed to make this method work in practice. For example, with most project management software the links between the different sub-networks (interfaces) must be entered from the planner's keyboard.

Standard macro networks

A method that requires some expert customization of the project management software was first used by a construction company specializing in industrial buildings. In hierarchical terms, it might be said that the planner draws a master or summary network (say at level 1), which the computer expands automatically to the next lower level of detail (level 2). Figure 12.3 illustrates the approach.

(a) Fragment of the complete network diagram, as drawn by the planner

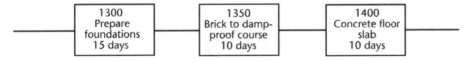

(b) The macro network for activity 1350 generated from the computer file

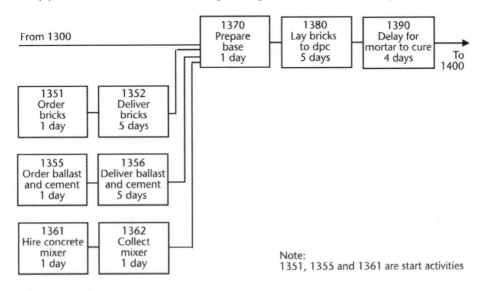

Figure 12.3   A macro network method used by a construction company

Whenever this construction company started a new project, the planning department drew a network diagram that, although it included every significant activity in the project, followed the usual and sensible practice of not going down to the smallest possible level of planning detail. So the planner could draw a network of perhaps 250 activities to cover the whole project. Figure 12.3(a) is a small fragment from such a network diagram. Had the planner attempted to show every small operation, and list all the small materials orders, the network might contain not 250 activities but an unwieldy 2500.

With the macro network method, the planning department compiles a library of standard macro networks that is made generally available for all projects. Each of these macro networks expands a commonly occurring activity from the usual project networks into its detailed components. This library of macro networks is stored in the computer.

In our example, activity 1350 in the project network is for a ten-day activity for constructing the lowest few courses of the brick walls for a new building. As this is an activity that is commonly found in this company's project networks, a corresponding standard macro network will be available in the macro library. The macro network file for activity 1350 is shown in Figure 12.3(b).

The computer is programmed to recognize part of the description field or ID code of every activity that has a corresponding macro network. It opens the relevant macro in each case and merges it into the network automatically. This creates a kind of virtual network, but the resulting work-to lists and materials requirements are real and practicable and have been achieved for relatively little planning effort.

Standard network modules or templates

There are only a few cases where companies are in the fortunate position of being able to use the same standard network diagram on two or more different projects. However, many more instances can be found where small parts of project networks in one project can be identified as patterns that repeat from one project to the next. It is sometimes even possible, with suitable analysis and imagination, to create a series of modules from which any future project network can be created.

Every company's case is different. There have been some hugely successful applications, with substantial savings not only in the costs of planning but also (because of the retained wisdom and logic embodied in the standard networks) in the time and costs of the projects themselves.

A SIMPLE CASE OF MULTIPLE STANDARD NETWORKS FOR WRITING ENGINEERING PROCEDURES

A London engineering company employing around 500 staff decided that, after a considerable internal reorganization, it was time to review, redesign and standardize its project management, engineering and general administration procedures. This company had a small organization and methods group and its manager was asked to initiate and coordinate the development of the new procedures as a uniform set of volumes. The main tasks of designing and writing the new procedures fell on the already busy chief engineers and managers who headed the various specialist functions in the new matrix organization. It soon became apparent that 20 loose-leaf volumes would be needed for each full set of procedures.

It was decided to conduct the establishment of these new procedures as an internal project, with the organization and methods manager appointed as project manager. The project objectives were to have all 20 procedures designed and implemented, and with a full set of procedures available in every engineering manager's office, in the company's library and at other central places for reference by all engineering staff. This was a considerable undertaking, and it was apparent that there would be resource bottlenecks in the conceptual design, preparation, approval and printing of all the procedures.

This project was planned and controlled from a series of standard sub-networks or templates, each network representing one of the 20 procedures. This standard network was similar to that shown in Figure 12.4. It was discovered that the same network was valid for every volume of procedures, although the names of the resources needed and the estimated activity times (not shown in Figure 12.4) had to be entered on the network templates to suit each case. Thus the entire project was seen as a set of 20 sub-projects, and these were entered from the templates into a multi-project computer module for time analysis and resource scheduling, using one of the many widely available project management packages. The resulting schedules required very little planning effort but were highly effective in controlling the project and smoothing the resource usage.

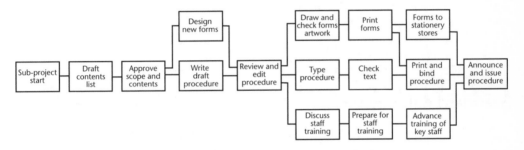

Figure 12.4   A standard network template used by a company to write each of 20 new engineering procedures

A MACHINE TOOL COMPANY EXAMPLE

A company in the British industrial Midlands produced high-value special-purpose machines and complex machining systems to the special requirements of large industrial customers, particularly in the automotive industry. Some of these machines were very large, weighing well over 100 tonnes. The company carried out an analysis of its past projects and discovered that all could be classified into one of three categories, which were:

1 one-off special-purpose machines for performing a single machining operation on a specific customer's workpiece
2 heavy milling machines (scalpers and plano-mills) for more general use
3 multiple machines combined into a system that could perform all machining operations on a raw casting to produce a finished component, such as a gear case, cylinder block or cylinder head.

This company designed a series of standard networks and network modules that, with only slight adaptation, could cover all its project activities. One standard network was devised that could be adapted for any project in category 1 (above). Another complete network was designed for category 2 projects. In each case the standard network diagram covered all possible customer options, so that when a network was applied to a particular project all that was necessary was for the project manager to strike out unwanted activities and review the estimates for the remainder.

Category 3 machines posed a more complex problem, but this was solved by devising a standard engineering design network module for every machine where the machining heads (for drilling, tapping and probing operations) could be purchased, and another standard network module for machines where the heads had to be designed in-house (typically for milling and boring). These templates were kept as preprinted self-adhesive films in a module library. These could be selected and stuck on to a large sheet of paper to suit the particular configuration of each new project. The templates were designed complete with interfaces that were connected on the large finished sheet simply by ruling in the lines.

For manufacture (as opposed to engineering design), a very simple module was devised that would link the standard engineering design and standard final assembly templates. One of these modules was used universally, without change, for each mechanical sub-assembly. This module is illustrated in Figure 12.5.

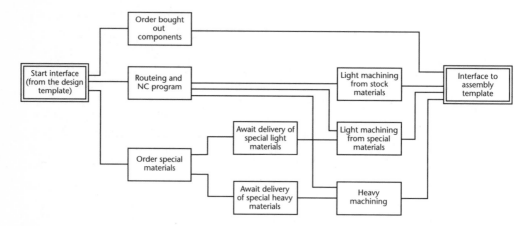

Figure 12.5   A template used by a machine tool manufacturer for machining every project sub-assembly

The system was developed to the point where all cost data, resource requirements and estimates were added to the networks by unskilled staff from a set of standard tables, devised by the planning manager. The only information that these unskilled staff needed for each new project was a schematic diagram of the machine produced before project authorization by the company's sales engineers.

No modules were held in the computer, so each project had to be keyed in. Further, because of the summary nature of the machining and assembly modules, the company's production engineers and production control staff carried out the detailed planning of manufacturing operations and the allocation of factory assembly space as functions separate from the project management scheduling. However, the multi-project model scheduled work so smoothly that demands for manufacture reached the factory at a steady rate, consistent with production and assembly capacity.

Although all this began in the early, mainframe, days of computers, a full multi-project model was maintained which allowed very accurate progressing and project control. Resource usage patterns were smooth and practicable. Every departmental manager had work-to lists tailored for the department. The model calculated project costs to within 5 per cent of the results obtained from the company's cost estimating department. All this was achieved in a company employing 600 people using a planning group comprising just one expert manager (part-time), one full-time planning engineer and one clerical assistant. This would have been impossible without templates. The system worked so well that it was eventually adopted, implemented and improved at the parent company's plant in the United States.

ADVANCED TELECOMMUNICATIONS PROJECTS

Another example of templating concerns an organization that, in the course of its work, constantly needs to design and build new radio communications receivers. Although each receiver is built for a specific purpose, all receivers have the common configuration of a main mounting frame, power unit and printed circuitboard assemblies.

This organization uses sophisticated modern software to house a library of templates. When each new project arises, it is only necessary to select the appropriate templates from the library browser. Then the computer automatically interfaces all the templates, 'draws' the network logic, carries out time analysis and finally performs full multi-project resource allocation.

A TURBOCHARGER PROJECTS EXAMPLE

This example concerns a British company, Holset Engineering Ltd, which always has a considerable number of special projects in hand to develop or modify automotive turbochargers for a number of customers in the motor industry. We are grateful to Holset Engineering Ltd for permission to describe this case, and especially for allowing us to include Figure 12.7.

The product and the problem

A turbocharger unit can be described as five basic components, as illustrated in Figure 12.6. Each of these components requires special design skills and considerable proving, through performance and safety tests, before it can be released to the customer. Typical projects range from a customer request that involves the design, testing and production of a turbocharger that is modified from an existing design to the development from scratch of a completely new unit. At any time, therefore, this company might be undertaking well over 100 projects, comprising a mix of new development projects and design change projects.

Such a large number of current projects would always pose a planning and scheduling problem of significant proportions but, in the case of this company, the situation is made more difficult by unpredictable customer-led changes in project scope, details and priorities. So, we have a very complex resource-scheduling problem, not made easier by the number of changes. Any solution has to be flexible to change, easy to administer and not too demanding in terms of planning effort.

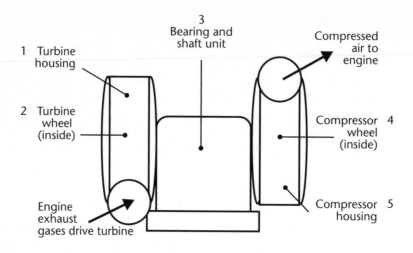

Figure 12.6   Five basic components of an automobile turbocharger

The solution

This company found that the clue to its scheduling solution lay in the modular nature of the product itself. Over a period of several months, intensive brainstorming sessions were held with the company's top engineers to design a network template for each of the following components:

- bearing and shaft unit
- turbine wheel
- turbine wheel housing
- compressor wheel
- compressor wheel housing
- performance and safety tests
- a standard template that would always interface all or some of these modules.

This whole collection of templates had to be designed twice – once for a design prototype and then for the preproduction unit, made from permanent tooling. In addition to the network logic, each template was designed complete with activity durations, resource usage estimations and budget data. All these data had to be accommodated within the template library.

Finding software that could handle such a library of templates and interface them automatically was a problem in itself, but this was largely solved using project management software from 4c Systems Ltd, a British company with a long pedigree whose website is http//www.4csys.com.

This is how the system operates in practice. A very small planning and coordination group, headed by a specialist, administers the system and safeguards the integrity of the multi-project model. When a new project is authorized, the appointed project leader is shown a template map (see Figure 12.7). The project leader ticks the templates that will be needed, according to the scope of the new project. For example, a project to modify an existing turbocharger design by changing the characteristics of just the turbine wheel and

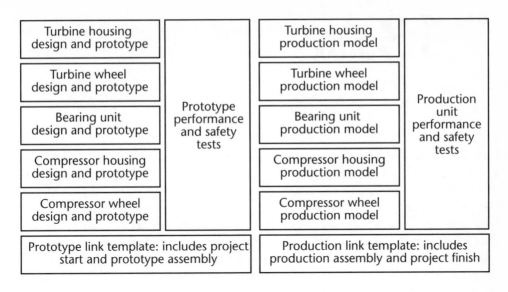

Figure 12.7   Standard template map for turbocharger projects

then building and testing a prototype would need only the template for turbine wheel design plus the obligatory templates for performance and safety tests and the prototype link.

The planning specialist enters the new project into the multi-project model in the computer, where the complete project network diagram can be plotted immediately simply by selecting the appropriate templates from the library browser. This first network is considered as a draft, not having validity until it has been checked and, if necessary, amended by the project leader. It is possible with this system to have a new project fully and very effectively scheduled in the multi-project model within one hour of the project being authorized.

Further, because each template has been designed for the optimum process by the company's best engineers and managers, the resulting networks are free from errors and make the best use of this company's considerable expertise.

Conclusion

Using the techniques such as standard networks or standard templates can bring several advantages. Planning effort is minimized but the effectiveness of plans is optimized. There is no better way of recording and exploiting a company's retained expertise. The economic benefits can be very significant, with more (if not all) projects completed to specification, within budget and on schedule.

13 *Risk*

No consideration of advanced project management would be complete without proper attention to the many risks that can beset projects and upset the carefully laid plans of their managers. The potential effects of risks range from trivial inconvenience to project disaster. Generally speaking, a risk event that occurs late in a project will have a greater effect and be more costly in terms of time and money than a similar event nearer the start of the project. That is because as time passes there will be a greater value of work in progress and higher sunk costs at risk of loss or damage. If, for instance, an engineer recognizes early in a project that his or her design is flawed and must be restarted, then the potential loss to the project might be significant, amounting to the cost of the wasted design salary and the loss of a week or two in progress. If the lost time cannot be made up, the indirect costs of the project will also rise as an inevitable result of the delay. If, however, the design error should not be discovered until late in the construction or manufacturing phase of the project, far greater costs will be incurred, many more people will be affected and possibly demotivated, and the setback to progress would be severe. Risk assessment must therefore be carried out early in the project life cycle. It should be accepted and performed as part of the project planning process.

Introduction

The purpose of risk management is to identify and assess as many of the potential risks as possible, as early as possible, and then develop a strategy for dealing with them. Projects are dynamic and, as they develop and evolve through their life cycles, so the potential for risk will change. The initial risk management strategy should therefore be reviewed from time to time throughout the project to ensure that it remains comprehensive and valid.

Project risk management is a particularly complex subject. Even the classification of risks is not straightforward and can be approached in different ways. There are several techniques for assessing and dealing with project risks, some of which are shared with other management disciplines (particularly quality management and reliability engineering). This chapter will outline a few of the methods commonly used.

Identifying and assessing risks

Risks can be foreseeable or totally unpredictable. For example, it is almost certain that some tasks will not be completed in line with their duration estimates and budgets. Some might exceed their estimates, whilst others could be finished early and cost less than expected. Indeed, statistical tools can be used to attempt an assessment of the probability of the project finishing by its target completion date. Earned value analysis can keep final cost forecasts under review. But the razing of project headquarters to the ground as a result of a gas explosion can hardly be predicted although, of course, if it did happen the effects of predictable departures from estimates would pale into insignificance.

IDENTIFYING AND LISTING THE POSSIBLE RISKS

Checklists, which grow in size and value as companies gain more project experience, are a good starting point for listing the foreseeable risks. Studying the history of similar projects can also highlight possible problems and help the project manager to learn from the mistakes and experiences of others.

Brainstorming is an effective technique for considering many aspects of risks. A brainstorming meeting of key staff is a particularly productive method for identifying all the possible risks, along with many of the improbable ones. Much depends on how the brainstorming session is conducted. The leader should encourage an atmosphere of 'anything goes', so that participants feel free to propose even the most bizarre risks without fear of ridicule.

It is desirable, even at the early listing stage, to attempt some form of risk classification. Perhaps the most practicable initial approach is to divide the list according to the stage in the project life cycle where each risk is most likely to occur. So, to give an example, risks might be grouped initially under the following headings:

1 risks most likely to occur at the start of the project
2 risks most likely to occur during the execution of the project
3 risks that can affect the final stages of a project, particularly during commissioning
4 risks occurring during the initial period of project operation, after handover to the customer
5 risks that can occur at any time in the project.

Once identified, risks can be ranked according to the probability of their occurrence and the severity of the impact if they should occur. For this, it is necessary to start by considering the possible causes and effects of every risk.

QUALITATIVE CAUSE AND EFFECT ANALYSIS

Fault-trees and fishbones

Fault-tree analysis (not described here) and Ishikawa fishbone diagrams are methods commonly used by reliability and safety engineers to analyse faults in design and construction. Figure 13.1, for instance, shows how an Ishikawa fishbone diagram might be compiled to analyse the numerous reasons why a car engine fails to start. Many items in this car engine example could be broken down into greater detail, leading to quite a complex diagram, with many branches to the 'fish skeleton'.

Fishbone diagrams can easily be used, without adaptation, to examine failures or poor performance in organizations. The process generally starts by thinking about the effect and then looking for the possible causes. Project risk management is, however, more often conducted from the opposite viewpoint, which means first listing all the possible causes (risks) and then assessing their probable effects. So, although often mentioned in connection with project risk management, these particular cause-and-effect diagrams arguably do not approach the risk management problem from the ideal direction.

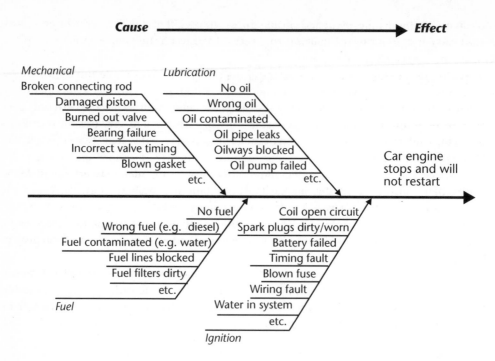

Figure 13.1   An Ishikawa fishbone cause-and-effect diagram

Failure mode and effect analysis (FMEA)

Failure mode and effect analysis (FMEA) has also been 'borrowed' by project managers from their reliability and quality management colleagues. Figure 13.2 shows a simple FMEA chart. Item 1 in this example considers structural failure risks in a building, during the course of a project for a new manufacturing or other processing facility. The scope of this project includes designing and constructing the building, and then installing and commissioning all the plant and machinery. During the initial brainstorming meeting, one person has asked what would happen if a floor structure collapsed during or after the installation of some of the very heavy machinery required for this project. The chart analyses possible causes of the

Item		Failure mode	Cause of failure	Effect	Remedy: recommended action
Main building	1.1	Building collapses during installation of heavy machinery	Errors in floor loading calculations	Personal injuries Project delays Loss of reputation	Ensure operatives get good training and instruction
	1.2	Building collapses during installation of heavy machinery	Floor slabs incorrectly poured	Personal injuries Project delays Loss of reputation	Employ competent site engineering manager
Security lighting	2.1	Some lights not operating	Lamps burning out	Reduced site security Risk of personal accident	Choose best-quality lamps Ensure correct voltage rating
	2.2	All lights fail to come on at correct times	Faulty time switchgear	Reduced site security Risk of personal accident Risk of fire in switch room	Use reliable brand of timer Ensure contacts correctly rated Ensure correct circuit protection

Figure 13.2   Part of a simple failure mode and effect analysis (FMEA)

risk event and then examines the possible consequences. The final column of the chart records pre-emptive measures that must be taken to prevent the failure happening, or to mitigate the effects if it should happen.

Security measures have been considered for the project in this example and these include high-intensity lighting around the perimeter of the building. The lighting is important not only for security but also for the safety of pedestrians who will use the adjacent footpaths during the hours of darkness. Two different failure modes for the lights have been considered in our example. The first (2.1) concerns random failures at individual lighting locations caused by the lamps burning out. The second fault condition (2.2) is more fundamental and would arise if the centrally controlled time switches were to fail. There are many high-intensity lights in the system, so the switches are handling high electrical currents with consequent risk of fire should the circuits not be properly protected.

Only four failure modes are shown in Figure 13.2 but there might be hundreds of items in a large, complex project. Another column is sometimes added to show when in the project life cycle the risk is most likely to occur.

The chart in Figure 13.2 illustrates a qualitative process in that the characteristics of each risk are examined. But there is no attempt to rank the risks according to their possible consequences. Consequently, a first glance at the chart might indicate that the failure of an electric lamp on a perimeter road would be just as significant as the collapse of a floor in the building. Thus we need to carry risk analysis forward to take account of the possible severity of any possible consequences. This should ensure that management effort is focused on the risks that pose the greatest threat.

Risk classification matrices

Figure 13.3 shows a risk classification matrix comprising nine sections. Although the chart in Figure 13.3 is labelled 'very simple', an even simpler four-section version is often used, containing the following quadrants:

- high chance – high impact
- high chance – low impact
- low chance – high impact
- low chance – low impact.

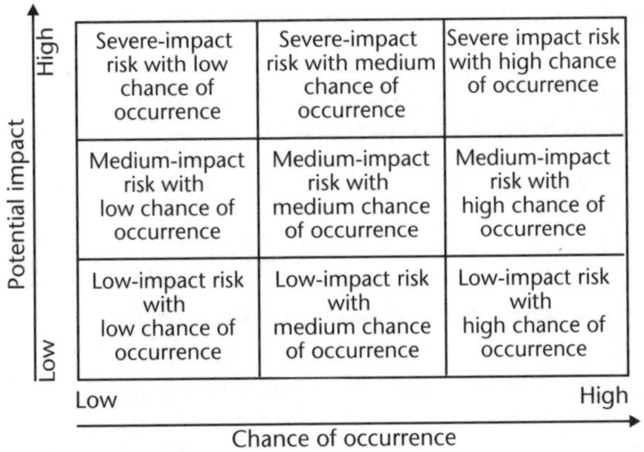

Figure 13.3   A very simple risk classification matrix

Risk event	Chance of happening	Potential harm to project	Difficulty of detection	Comment
Protests by environmentalists	High	High	Low	We shall offer land for a nature reserve.
Strikes or other industrial action	Low	High	Low	Loyal workforce with no previous problems.
Project manager struck by lightning	Low	Medium	Low	But she is a keen golfer.
Hairline cracks in structural steel	Low	High	High	Suppliers have high quality reputation.
Software bugs	Medium	High	High	Process safety depends on computer controls.
Exchange rate changes	Medium	Medium	Low	Not difficult to detect but very difficult to predict.
Materials shortages	Medium	Medium	Low	Preventable: must liaise with purchasing manager.

Figure 13.4   A qualitative risk assessment matrix

As with failure mode and effect analysis, this again is a qualitative method, in which no attempt is made to evaluate any risk numerically. Each risk item is considered for its likelihood of occurrence (chance) and for the relative scale of the impact on the project, should it occur.

Suppose, for instance, that a project is being planned to move a large company headquarters from a central city location to a country town. The possibility of some office equipment being lost, damaged or stolen in transit might be high, but the impact could be considered medium. The chance that some key staff might decide not to relocate with the company could be thought to be medium, and the effect could have a medium impact on the company's performance when starting up in the new location. The collapse of the new premises just before the proposed occupation date through an earthquake in Swindon would be a very low-chance risk, but the impact would be devastatingly high. The chance of moving day being made thoroughly miserable for all concerned through rain would be high, but with low practical impact.

Figure 13.4 shows a simple qualitative risk assessment matrix showing how the principles illustrated in Figure 13.3 might be applied in practice.

QUANTITATIVE ANALYSIS

Quantitative analysis methods attempt to assign numerical values to risks and their possible effects. They often examine the probable impact on project time and costs. Alternatively, for every identified risk, the evaluation process can produce a ranking number denoting the priority that a risk should claim for management attention and expenditure on preventive measures.

Although all quantitative methods produce 'actual' numbers, they can give a false sense of precision. It has to be remembered that the results are based on estimates, assumptions

Item		Failure mode	Cause of failure	Effect	Chance	Severity	Detection difficulty	Total ranking
Main building	1.1	Building collapses during installation of heavy machinery	Errors in floor loading calculations	Personal injuries Project delays Loss of reputation	2	9	5	90
	1.2	Building collapses during installation of heavy machinery	Floor slabs incorrectly poured	Personal injuries Project delays Loss of reputation	3	9	7	189
Security lighting	2.1	Some lights not operating	Lamps burning out	Reduced site security Risk of personal accident	1	4	1	4
	2.2	All lights fail to come on at correct times	Faulty time switchgear	Reduced site security Risk of personal accident Risk of fire in switch room	2	6	1	12

Figure 13.5   Part of a failure mode effect and criticality analysis (FMECA)

and human judgement. The contributing factors and estimates might be fundamentally flawed, mistaken or simply too difficult for any person to provide with any degree of certainty.

Failure mode effect and criticality analysis (FMECA)

The qualitative failure, mode and effect analysis method illustrated in Figure 13.2 can be adapted and extended to attempt risk quantification. The method then becomes failure mode effect and criticality analysis (FMECA). Figure 13.5 shows one version. In this example three assessment columns are provided, in each of which the risk analyst is expected to enter a number expressing the degree of significance on a scale of one to ten, with the higher numbers indicating the greatest degree of seriousness. The entries might be those of the risk analyst or, preferably, the collective opinions of a risk committee or brainstorming group.

The risk events shown in Figure 13.5 are the same as those included in the FMEA example of Figure 13.2. Looking at item 1.1, the assessor clearly thinks this event is unlikely to happen because he or she has ranked chance at the lower end of the one-to-ten scale. There is no doubt, however, that if this event did occur it would be extremely serious, so the degree of severity has been marked as nine.

Detection difficulty means the perceived difficulty of noticing the cause of this risk (design error in this case) in time to prevent the risk event. Here there is a considerable element of judgement, but the assessor thinks that although the chance of a design error is very low, the difficulty of spotting a mistake, if it did occur, would be greater (five on the scale of one to ten).

The product of these three parameters, $2 \times 9 \times 5$ gives a total ranking number of 90. Theoretically, when this exercise has been performed on every item in the list, the list can be sorted in descending sequence of these ranking numbers, so that risks with the highest priority for management attention are displayed at the top.

Although not usual practice, a case might be argued for allowing zero scores in the chance and severity columns. That could, of course, result in a total ranking factor of zero, and would be one way of disposing some of the more outlandish risk events identified during an 'anything goes' brainstorming session.

Sensitivity analysis

Sensitivity analysis is particularly useful in considering the effects of risks arising through incorrect forecasting of parameter values during project financial appraisal. The process involves repeating the appraisal calculations several times for stepped variations in the values of one chosen parameter to test the effect on the outcome. Suppose, for example, that the revenues (cash inflows) from a project in future years cannot be forecast reliably. After calculating the NPV of the project using the best estimates, the calculation can be repeated using a range of lower and higher cash inflows to test the sensitivity of NPV (or internal rate of return) to variations in revenue.

PERT

PERT (Programme Evaluation and Review Technique) is a critical path network planning method in which it is recognized that all activity duration estimates are at risk and might, in practice, take a shorter or longer time than the planner intended. For PERT, three time estimates are required for every activity:

t_o = the most *optimistic* duration that could be foreseen
t_m = the most *likely* duration
t_p = the most *pessimistic* duration

From these quantities a probable duration (the *expected* time) is calculated for each activity on a statistical basis, assuming that the errors will fall within a normal distribution curve when all the project activities are taken collectively as the sample:

$$t_e = \frac{t_o + 4t_m + t_p}{6} \quad \text{(where } t_e \text{ is the expected time)}$$

This calculation is repeated on all activities in the network and used to predict the probability of completing the project within the scheduled time. A computer removes the drudgery from these calculations and enables the results to be made available in time for appropriate action to be taken.

Monte Carlo analysis

Monte Carlo analysis is in effect a more sophisticated form of PERT, made possible by the power of modern computers. The input data, as in PERT, come from a network diagram in which the duration estimates for some or all of the activities are supplemented by additional estimates for the most optimistic and most pessimistic times. The computer is then asked to perform time analysis repeatedly – perhaps 500 or 1000 times. For each time analysis calculation the computer selects, at random, a different combination of the optimistic, pessimistic and most likely duration estimates. At one extreme, therefore, it is probable that the computer will carry out one or more calculations in which all the optimistic activity durations have been selected, and this will give the earliest possible completion time for the project. At the other extreme, one or more calculations will occur where the computer has selected all the most pessimistic times, so that the result is the most pessimistic forecast for the project completion date. In between these extremes, depending on the number of iterations performed, there will be a range of forecasts for project completion with all possible combinations of optimistic, pessimistic and most likely duration estimates.

If the computer can plot the expected completion time for the final activity in the network as a statistical histogram, a graph similar to that shown in Figure 13.6 will result.

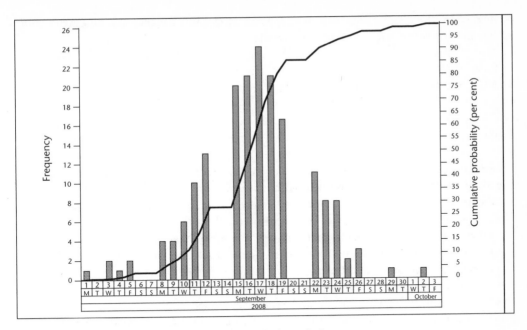

Figure 13.6   Typical histogram plot from Monte Carlo analysis

OPERA, which is part of the OPEN PLAN suite of project management programs, was one of the first systems with this capability. Today there are many others, such as PERTMASTER. All produce plots similar to that shown in Figure 13.6 (which we have simulated in this case, for clarity). Where resource scheduling is included in the calculations, the results can be related to either time-limited or resource-limited schedules.

The histogram needs some explanation. The left-hand vertical scale in this case shows the frequency, which is the number of times that a particular date has occurred as the completion date for the project. In some software this scale shows the frequency not as a number, but as a percentage of the total number of results. Interpreting the results from the graph, it is clear that the earliest possible completion date for this project is Monday 1 September 2008 (if all the critical optimistic times are achieved) and the latest possible date is Tuesday 2 October 2008. The expected date for completion is Wednesday 17 September. Notice that no results are scheduled on weekend dates, because this project was scheduled using a five-day week calendar.

The graph superimposed on the histogram is the cumulative probability of the project being finished at any of the dates on the timescale. Thus there is zero possibility of finishing the project before 1 September and 100 per cent probability of the project being finished by 2 October (this last result being one that can be taken with a huge pinch of salt by the realists among us, who know that even the most pessimistic estimates can be exceeded when things go wrong). There is a 66.7 per cent chance that this project will be finished on Wednesday 17 September.

There is no reason why the same method, using the same software, should not be used to predict project costs. All that is needed is to supply three cost estimates for some or all of the activities in the project and then select those data for the analysis.

The smoothest curve envelopes for these histograms will result from the projects having the highest number of activities in their networks, and where the number of iterations performed by the computer is the greatest. With modern computers, the time needed for (say) 1000 iterations is measured in milliseconds.

Methods for dealing with risks

When all the known risks have been listed, assessed and ranked it is time to consider what might be done about them. The manager has a range of options, which are as follows:

1 *Avoid the risk*. The only way to avoid a risk is to abandon the possible causes, which could even mean deciding not to undertake a project at all.
2 *Take precautions to prevent or mitigate risk impact*. This is a most important part of risk management, requiring the active participation of all managers and staff. It needs a high-level risk prevention strategy combined with executive determination to ensure that all preventive measures are always followed throughout all parts of the organization. It also requires the creation of a risk prevention culture, covering all aspects of project tasks, health and safety, and consideration for the environment. Here are a few examples of the many possible practical measures, listed in random sequence:
   * high-security fencing to reduce the chance of gatecrashers at an open air pop festival
   * provision of marquees at a garden party in case of rain
   * regular inspection and testing of electrical equipment to ensure safe operation
   * double-checking to detect errors in design calculations for vital project components or structures
   * provision of back-up electrical power supplies for vital operations, essential services and computers
   * frequent back-up and secure offline storage of business data
   * avoidance of trailing electric cables in offices
   * ensuring that means of escape routes in buildings are always clear of obstructions and that smoke screen doors are kept closed
   * regular fire drills, testing of fire alarms and emergency lighting
   * on-the-job training of back-up staff to understudy key roles in the organization
   * regular inspection and maintenance of lifts and hoists
   * provision of safety clothing and equipment to protect workers and enforcement of their use
   * restricted access to hazardous areas
   * provision of secure handrails to all stairways
   * choosing the time of year most likely to provide fair weather for outdoor projects
   * adequate training of all those operating potentially hazardous machinery
   * regular financial audits and the installation of procedures to identify or deter fraud
   and so on, and so on: the list is very long.
3 *Accept the risk*. Rain might make the day chosen for office relocation miserable for all concerned but the risk would have to be accepted. There are numerous small things that can go wrong during the course of any project, and most of these risks can be accepted in the knowledge that their effect is not likely to be serious, and that they can be overcome by corrective measures or replanning.
4 *Share the risk*. If a project, or a substantial part of it, appears to carry very high risk, the contractor might seek one or more partners to undertake the work as a joint venture. Then

the impact of any failure would be shared among the partners. Sharing a risk big enough to ruin one company might reduce its impact to little more than a temporary inconvenience.

5 *Limit the risk.* There are occasions when project risks should only be accepted with safeguards in place to limit their potential effect. A good example is an internal project, perhaps for pure research, that cannot be adequately defined at the outset. No one can tell how much the project will eventually cost or what its outcome might be. Yet the potential opportunities are too great to consider avoiding the risk altogether.

The usual and preferred solution to starting an ill-defined project is to limit the risk by authorizing work step-by-step. It may be possible to divide the project into a number of stages for this purpose: indeed the process is sometimes called stage gating. The stages might be determined by:

- the occurrence of significant events in the project that can easily be recognized when they happen
- the imposition of a time limit for each stage
- a budgetary limit for each stage or
- a combination of any two or all of these.

Funding or authorization of expenditure on each new stage of the project would depend on a critical review of the work carried out up to the review date, coupled with a fresh appraisal of the value of continuing with the project. This approach has the advantage of limiting the committed risk. Although it is not possible to define the entire project in advance, it should be possible to look the short way ahead necessary to define each new step. Each limited step so defined may then be amenable to the project management procedures that cannot be used for the whole project.

In the step-by-step or stage gate approach it always has to be borne in mind that it might become necessary to abandon the project at any stage and write off the expenditure already incurred.

6 *Transfer the risk through insurance.* Some risks, or substantial parts of them, can be transferred to another party on payment of a fee or premium. There are risks, however, which an underwriter will either refuse to insure, or for which the premium demanded would be prohibitive. Such cases arise in the following circumstances:

- where the chances against a loss occurring are too high or, in other words, where the risk is seen as more of a certainty than reasonable chance – for example, losses made through speculative trading or because of disadvantageous changes in foreign exchange rates
- where the insurer is not able to spread its risk over a sufficient number of similar risks
- where the insurer does not have access to sufficient historical data to be able to quantify the future risk
- where the insured would stand to gain as a result of a claim. Except in some forms of personal insurance, the principle of insurance is to attempt to reinstate the insured's position to that which existed before the loss event. A person cannot, for example, expect to benefit personally from a claim for loss or damage to property not belonging to him or her (property in which he or she has no *insurable interest*).

Planning for a crisis

Some risk events can have such a potential impact on a project that special crisis management contingency plans must be made. Such contingency plans can extend to projects that would need to be set up specially and rapidly to deal with a sudden crisis – for example, in areas that are particularly liable to epidemic diseases, famine, flooding, hurricanes, earthquakes or other natural disasters. Crisis contingency plans should also be put in place by process industries and other companies that carry out operations which, if they should go wrong, could be hazardous for people and the environment beyond the factory gates. One cannot always say when or where a disaster will strike, but at least plans can be put in reserve to be implemented immediately when the need arises.

Once the possibility of a crisis has been established, the first step in devising a contingency plan is to identify the key people who will take charge of the crisis management project. These people will constitute a sleeping organization, ready to awake at a moment's notice in case of need. The core organization might include senior representatives of local and national government, the emergency services, particular charities and relief organizations, and so on. Each person should have the authority to instruct others within his or her home organization and the permission to identify the relevant resources that could be made available should the crisis occur. A team leader or steering committee must be appointed that will manage the project should it become live. This group of key people might be called the 'crisis action committee'.

Once the key people have been elected or selected to serve on the action committee, they must meet to design appropriate contingency plans, and then meet again at regular intervals to ensure that the plans are kept up to date. The committee might have to arrange for emergency funds, stores and special equipment to be stockpiled or at least located against the time when they might suddenly be needed. Lists of secondary organizations and other helpers must be established, which, although not part of the action committee, could be called upon to give urgent and immediate assistance. These secondary associations might include, for example, specialist engineering or chemical contractors, explosives or decontamination experts, building and demolition contractors, caterers and a wide range of charitable organizations that could offer relief services. There might also be a need to plan for immediate advertising in the appropriate media to make public appeals for funds.

One thing that the action committee will need to do as early as possible is to assess what might happen should the crisis arise and use their collective imagination to consider, and be prepared in advance for, as many of the problems as possible. A tabletop exercise can contribute to this process, where the members of the action committee carry out a role-playing exercise to consider as exactly as possible what might happen and what they themselves and their subordinates might do should the crisis occur. Many crisis contingency plans can be tested by field exercises in which some or all of the services act out their parts as if the crisis had actually happened. Field exercises can reveal shortcomings in the contingency plans and test vital aspects such as mobility, response speeds and how to communicate and coordinate the various participants under emergency conditions, when power, water and telephones might all be out of action.

When the plans have been made and tested they must be documented, incorporating all the lessons learned from the tabletop and field exercises so that they are ready to be put into action effectively and with minimum delay. This is, in effect, creating a project handbook or project manual for a project that might never happen. When a crisis does cross from imagination to reality, however, contingency planning can save both time and many lives.

References and Further Reading for Part 3

Burke, Rory (1999), *Project Management: Planning and Control*, 3rd edn, Chichester: Wiley.

Chapman, C.B. and Ward, S.A. (1997), *Project Risk Management: Processes, Techniques and Insights*, Chichester: Wiley.

Chapman, C.B. and Ward, S.A. (2002), *Managing Project Risk and Uncertainty*, Chichester: Wiley.

Devaux, S.A. (1999), *Total Project Control: A Manager's Guide to Integrated Planning, Measuring and Tracking*, New York: Wiley.

Duffy, P. (1993), *Kluwer Handbook of Insurance*, 4th edn, Kingston-upon-Thames: Kluwer (loose-leaf).

Freeman, P.K. (1997), *Managing Environmental Risk Through Insurance*, Kingston-upon-Thames: Kluwer.

Grey, S. (1995), *Practical Risk Assessments for Project Management*, Chichester: Wiley.

Institution of Civil Engineers and the Institute of Actuaries (1998), *Risk Analysis and Management for Projects*, London: Thomas Telford.

Kerzner, H. (2000), *Applied Project Management: Best Practices on Implementation*, New York: Wiley.

Kerzner, H. (2001), *Project Management: A Systems Approach to Planning, Scheduling and Controlling*, 7th edn, New York: Wiley.

Kliem, R.L. and Ludin, I.S. (1997), *Reducing Project Risk*, Aldershot: Gower.

Lock, D. (2003), *Project Management*, 8th edn, Aldershot: Gower.

Lockyer, K.G. and Gordon, J. (1996), *Critical Path Analysis and Other Project Management Techniques*, 6th edn, London: Pitman.

4 *Managing Projects*

14 *Controlling Progress*

Previous chapters have dealt with various aspects of project planning, where the focus of attention is principally on project management activities that should take place before any work on the project starts. With this chapter the discussion moves forward to include the later stages of the project life cycle.

The planning and control cycle

The traditional planning and control cycle is shown in Figure 14.1. This is sometimes called the cybernetic form of control because it is similar in concept to the control systems that have long been familiar to electronic engineers.

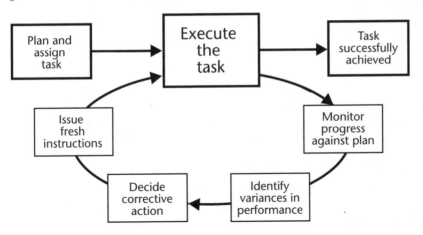

Figure 14.1   Traditional plan–execute–control cycle

The principle of cybernetic control is that the system starts with a planned result, which the working elements of the system attempt to achieve. During this process, the activity is constantly monitored to ensure that it conforms to the plan. Any detected deviation from the plan is analysed so that corrective action can be taken. In the electronic circuit such deviations are usually called distortion. In projects they are labelled as exceptions or variances. In any form of cybernetic control, data from a particular distortion, exception or variance is used either directly or indirectly to revisit the input to the system, make corrective changes, and so put the expected output back on course.

In project management, although planning and control for a single task follows along these lines, the cycle for a complete project is usually more complex than that shown in

Figure 14.1. Further, running through the cycle is the constant theme of integration through structuring. The principal elements, whose relationships are depicted in Figure 14.2, can be listed as follows:

1 project definition
2 change control
3 a WBS (see Chapter 8)
4 project estimate
5 planning, which includes:
   • expansion of the WBS into as much detail as possible
   • organization, particularly defining the OBS
   • design or selection of the project management systems to be used, as appropriate for the particular project
   • as part of system design, selection or design of the coding systems to be used for the WBS, OBS and cost accounts
   • a network diagram which is, in many cases, the precursor not only to simple scheduling but also to resource planning
   • translation of the foregoing into a schedule, resource budget and cost budgets.
6 the execution phase of the project
7 control, which begins as soon as the execution phase starts and includes:
   • data collection
   • analysis
   • reporting
   • management decision-making and executive action.

In many projects this is a multiple, reiterative cycle because the information available at the start is inadequate for full and accurate definition, estimation and planning.

PROJECT DEFINITION

Before a project can be planned or executed, it must first be defined as this determines what the project actually is along with work needed to deliver its objectives. Various terms are used to describe this project definition, such as project scope, statement of work (SOW), statement of requirements, specification, contract brief or documentation and so on.

The project definition may be different for different phases and companies involved in a project. For example, the project definition for a construction contractor may consist of a fully defined project design. For an architect it will probably consist of a design brief. The definition for a company's board of directors might be an outline proposal, supported by a technical summary and financial data, including the expected rate of return.

Defining the project is probably the most critical element in the control cycle. It determines all that follows. If a project is incompletely or confusingly defined, the actual project deliverables might be very different from those that the client or project sponsor expected and wanted. At the very least, a poorly defined project can lead to additional costs and delays in completion. Therefore considerable care must be taken in defining a project and in obtaining the agreement of all parties who have a stake in this definition.

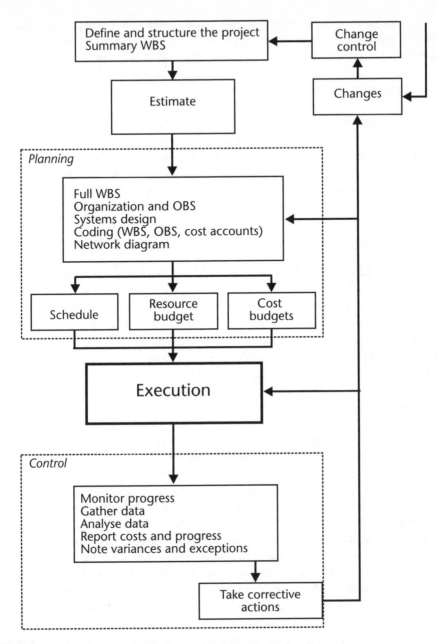

Figure 14.2   A more comprehensive view of the project control cycle

The project definition should include the following factors:

1 the project objectives or deliverables
2 the project strategies, including the contracting strategies
3 a scope of work statement
4 a summary WBS, if possible with its initial coding
5 specifications, sketches and preliminary drawings

6 a summary schedule showing the proposed start date, target complete date, and timings for milestones and WBS elements
7 indicative budgets or estimates, and any special financial constraints
8 health and safety policies for the project execution and, where relevant, for post project operating and maintenance.

The SOW, or technical scope of the project (depending on the industry or jargon used) describes the work required for the project and the intended end product. In conjunction with this description, the first two or three levels of the WBS should be established, including the project's WBS dictionary and coding. This should ensure that each important WBS element is defined and that the work need for each element is determined at the very first control cycle stage.

CHANGE CONTROL

All too often, as a project progresses through its life cycle, changes are made that affect the project scope, cost, schedule and economics. Many projects start life as a sound economic proposition but, before anyone has realized, the cost has increased by 20 per cent or by far more dramatic proportions without any conscious decisions being taken. Therefore as soon as a project is defined, even in the most elementary way, a system for monitoring and controlling changes must be put into place. The important (but often neglected) subject of change control is considered more fully in Chapter 18.

PROJECT ESTIMATE

The project estimate contains most of the information required to plan the project in the project dimension, including schedule, resource plans and expenditure budget. Effective control requires the comparison of actual costs, resources and times with those used in the estimate and plans based on it. Yet in many projects, the schedules, resource plans and budgets, and the actual outcomes of these factors, cannot be directly related to the estimate. This, in turn, creates the problem that estimating rates cannot be confirmed because the feedback of actual performance cannot be directly compared to the estimate.

The principal reason for this state of affairs is that the estimate and the plans are structured differently. Each uses a different breakdown of the project work. Often the structure and breakdown of a project estimate bears no relation to how the project is planned, or to how the work is carried out. Among the reasons for this are the following:

1 The excuse is made that 'It is more convenient', or 'The estimate can be done much more easily and quickly that way'.
2 Pressures to produce tenders before a submission deadline cause the estimating process to be rushed.
3 The client has specified the format of a tender, perhaps on a bill of quantities basis, which cannot easily be related to how the work is planned or carried out.
4 There is stubbornness or resistance to change on the part of the estimator.

Whatever the reason, the results of an inappropriately structured estimate can be catastrophic for the project. It is critical that the estimate can be related to the plans, to the control data and to subsequent reports. The converse is also true, so that the plans, control data and reports must be relatable to the estimate. Thus the structure of the estimate must match the structure of the project, the plans and the control system. In other words, these should all be structured using the project's WBS as the basis. If the estimate is arranged in any other way, it must be restructured or translated so that it matches the WBS, and makes the information contained in the estimate useable in the planning and control processes. This can usually be achieved using spreadsheets or specialized transformation programs.

Thus the project estimating process should price the elements of the WBS, based on the definition of these elements during the project definition stage. As more detail becomes available during the course of the project, this often requires extending the initial summary WBS into greater detail and more breakdown levels. However, consistency is maintainable, because the consolidations (roll-ups) of these lower breakdown levels will correspond with the elements of the initial summary WBS. This enables the coding, dictionary and cost–resource–time (CRT) catalogue to be prepared for the WBS elements.

PROJECT PLANNING

Although the estimate provides data necessary for the project schedule, resource and budget plans, there are a number of other elements needed to carry out the modern planning and control process. These are necessary to ensure integration, two-dimensional planning and control, and the design of the project systems. They include the following:

1 *Project organization design*
   This establishes the relationships between groups, defining the OBS and providing a basis for its coding. It also includes the merging of the WBS and OBS to identify work assignments and the responsibilities of organizational groups: that is, the cost accounts, or 'who does what?' questions. In addition, this stage allows the disaggregation of the project's objectives across the same framework.

   This stage will include the preparation and issue of the project coordination procedures and responsibility matrix, which will identify the key individuals from the organizational elements, responsibilities and interrelationships. This is an essential step to ensure communication and coordination, particularly (but not only) between client and contractor.

2 *Project systems design*
   The project systems can now be designed and integrated using the code of accounts based on the WBS, OBS and cost accounts. These will also include various internal coordination procedures, as well as contract coordination procedures between client and contractor.

3 *Network diagram*
   A network diagram is needed now to determine the sequence, timing and priorities of all activities. This information is essential for producing the schedule and the resource plan.

4 *CRT catalogue/WBS dictionary/active database*
   The CRT requirements for all elements, cost accounts and activities will have to be determined. This may be formally constructed on a WBS basis, or it could be in a database or spreadsheet. Whatever its format, a CRT catalogue, WBS dictionary or some form of database holding roughly the same type of information will be required at this stage.

Unfortunately these essential steps have often been implicit, or left to accountants and other staff groups to carry out, instead of being the concern of project management. But they are vital steps in the planning and control process. These steps and the planning of the schedule, resources and expenditure are based on the project structures developed from the initial summary WBS of the definition stage. Thus the WBS is extended in the estimating and planning stages, and combined with the organization structure and coding. Thereafter the project is planned on a hierarchical, two-dimensional basis, integrating schedule, resources and budgets, using these structures as previously described.

CONTROL

Control must be exercised at many levels in the organization and in the WBS. At the level of individual tasks or activities, this is a direct and immediate process. It depends on the supervision of group and departmental managers who, once tasks are assigned to people, small groups or external contractors, will check progress at regular intervals, offer encouragement, solve local difficulties and generally ensure compliance with the schedule.

At higher levels in the WBS, up to and including the level of the whole project, exceptions and variances are more difficult to detect in their early stages. But if these are not discovered early, corrective actions might come too late to be of any use. So some form of measurement and analysis is required that can identify adverse trends early. The earned value method is commonly used in this context, and this is described later, in Chapter 16. Reports are then produced for the managers involved, as appropriate to their areas of responsibility. Thereafter action must be taken to deal with the deviations and problems highlighted, or all the previous work will have been done for nothing.

Multiple control cycles

The planning and control cycle so far described identifies the planning and control process required for any project. However, it will probably only apply in its basic form to a developed project at the stage where contracts could be placed, and not over the total project life cycle. The reason for this is that a project cannot generally be defined in terms of the work required to complete it until a considerable amount of work, time, resources and money have been expended on it.

The problem is that there is simply not enough information available at the early stages in the project life cycle to define, estimate and plan the project with any degree of detail or accuracy. Yet, in these early stages, statements – even commitments – are often made regarding completion dates, costs and rates of return. These can really only be targets, or expressions of hope, based as they are on insufficient information. Nevertheless, despite the lack of information, the project must be planned and controlled from the very first stage of its life cycle if there is to be any chance of fulfilling the stated objectives.

In addition, many projects have contract tendering processes between many of their stages, resulting in the subsequent employment of external contractors to carry out the following stage or stages. Often projects cannot be fully defined, estimated and completely planned until the design stage has been completed. Project definition is almost a continuous process, with the picture becoming steadily more accurate and complete as work proceeds until the final definition in the as-built condition of the project. For planning and control purposes, however, we can identify the following three points of particular significance in the project life cycle, which lead, in their turn, to three or more planning and control cycles within the overall planning and control cycle:

1 the conceptual definition of the project, produced at the end of the conception stage of the project life cycle
2 the definition of project requirements produced at the end of the definition stage in the life cycle
3 the more fully detailed definition of the project produced at the end of the design stage.

Nevertheless, each stage of the project must be planned and controlled, and all stages must be planned and controlled in one integrated overall project control cycle. The problem of lack of information necessitates a multi-stage or phased control approach to both planning and control, as summarized in Figure 14.3.

In this multi-phase approach, the conception stage of the project life cycle will result in the following:

- level 1 plans and estimates for the project as a whole
- level 2 or 3 plans and estimates for the definition stage, which is in effect the 'execution' stage for these plans.

The level 1 project plans will be used to establish the overall planning and control cycle, whilst the level 2 or level 3 plans will become the basis of the phase control cycles for the definition stage. In addition, as soon as the first conceptual definition of the project is crystallized, no matter how tentatively, it is imperative that the change control system be put in place.

The output from the definition stage will produce the plans for the execution stage – that is, the design stage. This will have its own phase control cycle, within the overall project cycle and change control system. This process will be repeated, with some overlap, for the subsequent stages of the project life cycle, as outlined in more detail below.

CONCEPTION STAGE

The conception stage in a project takes an idea and turns it into a formal proposal. It will define the project conceptually, develop the project's objectives and initial ideas on strategy, and it will define roughly what is required to complete the project. It will also prepare an initial level 1 summary plan, plus a level 1 approximate estimate of cost and the resources required to complete the project. All these will be structured and coded to two levels of a WBS. This stage evaluates alternatives, strategies and the economics of the project proposal and thus involves an iterative process which evaluates different alternative proposals and strategies, based on the approximate estimates of cost, resource and time developed during the process.

The planning and control cycle for the conception phase is thus somewhat different from the basic cycle. The conceptual definition of the project is followed by estimating and planning stages, as before, but the various project alternative proposals, their rough estimates, plans and overall economics are then evaluated in the 'control' stage. This involves an

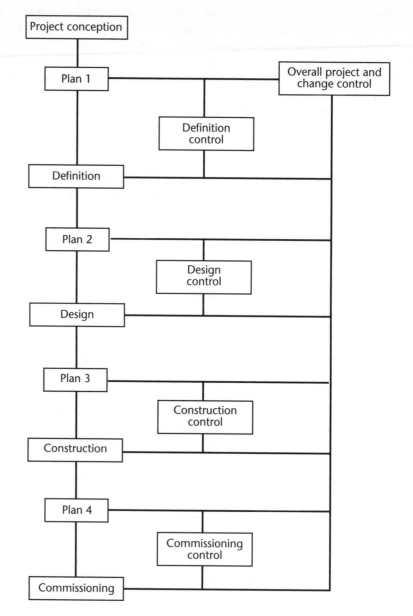

Figure 14.3   The multi-stage project control cycle

iterative process as the alternatives are compared and refined until one or more conceptual definition, plan and estimate are put forward to the decision-making body for approval to proceed. The control element of the conceptual cycle is of the 'go' or 'no-go' category, rather than cybernetic and can thus include the following:

- a revision option
- a 'no-go' option
- a 'go' option, which will trigger the move to the formal definition stage.

The conception stage will also include the planning and estimating of the resources and cost of the definition stage, to level 2 or 3. Additionally, it may include a tendering process to employ consultants or contractors to assist in the preliminary design work that may be needed to develop the conceptual project proposal into the formal definition of the project.

The output from this conception phase will then include the first summary, conceptual or approximate of the following:

1 project definition
2 a summary project WBS
3 project objectives and strategy
4 estimates and plans for the overall project on a level 1 (summary) basis
5 estimates and plans for the definition stage of the project at level 2 or 3 (that is, on a detailed basis).

DEFINITION STAGE

In the second, or definition, stage of the project life cycle, the project requirements will be defined to take the project to the stage at which design work can start – that is, to the point where the design staff know exactly what they have to design. In the context of contracts, for instance, it will give an architect a brief for a building or, in the case of a North Sea oil platform, contracts can be let to design the modules.

An estimate and the second stage of plans will be produced for this definition, and the 'go, no-go' process repeated. Where design, or design and build contracts are involved, there will be a tendering process towards the end of this stage. There could be another 'go, no-go' or revision decision if tender prices are significantly different from the estimates. The work in this development stage will have to be controlled against its input stage plans, and change control must be maintained within the overall project control cycle.

The output from this stage will be that detailed as for the basic control cycle, with the plans and estimates being more or less as follows:

* level 2 for the project as a whole
* level 3 for the design stage.

The execution stage will still be somewhat uncertain, as it cannot be fully defined, estimated or planned in detail until substantial parts of the design have been completed.

DESIGN PHASE

The design phase will follow the same pattern as the definition phase and, as design work progresses, plans and estimates for the subsequent stages can be completed in more detail. In some industries, where design and execution are typically overlapped, activities for procurement and fabrication or construction will be started part-way through the design stage. In other cases, where execution, manufacture or construction must wait for complete designs, the tendering process will be repeated as before and this, again, might lead to a 'go, no-go' or revision decision. The design stage will be subject to its own control cycle, set within the overall project control cycle and change control system. Output will include the following:

- the detailed design
- the definitive estimate
- plans for the execution and commissioning stages.

This process is repeated for subsequent stages, with the various phases tending to overlap.

SUMMARY

The rolling wave project planning for large or complex projects thus follows the pattern listed below:

1 Project:
   - level 1 at the end of the conception phase
   - level 2 at the end of the definition phase.
2 Each stage:
   - the level 3 (detailed) plan for each stage following the conception stage is developed towards the end of the preceding stage. Thus the crest of the rolling wave (level 3 planning, with level 4 short-term detailed or work packages) occurs within each stage as it proceeds. In general, therefore, the detailed planning for each stage will start part-way through its preceding stage.

Further reflections

In the 1960s project planning was revolutionized by the adoption of computer methods based on critical path networks. Since then, other significant changes have evolved in the project planning and control process, not the least of which is that project planning and project control are no longer regarded as separate entities. Project control is no longer concerned only with planning techniques such as Gantt charts or critical path networks to prepare a project schedule. A structured methodology is now required, which must involve incorporating these planning techniques into a system that also embraces the organization, planning, control, the human element and integrated management information systems.

A principal catalyst in these developments is the widespread availability of powerful computer systems, with their networked communications, relational databases and user-friendly, but very capable, project management software suites. However, it is the widespread acceptance and adoption of this structured methodology for project control, backed up by these integrated project management systems, that has revolutionized project management, planning and control.

STRUCTURED METHODOLOGY OF PROJECT CONTROL

The methodology of project control used is more important than the particular planning technique chosen. There are several effective methodologies, such as C.Spec (mentioned in some detail in Chapter 16) and PRINCE2, which is a UK government-sponsored framework. PRINCE (PRojects In Controlled Environments), the forerunner of PRINCE2, had its origins in IT projects. Prince2 is now widely promoted for all projects and is mandatory for some UK government-sponsored projects. However, the PRINCE2 methodology is considered too prescriptive and management top-heavy by some professionals and may not be suitable for all projects. It does, however, have many advocates and a growing number of practitioners. There are several useful websites but http//www.ccta.gov.uk and http//www.prince2.org.uk are recommended for those wishing to tread this path.

All structured methodologies, whether imported or 'home-grown', should have the following characteristics:

- Organization, planning, control, systems and the human element are integrated.
- The project is structured in one, two or more dimensions.
- Planning and control tends to be structured, two-dimensional, hierarchical, multi-level, rolling-wave, modular and personalized.
- There is an emphasis on personal accountability, right down to the lowest levels of management.
- Planning tends to be distributed, but integrated.
- Performance is analysed based on earned value methods.
- The control cycle is multi-stage, and the project is structured during the initial stages.
- There is an integrated PMIS.

TOTAL INTEGRATION

The modern project plan is an integrated set of three plans, which are the work schedule, the resource or manpower plan and the expenditure budget. This integrated plan covers all activities, work groups, companies and stages of the project from its conception to completion and beyond. This plan and the consequent control function are integrated with the organization of the project, the project management systems, and the people involved to give the concept of 'total' integration. This total integration is essential to the effective management of a project. Its absence can be a principal cause of project failure.

STRUCTURING THE PROJECT

Project structuring is central to the achievement of integration, and is the basis of the modern approach to project management, planning and control. Structuring, in one, two or more dimensions provides the framework for project integration. This structuring performs many functions and has several benefits, including the following:

- It is an aid to the organization of the project.
- It provides the basis for the design of the project management systems.
- It establishes the hierarchy of plans and control reports.
- It is an aid to managing people in the project.

This approach provides a formal and systematic method for structuring a project and its organization, coding the project elements and activities, and integrating all the project systems. It has developed along two lines:

1 a single-dimension WBS that breaks a project down into its principal elements.

2 a two-dimensional approach that combines the WBS with an OBS to identify the individual work assignments or organizational elements on WBS elements.

Thereafter, other structures (such as the CBS) can be used in conjunction with either of these two approaches.

The 'classical' two-dimensional approach originated in the C.Spec methodology developed by the US government in the 1960s, but found little general acceptance outside government projects until the 1980s. The single-dimensional approach was adopted for some large industrial projects as a somewhat simpler derivative of C.Spec. However, from the late 1980s onwards, the wide availability of low-cost, but effective, project software supporting a multi-dimensional approach has led to a merging of the two methodologies.

Integral to all these systems is the use of a standardized coding system that can identify uniquely each element of work and the structural relationships. The use of these structure-based codes extends throughout the project management systems and is critical to their integration.

STRUCTURED PLANNING AND CONTROL

Project planning and control follows the structures used and is modular: that is, it is based on the elements of the WBS and the OBS, and on the assignments or cost accounts defined by the intersection of these structures in the two-dimensional approach. In the single-dimensional approach it is based on the WBS elements and work packages, plus plans for the individual disciplines.

Large, monolithic plans are considered to be outdated, cumbersome and no longer necessary. Instead, project plans are made in a hierarchical, multi-level manner, with the level of detail being consolidated (rolled up) the hierarchy. The number of levels may vary and these may or may not correspond to the levels used in the structures. However, a common hierarchy used in many projects is as follows:

- level 1 – summary plan
- level 2 – intermediate level plan
- level 3 – detailed intermediate level plans
- level 4 – short-term plans, perhaps involving the use of job cards.

Within this hierarchy, the lack of information at the beginning prevents sufficiently detailed planning of the project in its entirety, particularly when attempting to look ahead to the later stages. This difficulty is overcome using the rolling wave concept. This uses the level 1 or level 2 plans to integrate all stages of the project from its start, developing the more detailed level 3 and level 4 plans later, when the necessary information becomes available.

PERSONAL ACCOUNTABILITY AND RESPONSIBILITY

Planning and control have become much more personalized, with each manager, group and company having their own plans and control reports within the overall framework created by the various levels of planning and project structures. These modular and personalized plans and control information are used to reinforce the delegation of personal accountability and responsibility to each manager and group involved. This, combined with the contractor–consignee principle for in-house work, greatly enhances motivation and teamwork within the project group.

DISTRIBUTED, BUT INTEGRATED, PLANNING AND CONTROL

Within the context of the above personalized planning, accountability and responsibility, both planning and control now tend to be distributed to these managers and groups. At the same time, they are integrated within the framework of the structures and hierarchy of plans.

PERFORMANCE ANALYSIS

Whatever the method adopted, there is now a widespread and growing adoption of performance analysis based on earned value (Chapter 16), as well as the more traditional use of variance analysis of progress. Thus each manager and group has individual measurement of performance of both time and cost, which gives greater control and increases motivation.

INTEGRATED PROJECT MANAGEMENT INFORMATION SYSTEMS

No project can be effectively managed without a PMIS to plan, control and integrate the people and the work. This information system will consist of several information subsystems, of which planning is only one. It is essential that these subsystem information modules be integrated. This integration is far easier than it used to be, with a large, quickly accessible relational database at the heart of the information system. Within this system, any of the better modern project management software packages can play a vital role in that, when appropriately chosen and operated, it can consolidate several information subsystems (such as cost management, earned value analysis and reporting) into one.

15 *Controlling Costs*

Much that is said and written about controlling project costs is about cost measurement, cost analysis and cost reporting. However, although necessary and important, none of those processes deals directly with cost control. Control implies taking action – not dwelling upon costs that have already been incurred. Cost control is not for historians. So this chapter concentrates solely on measures that can, and should, be taken to keep project costs within their budgeted limits.

Estimates and budgets

The structured project estimate will enable budgets to be established for all categories of expenditure for every department and other organizational element of the project. Coding is essential for all budgets and cost elements, so that every item of cost can be related to its budget and to its place in the structure of the project.

TREATMENT OF BELOW-THE-LINE ITEMS

Project estimates should always contain allowances for contingencies and other unforeseen circumstances. These allowances, always known as below-the-line items (because they come below the line of the initial total project estimate) might include the following:

- escalation allowances, which provide for increased costs with inflation on projects of long duration
- contingency allowances, which cover, partly or in full, deficiencies in the original estimate, serious scrap and rework events and unfunded changes
- exchange rate allowance, for international projects priced in a single currency, where changes in the foreign exchange rates could result in increased project costs
- provisional sums (pc sums), which are sums notified to the project purchaser but not included in the basic price, to be realized only if a named suspected risk should materialize. For example, a customer requests that all existing doors in an old building are to be re-used in a new building, but the contractor has doubts about their suitability and nominates a pc sum that will be added to the contract price if, in the event, it should prove necessary to purchase new doors.

In general, all such allowances will be held as reserve budgets and will not be included in the budgets initially issued to the relevant managers. Should it become necessary, the project manager or other senior manager may authorize a budget supplement by 'drawing down' funds from these reserves. Naturally, projects won against competition often allow only low reserves to be set aside.

Understanding the nature of project costs

All project managers should communicate regularly with their project accountants and be familiar with the fundamentals of cost and management accounting. Figure 15.1 shows the principal cost components of a project. Although there are a few other cost categories that could be included (such as indirect bookings by direct workers), those shown in the diagram are sufficient for the purpose of our discussion. Indeed, Figure 15.1 can be regarded as the keystone for this chapter.

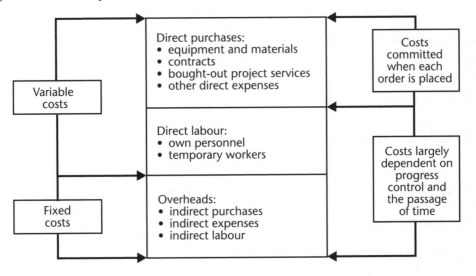

Figure 15.1   Principal project cost components

Project costs can be categorized in several different ways. One of these is to classify costs as either fixed or variable. Costs can also be classified as labour, materials and expenses. Many permutations and combinations of these classifications are possible.

Variable costs are those costs that vary according to the rate of working on the project. If no work is done, then no variable costs are incurred. Variable costs are also, more commonly, classed as direct costs, because they can be associated directly with project tasks.

Fixed costs must be incurred by the project organization regardless of the rate of working. These include the costs of management, accommodation, test equipment, production facilities and all other infrastructure costs needed to keep a modern business running. These fixed, indirect or overhead costs cannot be directly related to a single project, unless the organization is only undertaking one project.

Direct purchases

All equipment and materials bought for incorporation into a project are direct purchases. Some bought-out services can also be included under this heading, as can most contracts let for a fixed price. All these purchases share a few common factors that are important in the context of project cost control:

1 The sum total of all project purchases will typically account for a very high proportion of project expenditure, often exceeding half the total project costs. Effective purchasing controls are therefore essential if project costs are to be controlled.

2 All high-value purchases should be made against competitive bidding. A formal bid evaluation procedure is essential. Remember that the purchase costs are committed when the purchase order is issued, or when the contract for bought-out services is signed. Cost control therefore requires making every effort to eliminate errors at the purchasing stage and being certain that the price and scope of each purchase are understood and agreed by all parties.

3 All those working on a project must be told the limits of their authority in regard to authorizing purchases. In most cases, the limit will be zero, with only one or two nominated people allowed to approve the issue of purchase orders or to sign contracts.

4 Amendments to purchase orders and any other changes to bought-out services should be avoided as far as possible. When a change is made to an existing order, the competitive bidders who were around before the order was placed are no longer in the picture because a one-to-one contract now exists between seller and purchaser. Thus, for every active purchase order the seller has become the sole supplier, with a monopoly. In principle (but, fortunately, rarely in practice) the seller could increase the price of the original order by any amount of his choosing when the purchaser requests a change of scope or other amendment of any significance. It is even said, with some truth, that some suppliers and contractors pitch their initial price bids low because they reckon on making their real profits on the inevitable changes that can be expected from their customers.

5 Administrative and inspection controls must be in place so that when goods are received the supplier's invoice will only be paid if the goods supplied are in accordance with the purchase order and are received undamaged.

DAYWORKS AND CONTRACTORS' CLAIMS FOR PAYMENT

All contractors' claims for payment should be certified to show that the work claimed for has actually been performed. Construction managers are familiar with the practice of having quantity surveyors measure the work done by contractors and issuing the relevant certificates to support the contractors' claims.

A problem and opportunity for cost leakage sometimes arises when contractors on a project site are given sundry additional tasks, and these are typically recorded on dayworks sheets that are eventually costed and arrive back at the project manager's offices as invoices. Dayworks should only be authorized by senior, nominated personnel, and all copies of dayworks sheets must be retained to be checked against the contractors' eventual invoices. One London company employed a well-known City of London contractor to carry out a number of office alterations and improvements over a period of about six months. Dayworks sheets were signed regularly for additional jobs and for the provision of rubbish skips and so on. A site hut was maintained on the premises for longer than intended, simply because of the amount of dayworks carried out. The work of this contractor was of a high standard and their charges were reasonable. Their office efficiency, however, left much to be desired and, some six months after the contractors had left the site, the customer was suddenly faced with one enormous bill covering all the main project and additional dayworks. The customer had to employ its own quantity surveyor for about three months to sort out the administrative muddle and certify all the amounts claimed.

COST COLLECTION AND REPORTING METHODS FOR PROJECT MATERIALS AND DIRECT PURCHASES

There are three possible methods for collecting the costs of materials used on a project. Each has its advantages and disadvantages in the context of cost control and cost reporting.

The most common method used by accountants for manufacturing projects is to collect and price all stores issue notes, or bills of material or stores requisitions after the materials have been issued from stores for use on the project. This method has two disadvantages for the project manager. First, the cost data become available very late, after the materials have been used and far too late to measure cost trends. Second, materials bought for the project in error or in excess of requirements will remain in the stores, and their costs will not be taken into account.

Perhaps the most accurate method for collecting materials costs would be to sum the amounts incurred each week or each month against relevant suppliers' invoices. This will certainly take account of purchasing errors and surplus quantities. But some suppliers are slow to submit their invoices, and there will be further delays while the invoices are processed.

The recommended and earliest possible method for collecting materials costs is for the project manager to ask the purchasing agent or purchasing department to make a weekly return of the value of purchase orders and purchase order amendments placed. This means that the data are available to the project manager at the time when the costs are committed. For individual orders it is still too late to do anything about over-budget purchases, but at least adverse trends can be picked up in time to tighten controls on purchases yet to come.

Controls for direct labour costs

It is sometimes said, with good reason, that labour budgets should only be issued to managers in terms of time units (that is, man-hours) and not as amounts of money. The argument here is that managers can generally be held accountable for progress, and for the time spent on jobs, but they cannot be responsible for industrial wage awards, escalation and the like.

The most effective control for direct labour costs is good supervision, which includes providing the workforce with expert advice and adequate information, avoiding materials shortages and generally encouraging good performance through teamwork and motivation. It is generally true that a job which runs late will overrun its budget, whilst every job finished on or ahead of schedule is more likely to cost less than the budget.

Collecting labour costs

The universal method for collecting direct labour costs is to have everyone involved in the project complete a timesheet at the end of each working week. These provide for the hours worked against each cost account to be recorded. The accounts department will translate the times recorded into costs, most likely using standard cost rates. Briefly, each standard cost rate is an average hourly rate applied across all staff of a particular grade. Among the advantages of using standard costs is that of confidentiality – if the rates used are averages for a group, no one who sees these rates can know the actual wage or salary of any individual.

Standard costs are also very helpful when estimating and setting budgets, because it would be foolish to attempt such calculations using real names and real salaries when no one can possibly say who will actually perform the tasks when the time comes.

Again, coding is essential. Every task must have a cost account code. The accounts department can analyse the timesheets at the end of each week, and their computer will allocate the standard costs across all the relevant accounts codes.

Timesheets should be completed by all staff doing direct work on the project, which includes temporary staff imported from agencies. These temporary staff will typically fill in two timesheets each week, one for the project employer and one for their agency.

Timesheet entries should be checked by the relevant managers for accuracy. This is particularly important when agency invoices relate directly to the times entered on timesheets by temporary staff. It is also important, and ethical, to ensure timesheet accuracy where the times booked result directly in invoices to clients on cost-reimbursable or cost-plus contract terms.

From time to time most timesheet systems will also need to be audited by independent auditors, again to check that the bookings are equitable and soundly based.

In recent years timesheet administration has, to some extent, moved away from the direct supervision of accountants with the advent of timesheet capabilities in some project management software. With these systems, staff are able to key their timesheet data into the computer system directly. Checking and auditing is more difficult, but just as necessary, for these online methods.

Controls for indirect costs

Many indirect cost items will fall well outside the responsibility of the project manager but, whoever is responsible, the level of indirect costs must be kept as low as possible. It could be said that indirect costs add cost but no value to a project. Further, as Figure 15.2 illustrates, they can penalize a project that overruns its schedule, because indirect costs for many

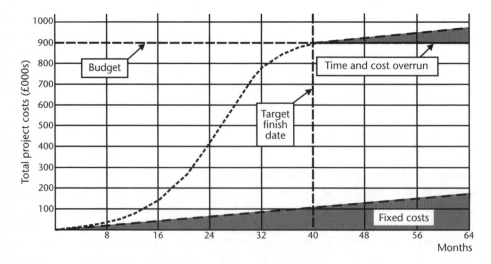

Figure 15.2   The effect of fixed costs on late project completion

projects must continue to be incurred for as long as the project remains unfinished and undelivered. These costs will continue to accrue, even if there is no work actually taking place on the project, or if there are just a few people engaged in final debugging work during commissioning and final testing.

Some contracts will allow for costs that might be considered as indirect in many organizations to be charged to the client as expenses. These costs can include telephone charges, special stationery and printing costs and so on. Although this might sound trivial, one London organization reduced its annual communication bills from over £100 000 to just £25 000 by the simple process of installing a call logger and charging out all calls that could be identified against projects.

Other ways of minimizing indirect costs can be more fundamental and involve running a lean organization with no unnecessary indirect staff (including managers). It is sometimes possible to have at least part of the time of indirect staff recognized as direct project work, in which case they should be asked to complete weekly timesheets so that the relevant hours can be booked to the particular client or project.

Cost reporting

Cost reporting, usually on a periodical basis, must always be carried out at several levels in the project structure, and sometimes between the main contractor and the project purchaser. But cost reports by themselves mean nothing unless they can be related to the work achieved or value earned. The following chapter, therefore, discusses various earned value methods.

16 *Earned Value Analysis*

Perhaps the most common questions that a project manager will have to answer during the course of any project will be along the lines of 'How are we doing? Are we still set to deliver on time? Shall we finish within budget?' Getting answers to these questions will usually require a certain amount of analysis, especially on a large project. If progress is being monitored constantly against good critical path network data, then it should be fairly easy to answer the question about completion on time. At least, if any critical task is running late, then the project must be running late by that amount. But what about the costs? Provided that the organization has competent accountants and a good cost collection system, the actual expenditure to date (or at least to the end of the previous accounting period) should be known. But how can the costs incurred be related to the progress achieved? The answer to that question is usually more difficult to answer and is complicated on any project of significant size by huge amounts of work in progress. This chapter discusses some methods for examining the relationships between expenditure and achievement throughout the project life cycle and assessing the implications.

Variance analysis

One method of control analysis – once the only common method – is variance analysis. This remains an important tool and relies on simple subtraction to evaluate the difference (variance) between a planned result and an actual measurement. Variance analysis can be used to show differences between planned and actual progress, or between budgeted costs and actual costs. In other branches of management, deviations from plan are also called 'exceptions' and 'management by exception' is the process of maximizing management effectiveness by concentrating on things that need attention rather than wasting time on things that do not. The following are common sources of variances (or exceptions) in the context of projects:

- scheduled start versus actual start
- scheduled finish versus actual finish
- scheduled time for an activity versus actual time
- scheduled achievement time for a milestone event versus the actual achievement time
- budgeted cost versus actual cost
- measured value versus actual cost
- budgeted man-hours versus actual man-hours
- budgeted unit cost versus actual unit cost
- budgeted percentage complete against actual percentage complete.

Although still used extensively, variance analysis can, however, be inadequate or even misleading. It can be a meaningless guide to progress and performance. For example, consider a simple case where the budgeted expenditure to date on a project is £820 000 and the actual expenditure is £850 000. This gives a positive variance of £30 000 (an apparent overspend of £30 000). Yet, although this tells you that expenditure is over-budget, it does *not* tell you:

- whether the project is on, above or below the expected cost performance
- what the probable final cost of the project will be
- whether work is on, behind or ahead of schedule
- what the probable project completion date will be.

To answer these questions, a subjective assessment of the 'percentage complete' can be made for comparison against these cost figures. Almost inevitably this will be optimistic and influenced by the actual figures. Subjective estimates are usually unreliable, to say the least.

Thus variance analysis, used alone and not supplemented by a more reliable assessment method, suffers from the following deficiencies:

- It is purely historic and not sufficiently predictive.
- It does not indicate performance clearly and simply.
- It is insufficiently sensitive to identify problems early.
- It does not effectively use all the data available.
- When used with 'percentage complete' assessments it tends to be highly subjective and unreliable.
- It does not indicate trends.
- It does not integrate schedule and cost. Thus it confuses the effects of cost and schedule variances and their interactions.

In sum, variance analysis, when used on its own, is an ineffective way of analysing and reporting project progress and performance.

Principles of performance analysis based on earned value

Project progress and performance analysis based on 'earned value' concepts integrate cost and schedule on a structured and personalized basis. With earned value analysis there are three elements of data required to analyse performance, which are:

1 the budgeted cost scheduled up to the time of measurement
2 the actual cost at the time of measurement
3 the corresponding earned value.

The earned value is simply the budgeted value (cost or man-hours) of the work actually completed. If a job was budgeted to cost £500 000, when that job is completely finished its earned value is £500 000, even if the actual cost to complete the work happened to be £400 000 or £900 000. Subjectivity problems are minimized in the structured earned value approach, where the work is broken down into WBS elements, cost accounts and work packages, as outlined in previous chapters. The total earned value of the work completed at the time of measurement is then based on the budgeted value of all these completed segments of work, plus an estimate to allow for active work in progress.

A VERY SIMPLE CASE

Consider a case with the following data:

- Budgeted expenditure to date   = £820 000
- Actual expenditure to date   = £850 000
- Earned value to date   = £750 000
- Total budgeted cost of the project = £2 million
- Planned project completion time   = 50 weeks.

Cost analysis

Results based solely on variance analysis would be calculated as follows:

> Cost variance = budget to date minus the actual costs to date, which in this case gives –£30 000.

Note that the adverse variance here is negative. Some accountants and managers reverse the sign, and treat adverse variances as positive quantities and under-budget variances as negative.

Without further analysis, we know that this tiny project appears to be overspent by £30 000, but that result is inadequate for assessing true cost performance because it does not take earned value into account. Now consider the case, using the same data, where the earned value is assessed.

> Cost variance = earned value minus actual expenditure, which is £750 000 – £850 000 = –£100 000.

This project is therefore effectively £100 000 over-budget, not the £30 000 indicated by simple variance analysis. For every £850 000 spent, only £750 000 value is being earned, which is equivalent to a value of only 88.2p value earned for every pound spent. Using simple proportional arithmetic, if this trend were allowed to continue unchecked for the remainder of this project, the original budget of £2 million will not be held. The final total project cost is likely to be £2 million divided by 0.882, which is £2 267 000 – a predicted overspend of £267 000.

Schedule analysis

For this very simple case we are not given the data for straightforward schedule comparison by variance analysis but, even if that information were to hand, it would mean little. Using earned value concepts, however, we can make a prediction of progress to completion. All data are the same as above.

> Earned value to date minus the budget value to date = £750 000 – £820 000, which is –£70 000.

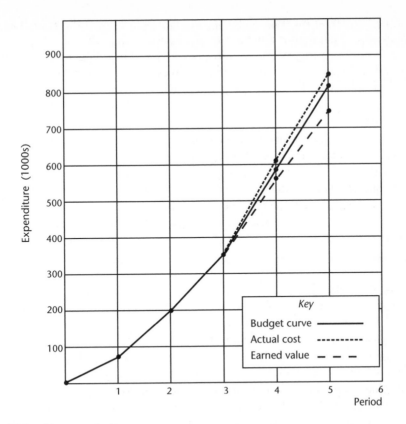

Figure 16.1   S-curve analysis

	Cumulative data			Data for each period			Performance indices (per period)	
Period	Budget (£)	Actual cost	Earned value	Budget (£)	Actual cost	Earned value	Cost	Schedule
1	100 000	100 000	100 000	100 000	100 000	100 000	1.00	1.00
2	200 000	200 000	200 000	100 000	100 000	100 000	1.00	1.00
3	330 000	330 000	320 000	130 000	130 000	120 000	0.92	0.92
4	500 000	520 000	480 000	170 000	190 000	160 000	0.84	0.94
5	820 000	850 000	750 000	320 000	330 000	270 000	0.82	0.84

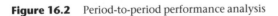

Figure 16.2   Period-to-period performance analysis

This means that the project is behind schedule by £70 000 in terms of the value that should have been earned. Simple proportional arithmetic indicates that, should this performance ratio of 7.5/8.2 continue, the project will most likely exceed its original target of 50 weeks and run instead for 54.7 weeks. So, unless action can be taken to reverse the poor progress performance, the project will be nearly 5 weeks overdue.

S-curve analysis

Additional information can be obtained, particularly on trends, by the interpretation of S-curve graphs. These can compare budgeted, actual and earned value, as shown in Figure 16.1 (p. 215). The curves show that the work progressed as planned up to the end of period 3. The rate of working then accelerated in periods 4 and 5, but did not achieve the planned rate of working. In particular, the slope of the earned value curve is significantly less than the slopes of the budgeted and actual expenditure curves. Unless the slope of the earned value curve can match that of the other factors, overexpenditure and schedule slippage will continue to increase.

Period-to-period analysis

There is a danger of underestimating trends if cumulative analysis only is carried out. Figure 16.2 (p. 215) shows the period-to-period data and the graphs of period-to-period cost and schedule performance. These show the position in this project to be more serious than that shown in the cumulative analysis. The cost performance ratio in period 5 was only 0.82, indicating a final project cost of £2 374 000 (compared with the forecast of £2 267 000 predicted using cumulative data). That would be 18.7 per cent over-budget if performance were to remain unchanged. Similarly, the period 5 schedule performance indicates that the project will be 8 weeks late, whereas cumulative data yielded a forecast of less than 5 weeks' delay.

Although this simple case used project expenditure as the basis, the same methodology can be applied to labour cost on its own, or simply to the man-hours worked and budgeted (which are often the alternative currency used in analysis).

C.Spec. performance analysis principles

Earned value performance analysis and reporting can be used with any structured methodology of project control but finds its fullest expression (and widest use) with the C.Spec. methodology that can be traced back to defence projects in the US and comes complete with its own terminology. Among the jargon are three basic terms for the three elements of data discussed above. These can be used for cost units or man-hours and are as follows:

- BCWS – budgeted cost for work scheduled
- BCWP – budgeted cost for work performed (the earned value)
- ACWP – actual cost of work performed.

Using these three elements, it is possible to evaluate the following for each cost account and WBS/OBS element:

- Cost variance   = BCWP – ACWP
- Cost performance index (CPI)   = BCWP/ACWP

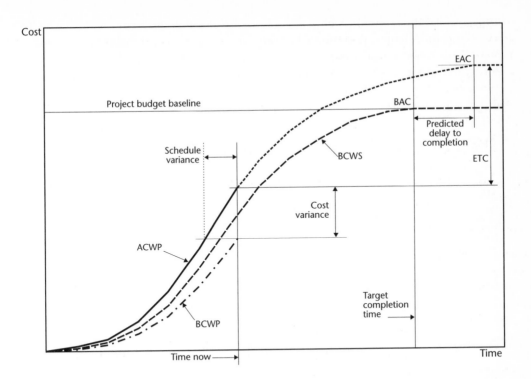

Figure 16.3   A typical project S-curve in the context of earned value analysis

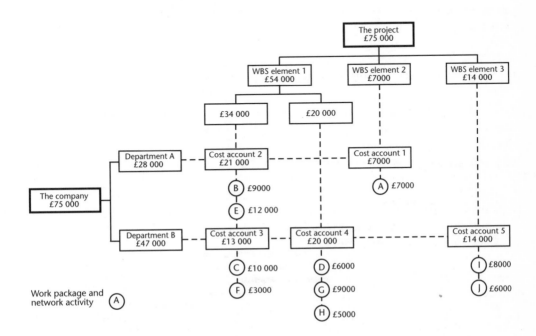

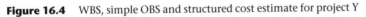

Figure 16.4   WBS, simple OBS and structured cost estimate for project Y

- Schedule performance index (SPI)   = BCWP/BCWS
- Remaining estimated costs to completion (ETC)   = (BAC − BCWP)/CPI
  (where BAC is the budget at completion)
- Forecast final cost or 'estimate at completion' (EAC)   = ACWP + ETC

Figure 16.3 (p. 217) is a graphical, S-curve, illustration of these quantities for a typical project.

C.Spec. earned value analysis for project Y

The use of the quantities listed above can be demonstrated using a very simple project example, which we have called project Y. Figures 16.4 (p. 217) and 16.5 contain some of the details for this imaginary project which, although not complete, are sufficient for our purposes.

Network

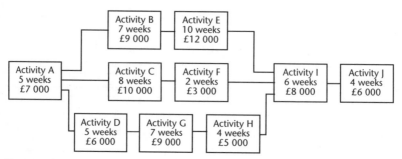

Time analysis

Activity ID	Duration	Early start	Late start	Early finish	Late finish	Free float	Total float
A	5	0	0	5	5	0	0
B	7	5	5	12	12	0	0
C	8	5	12	13	20	0	7
D	5	5	6	10	11	0	1
E	10	12	12	22	22	0	0
F	2	13	20	15	22	7	7
G	7	10	11	17	18	0	1
H	4	17	18	21	22	1	1
I	6	22	22	28	28	0	0
J	4	28	28	32	32	0	0

Gantt chart

Acitivity ID	Week 1–4	5–8	9–12	13–16	17–20	21–24	25–28	29–32
A								
B								
C								
D								
E								
F								
G								
H								
I								
J								

Figure 16.5   Schedule information for project Y

BUDGETED COST FOR WORK SCHEDULED (BCWS)

BCWS is simply another name for the time-phased budget against which performance is measured for the project and for the individual cost account. It is generally determined for each individual cost period on a cumulative basis, although in small projects it may be determined on only a cumulative basis. For any given time period, budgeted cost for work scheduled is calculated at the cost account level by totalling the budgets for all work packages scheduled to be completed plus the budget for the proportion of work in progress (open work packages) scheduled to be accomplished. To these figures are usually added the appropriate overhead costs. Figure 16.6 shows the detailed BCWS for each period of project Y.

Control centre	Estimate £	Budget (£) per four-week period							
		1	2	3	4	5	6	7	8
Cost account 1									
Work package A	7 000	5 600	1 400						
Total	7 000	5 600	1 400						
Cost account 2									
Work package B	9 000		3 857	5 143					
Work package E	12 000				4 800	4 800	2 400		
Total	21 000		3 857	5 143	4 800	4 800	2 400		
Cost account 3									
Work package C	10 000		3 750	5 000	1 250				
Work package F	3 000				3 000				
Total	13 000		3 750	5 000	4 250				
Cost account 4									
Work package D	6 000		3 600	2 400					
Work package G	9 000			2 571	5 143	1 286			
Work package H	5 000					3 750	1 250		
Total	20 000		3 600	4 971	5 143	5 036	1 250		
Cost account 5									
Work package I	8 000						2 667	5 333	
Work package J	6 000								6 000
Total	14 000						2 667	5 333	6 000
Department A									
Cost account 1	7 000	5 600	1 400						
Cost account 2	21 000		3 857	5 143	4 800	4 800	2 400		
Total	28 000	5 600	5 257	5143	4 800	4 800	2 400		
Department B									
Cost account 3	13 000		3 750	5 000	4 250				
Cost account 4	20 000		3 600	4 491	5 143	5 036	1 250		
Cost account 5	14 000						2 667	5 333	6 000
Total	47 000		7 350	9 971	9 393	5 036	3 917	5 333	6 000
Total project	75 000	5 600	12 607	15 114	14 193	9 836	6 317	5 333	6 000

Figure 16.6   Calculation of cost account budgets for project Y

BUDGETED COST FOR WORK PERFORMED (BCWP)

BCWP comprises the budgeted cost of all the work actually accomplished, either during any given time period or on a cumulative basis. At the cost account level, BCWP is determined by totalling the budgets for work packages actually completed, plus the amount of budget applicable to the amount of work in progress on all other work packages that have been started, all with their overhead budget costs included.

The main difficulty encountered in determining BCWP is the evaluation of work in progress. The use of short-span work packages or the establishment of value milestones within work packages will significantly reduce difficulties and errors here. The procedures used to evaluate work in progress will vary, to some extent varying according to the average work package length. For example, some contractors prefer to assume 50 per cent completion

Control centre	Estimate £	Percentage of work completed	Cumulative BCWP	Previous BCWP	BCWP this period
Cost account 1					
Work package A	7 000	100	7 000	7 000	0
Total	7 000	100	7 000	7 000	0
Cost account 2					
Work package B	9 000	85	7 650	3 240	4 410
Work package E	12 000	0	0	0	0
Total	21 000	36	7 650	3 240	4 410
Cost account 3					
Work package C	10 000	85	8 500	3 800	4 700
Work package F	3 000	0	0	0	0
Total	13 000	85	8 500	3 800	4 700
Cost account 4					
Work package D	6 000	100	6 000	3 600	2 400
Work package G	9 000	0	0	0	0
Work package H	5 000	0	0	0	0
Total	20 000	30	6 000	3 600	2 400
Cost account 5					
Work package I	8 000	0	0	0	0
Work package J	6 000	0	0	0	0
Total	14 000	0	0	0	0
Department A					
Cost account 1	7 000	100	7 000	7 000	0
Cost account 2	21 000	36	7 650	3 240	4 410
Total	28 000	52	14 650	10 240	4 410
Department B					
Cost account 3	13 000	65	8 500	3 800	4 700
Cost account 4	20 000	30	6 000	3 600	2 400
Cost account 5	14 000	0	0	0	0
Total	47 000	31	14 500	7 400	7 100
Total project	75 000	39	29 150	17 640	11 510

Figure 16.7   Calculation of BCWP at period 3 for project Y

for any work package as soon as it starts, taking the other 50 per cent upon its completion. Others use formulae which approximate the time phasing of the effort, while others prefer to make a physical assessment of the amount of work completed (the use of quantity surveyors in construction contracts being a good example of this). For assessing achievement on work packages of longer duration, other contractors identify the amount of work done according to discrete, easily identifiable milestones, each of which has a pre-established budget or progress value.

Thus the achievement measurement method depends largely on the work package content, size and duration. However, arbitrary formulae should be limited to the very short duration work packages. Figure 16.7 shows the BCWP calculation for project Y at the end of period 3.

ACTUAL COST OF WORK PERFORMED (ACWP)

Calculation of the ACWP is principally an accounting function. It simply means collecting and collating all the costs incurred for accomplishing the work performed, both cumulatively and within a given period. These costs may be collected at cost account level, although more commonly they are collected at the level of work packages or individual activities (depending on the size of the activities).

COST–PERFORMANCE ANALYSIS

Using these elements of data, it is possible to carry out an analysis of performance that integrates schedule and cost. If this analysis is combined with the WBS it can be carried out at will, for any part of the project, for any contributing organization and for the project as a whole. On larger projects, these comparisons are carried out both for the latest time period and for the cumulative performance to date. On smaller projects the comparisons are sometimes carried out only on a cumulative basis.

Cost variances show whether the work done has cost more or less than the corresponding estimate, while schedule variances show the deviation from schedule for the cost account, WBS item or the whole project. Although estimates to complete (ETCs) and the estimate at completion (EAC) produced by this method are mechanistic ways of forecasting the final costs, they do tend to show what the outcome will be if no corrective action can be taken to reverse the trend. In essence, these forecasts pose the challenging command 'Show why we should not believe these figures to be the likely results'.

Cost and schedule variances (when considered together) give an integrated picture of the project or individual cost account. This is illustrated in Figure 16.8 (p. 222).

Figures 16.9 (p. 222) and 16.10 (p. 223) are the project Y performance analysis reports for periods 2 and 3, respectively, and these reports show how the C.Spec. terms are applied in practice.

COST VARIANCE ANALYSIS

The comparison of BCWP and ACWP shows whether completed work has cost more or less than the amount budgeted for that work. For example, consider cost account 2 for the project Y period 3 report in Figure 16.10. This is seen to be costing £690 more than its budget, as found by the following subtraction:

BCWS	BCWP	ACWP	Cost variance	Schedule variance	Analysis
4000	4000	4000	0	0	On schedule, on cost
4000	4000	3000	1000	0	On schedule, under cost
4000	4000	5000	−1000	0	On schedule, over cost
3000	4000	4000	0	1000	Ahead of schedule, on cost
3000	4000	3000	1000	1000	Ahead of schedule, under cost
3000	4000	5000	−1000	1000	Ahead of schedule, over cost
5000	4000	4000	0	−1000	Behind schedule, on cost
5000	4000	3000	1000	−1000	Behind schedule, under cost
5000	4000	5000	−1000	−1000	Behind schedule, over cost

Figure 16.8   Interpretation of cost and schedule variances

(a) Performance analysis for period 2

Cost account number	BCWS	BCWP	ACWP	Variance Schedule	Cost	Performance index Schedule	Cost	Project costs at completion BCWS	EAC	Variance
1	1400	1400	2150	50	− 700	1.03571	0.674418			
2	3857	3240	3270	− 617	− 30	0.84000	0.990825			
3	3750	3800	3825	50	− 25	1.01333	0.993464			
4	3600	3600	3672	0	− 72	1	0.980392			
5	0	0	0	0	0	0	0			
Project	12 607	12 090	12 917	− 517	− 827	0.95899	0.935875			

(b) Cumulative performance analysis

	BCWS	BCWP	ACWP	Schedule	Cost	Schedule	Cost	BCWS	EAC	Variance
1	7000	7000	7700	0	− 700	1	0.90909	7 000	7 700	− 700
2	3857	3240	3270	− 617	− 30	0.84000	0.990825	21 000	21 194	− 194
3	3750	3800	3825	50	− 25	1.01333	0.993464	13 000	13 085	− 85
4	3600	3600	3672	0	− 72	1	0.90392	20 000	20 400	− 400
5	0	0	0	0	0	0	0	14 000	14 000	0
Project	18 207	17 640	18 467	− 567	− 827	0.96885	0.955217	75 000	78 516	− 3516
Department A	10 857	10 240	10 070	− 617	− 730	0.943	0.933	28 000	30 010	− 2010
Department B	7 350	7 400	7 497	50	− 97	1.001	0.987	47 000	47 610	− 619
Project (by department)								75 000	77 679	− 2629

(c) Work package analysis

Work package	Budget	Actual cost	Cost variance
1	7000	7700	− 700

Figure 16.9   Project Y performance report for period 2

$$\text{Cost variance} = \text{BCWP} - \text{ACWP}$$
$$= £4410 - £5100$$
$$= -£690$$

The discovery of adverse cost variance analysis should prompt a search for the causal factors. These might include poor initial estimates, delays through material shortages of lack of

(a) Performance analysis for period 3

Cost account number	BCWS	BCWP	ACWP	Variance Schedule	Cost	Performance index Schedule	Cost	Project costs at completion Budget	EAC	Variance
1	0	0	0	0	0					
2	5143	4410	5100	– 733	– 690	0.857476	0.864706			
3	5000	4700	6000	300	– 1300	0.94	0.783333			
4	4071	2400	3540	– 2571	– 1140	0.482759	0.677966			
5	0	0	0	0	0	0	0			
Project	15 114	15 510	14 640	– 3604	– 3130	0.761535	0.786202			

(b) Cumulative performance analysis

	BCWS	BCWP	ACWP	Variance Schedule	Cost	Performance index Schedule	Cost	Project costs at completion Budget	EAC	Variance
1	7000	7000	7700	0	– 700	1	0.90909	7 000	7 700	– 700
2	9000	7650	8370	– 1350	– 720	0.85	0.913978	21 000	22 976	– 1970
3	8750	8500	9825	250	– 1325	0.97142	0.865139	13 000	15 027	– 2026
4	8571	6000	7212	– 2571	– 1212	0.7	0.831947	20 000	24 040	– 4040
5	0	0	0	0	0	0	0	14 000	14 000	0
Project	33 321	29 150	33 107	– 4171	– 3957	0.874813	0.880478	75 000	85 181	– 10 181
Department A	1 600	14 650	16 070	– 1350	– 1420	0.916	0.912	28 000	30 702	– 2702
Department B	17 321	14 500	17 037	– 2821	– 2537	0.837	0.851	47 000	55 229	– 8229
Project (by department)								75 000	85 931	– 10 931

(c) Work package analysis

Work package	Budget	Actual cost	Cost variance
1	7000	7700	–700
4	5000	7712	–1 212

Figure 16.10   Project Y performance report for period 3

information, technical difficulties requiring additional resources, materials price increases, or a combination of these and other factors.

SCHEDULE VARIANCE ANALYSIS

Comparisons of BCWS with BCWP relate the work scheduled to the work completed during a given period. This can be illustrated by referring again to cost account 2 in period 3 for project Y (Figure 16.10). The schedule variance, which is expressed here in terms of cost, is calculated as follows:

$$\text{Schedule variance} = \text{BCWP} - \text{BCWS}$$
$$= £4410 - £5143$$
$$= -£733$$

Thus the work for cost account 2 is significantly behind schedule. Although this provides a valuable indication of schedule status (expressed in the monetary value of the work performed) it may not indicate clearly whether or not milestones are being met, since some work might have been performed out of its planned sequence. A formal time scheduling system must therefore be used to provide the means of determining the status of specific activities or milestones. For example, Figure 16.11 (p. 224) shows the integration of the project Y schedule analysis at the end of period 3.

PERFORMANCE INDICES

On scanning a performance report, the cost and schedule variances seen might not, at first glance, indicate their relative significance because they will depend on the overall magnitude

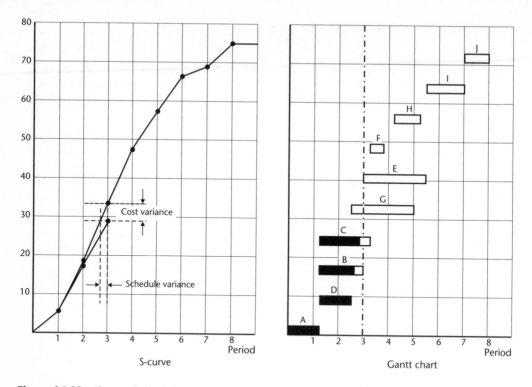

Figure 16.11   Cost and schedule integration for project Y at the end of period 3

of the figures involved. For example, a cost variance of –£20 000 on a cost account with a BCWP of £200 000 is clearly not as significant as it would be on a cost account where the BCWP is £100 000. The use of cost and schedule performance indices overcomes this difficulty and can provide a more reliable at-a-glance indication of danger spots. The indices are calculated as follows:

Cost performance index (CPI)   = BCWP/ACWP
Schedule performance index (SPI) = BCWP/BCWS

A performance index of 1 represents par performance in each case. Anything less than 1 indicates performance below that expected. Returning to the period 3 performance report for project Y (Figure 16.10) it can be seen that the cumulative performance indices for cost account 2 are as follows:

CPI = 7650/8370 = 0.914
SPI = 7650/9000 = 0.85

We note that the compilers of the reports in Figures 16.9 and 16.10 have expressed the index values in too many places of decimals, given that much of the data in these reports originates from estimates.

CONSOLIDATION OR ROLLING UP

All variances and performance indices are required not only at the cost account level, but also at higher levels in the project structure. Performance analysis at the higher levels mean summarizing the lower-level results (a process often called rolling up). Carrying this through to the top, it is thus relatively simple to determine project status and organizational performance at all levels of both the OBS and the WBS. Positive (favourable) variances in some areas may, of course, be offset by negative variances in other places. Higher-level managers will normally see only the most significant variances at their own level. However, the cumulative effect of many small variances (that are in themselves insignificant and might arise from a variety of causes) could amount to a large cost problem at the project level. Rolled-up reports, such as those shown here for project Y in Figures 16.9 and 16.10, should make such problems apparent.

In the simple example of project Y the project itself is the only higher-level cost account, on the vertical consolidation axis, for which performance analysis is carried out. On the horizontal axis, performance analysis is carried out for the two departments involved. Figure 16.10 shows this analysis carried out for these three higher-level cost accounts.

Forecasting the final cost

Forecasts of the final project cost and parts of it (cost accounts and WBS items) are often requested by anxious senior managers. Such forecasts are vital to the project cash flow and sometimes even for decisions on whether to close and abandon a running project. Of course, the first answer to these questions, before or soon after the project starts, must come from the original project estimates. Subsequent forecasts, made during the progress of a project, effectively update the original estimates. This updating process should be continuous throughout the project life cycle.

A great deal of management judgement should go into all these estimates, but the earned value method does provide a mechanistic way of estimating the final costs and also offsets the risk of placing too much reliance on subjective estimates. Earned value results can be regarded as a starting point from which to make more judgemental estimates and as a comparative benchmark. The earned value method used is a simple extrapolation of the performance measured to date. The forecasts are calculated for each cost account and for higher-level accounts. These forecasts include a full performance analysis for the whole project, made by dividing the budget for the remaining work by the cost performance index and adding the result to the actual costs incurred to date. The process is as follows:

Cost performance index (CPI)   = BCWP/ACWP
Budgeted cost for work remaining = BAC – BCWP
Estimate to complete (ETC)   = (BAC – BCWP)/CPI
Forecast cost at completion   = ACWP + ETC

Using this method, forecasts of the final costs can be made for the following:

1 individual cost accounts that have been started
2 WBS items that have been started
3 organizational cost accounts that have been started.

The forecast final costs for project Y, made at the end of the third working period, are shown in Figure 16.10. The relevant data are as follows:

Cost performance index (CPI)	= 0.88
Budgeted cost for the remaining work	= £75 000 – £29 150
	= £ 45 850
Estimate to complete (ETC)	= £ 45 850/0.88
	= £52 073
Estimated cost at completion (EAC)	= £33 107 + £52 073
	= £85 180

One apparent drawback is that no forecast can be made for those segments not started, except to take into account the average overall performance. This is where the hierarchical cost account structure permits a logical extrapolative forecast for many cost accounts not yet started. For example, where an organization is responsible for several cost accounts, performance on their first few cost accounts can be used to forecast performance in later cost accounts. Admittedly there are many factors to take into account, but the extrapolative forecast is a good starting point, and any departure from it must be justified. Similarly, forecasts of final costs on higher-level WBS items can be based on performance in the earlier work.

In the project Y example at the end of period 3 (Figure 16.10) it can be seen that cost account 5, the responsibility of department B, is not started. That department is also responsible for cost accounts 3 and 4, both of which are in progress at the end of period 3. That allows a CPI to be calculated for department B, extracting data from the performance report (Figure 16.10) as follows:

Cost account	BCWP(£)	ACWP(£)	CPI
3	8 500	9 825	
4	6 000	7 212	
	14 500	17 037	0.851

Using this as an indicator of future performance, the EAC for cost account 5 (original budget £14 000) becomes £16 451.

Thus there are three methods for forecasting the final project cost:

1 the average overall performance to date
2 organizational performance
3 WBS performance to date.

For this project Y example, the first two of these methods have been used. The results, seen in Figure 16.10, are respectively £85 181 and £85 931, against the original budget of £75 000.

A hypothetical analysis for the first three periods of project Y now follows.

PERIOD 1 ANALYSIS

The performance report for period 1 is not shown, as the only work done during that time was on cost account 1. Data for this cost account are as follows:

Budget at completion (BAC) £7000 (the baseline budget)
BCWS at end of period 1 £5600
ACWP £5500
Estimated completion 80 per cent
Derived BCWP £5600 (earned value, 80 per cent of the total budget).

Thus the work is shown to be on schedule and within the budget.

PERIOD 2

The performance report for period 2 in Figure 16.9 gives the data on both periodic and cumulative bases. In both, the expenditure is approximately as budgeted and the performance indices are only marginally below par. The forecast final cost, that is the estimate at completion (EAC) is slightly more than the budget at completion (BAC). So, there appears to be no serious cause for alarm. But, in fact, there are signs of several small problems:

1 The schedule performance index (SPI) for cost account 2 is only 0.84, which was due to a delayed start. However, the momentum of work seems to be approximately as planned and budgeted, so the effects of this slow start appear to have been overcome.
2 The cumulative cost performance index is established at 0.91, based on a completed work package. If this is used for the whole of department A's performance, it raises the EAC for that department to £30 010. If extended to the project as a whole this would forecast an EAC of £82 417, which is rather more worrying.
3 The CPI for cost account 1 in period 2 is 0.67 and this abnormally low value is caused by the system correcting for the previous period's optimistic estimate of 80 per cent completion, when it transpires that a more realistic value would have been (with hindsight) 72 per cent. This demonstrates how the system rapidly corrects and highlights previous optimistic, subjective estimates of progress. It also calls into question the reliability of percentage completion estimates made for the other work packages open in this period. However, it is early days yet, the signs are not conclusive, and the project manager would have difficulty in convincing other people of their accuracy. But at least some alarm bells have been rung.

PERIOD 3

The performance report for period 3 (Figure 16.10) reveals more obvious problems. Although the rate of expenditure is only slightly below budget, the work achieved for this expenditure is far less than expected. The significant pointers are as follows:

1 Both the SPI and the CPI for work done during the period are very low, indicating that work on the project is not going well and that previous estimates of completion percentages were highly optimistic.
2 The forecast final cost of the project (EAC) is now £85 181 if based on overall performance, or £85 931 when based on departmental performance.
3 Both departments' performances are well below par, with department B being especially poor with an SPI of 0.837 and CPI of 0.851.
4 Work on cost account 4 is well behind schedule and well over budget, with a SPI of 0.7 and a CPI of 0.83.

Conclusion

Performance analysis using the earned value concept on cost centres (termed work packages), each looked upon as a discrete subcontract, and structured into cost accounts using the WBS, can provide effective control information for projects. The size of the work package can be varied according to the size of the project and the sophistication of the information system available. The schedule and cost variances, coupled with the schedule and cost performance indices, give sensitive and reliable indicators of progress achieved against budget. The system also automatically produces forecasts of final cost for parts of the project and for the project as a whole. The performance of contributing organizations is automatically monitored and gives effective feedback to those responsible.

However, it is quite apparent from the foregoing that none of this analysis can be made without considerable effort. Many find the terminology difficult and illogical. The Project Management Institute now gives the following alternative terms (PMI, 2000):

BCWS becomes PV (planned value).
BCWP becomes EV (earned value).
ACWP becomes AC (actual cost).
CV is used for cost variance (EV – AC).
SV is used for schedule variance (EV – PV).
CPI (cost performance index) is EV/AC.
SPI (schedule performance index) is EV/PV.

All the work performed in earned value analysis will be wasted if the results are not sorted, filtered and communicated rapidly to the managers responsible for taking action on each work package. This will be discussed in the following chapter in the general context of information handling and communications.

17 *Handling and Reporting Information for Project Management*

All project activities, from the earliest conceptual stage right through to the end of the project life cycle, generate information. The bigger the project, the greater the amount and diversity of information that has to be managed. Information has been described countless times as the lifeblood of organizations (and of many other things). Projects depend on the appropriate handling, storage and communication of vast quantities of the stuff. Hartman (2000) even declares [poor] communication to be 'the only cause of failure'.

Introduction

Information takes many forms, carried in many channels and media, and the world is awash with it. Yet the average manager is concerned only with the tiny fragment of all that data which is relevant to his or her activities. There is a clear analogy for project management information in radiocommunications, where the world around us is rich in radio, telephony and television signals of all kinds, only a small part of which is of any interest to a particular individual. In broadcast radiocommunications, the signals are transmitted to a section of the population at large, but in channels that are defined by the carrier frequency and, with modern technology, digital coding. Each person in the wider population selects the signal that he or she needs by tuning in to the appropriate channel, which is in fact a process of filtering. An additional stage of selection takes place by sorting – namely by choosing the appropriate date and hour when the particular information wanted is due to be broadcast.

Project data have to be filtered and sorted in similar fashion so that each person who has to take responsibility gets the information that he or she needs, at the right time, and with irrelevant data filtered out. When a project has been correctly structured, the necessary filtering and sorting can be carried out by a computer system provided that each piece of data carries a suitable identifying code. In other words, any company that undertakes projects as part of its normal business operations needs to establish an integrated project management system, based on the following:

* a structured approach to the project, its organization and its systems
* a uniformly applied and logically designed coding system that mirrors the project structure and organization
* an earned value method of performance measurement and analysis
* a suitable computer system loaded with appropriate software and operating as a database.

Every project manager must rely on an effective project management information system (PMIS). It is not possible to manage a complex entity, such as a modern project, by the 'seat of the pants' method. Systems for planning, budgeting, monitoring, analysing data and selective reporting have become essential. If project managers are not given this back-up, their planning and decision-making will be slow and laden with errors. Without a good information system, managers cannot control their project, and will not know until too late what is happening or even what is expected of them. They must spend much of their valuable time (the scarcest resource) searching for information. Any information they do get will inevitably be too little, too late.

Primary and secondary information modules

Any PMIS will be built from a number of subsystems or modules. These modules will vary with the industry, individual project requirements and the particular company. Information modules can be divided into primary and secondary, on the simple basis that the primary modules are essential, to be used on every project, whilst the secondary modules are optional, to be used only on selected projects. Opinions will differ on which modules should be primary and which secondary, and there will be no correct division as such because everything will depend on the circumstances.

Primary modules could include the following:

- project structuring and coding
- change control
- design
- estimating
- materials management
- planning
- budgeting or cost management
- quality
- data acquisition (accounting, payroll, measurement)
- analysis and reporting.

Secondary modules might include:

- risk analysis
- contract administration
- correspondence
- safety
- work packs
- contract brief.

Within any individual project information system, several modules might be combined into one. For example, budgeting, planning and reporting may be combined with the planning module in the software. Although the above list of information system modules might seem large, all the primary and most of the secondary modules will exist explicitly or implicitly on every project in some form or another. They may not be described anywhere, but the functions they represent will be carried out, and some sort of data files will be kept, even if only in cardboard folders.

The effectiveness of individual modules and of total OMIS varies considerably. Too often, the project manager has to accept existing company systems that were not designed to cope with the dynamic requirements of project management. As a result, the PMIS could be a hotch-potch of existing purchasing, accounting and financial systems that are not integrated in any way, plus whatever project planning package (or even packages) the company happens to have purchased in the past. This is inadequate for the management, planning and control of large projects and is a recipe for failure. Examples of the problems that arise from these system incompatibilities are as follows:

- Any structuring and coding that exists will be limited and not used to integrate all the project systems.
- In some cases, budgeting will not be carried out, so that there can be no expenditure plan. Cost control will be severely impaired.
- Change control will be simplistic and ineffective, leading to the breakdown of project control.
- The usefulness of analysis and reporting might be too limited to guarantee project success.
- The information system may be too slow for generating effective corrective actions.
- In general, the modules will not be integrated, with all the difficulties and problems which that entails.

All information system modules are integrated to some extent, particularly the primary modules, as shown in Figure 17.1 (p. 232). Each module produces data and information that are used in other modules, or uses information produced by other modules, or very often both. Thus, as previously outlined, integration of these information system modules into an integrated PMIS is of great importance for effective project management.

Design of the project management information system (PMIS)

The PMIS needs to be purpose-designed to ensure that the individual modules are effective and integrated. This design and implementation should be relatively easy compared with the same task a few years ago, owing to the following factors:

- The methodology of project management is well established.
- Computer hardware and software is relatively cheap, user-friendly, with adequate speed and power.
- There is a wider choice of project management software packages, many of which are versatile, multi-functional and reasonably priced.
- Communications between computers is easier and there is more compatibility between different software packages.
- Experience in the design and implementation of systems is widespread and help can be obtained from package suppliers and consultants.
- Database management information packages are widely available, used by many firms, and most modern project management packages are designed to interface with them.

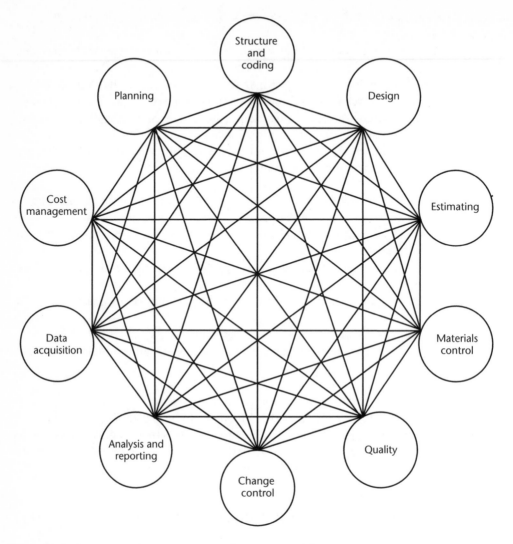

Figure 17.1   Interactions between primary information modules

- Standard report templates available from most systems mean that sorting, filtering and design of report formats, once the province of programming experts, can now be carried out effectively by any competent user, needing little or no specialist training.

The PMIS and database management packages

The IPMS should be a database management system, with all files on a database that is common to all the information modules. Some of the higher-end (and higher-priced) project management software packages come complete with such databases. Project planning and scheduling, once the only capability of so-called project management packages, is just one of the modules of the total system. This is illustrated in Figure 17.2. However, moving from a hotch-potch of information modules to a fully integrated database approach can sometimes be

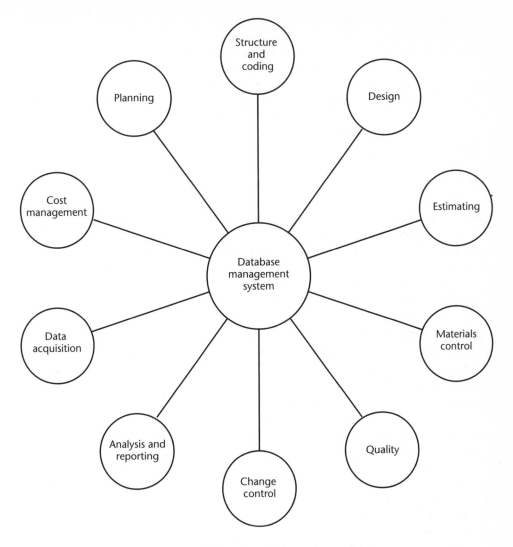

Figure 17.2   Database management and the primary information modules

too large a step for a company, especially where departmental managers have long used their own preferred systems and are resistant to change. Further, designing a fully integrated and completely compatible system is a considerable undertaking, requiring much analysis of existing methods across the organization and clear, logical thinking if order is to be created from the previous chaos. Failure to implement changeover to a new system can be an expensive disaster, in terms of cost, time and the creation of frustration, apathy or open hostility among the system users. Parallel running of the old and the new for a proving period is a common and prudent approach.

There are several states of nature or steps that can facilitate integration. These include the following:

- The use of a WBS approach and coding in all the modules, even though they might be independent entities. All modules must, as far as is practicable, use the same structures and a common system of coding. Coding is one of the most important, if not *the* most important, aspects of PMIS design.

- Partial integration, involving the linking of several modules in one software package. Modern project management packages have come a long way from their origins as simple scheduling tools. Many can combine several primary modules, such as cost management and materials management. Facilities are widely available for dealing with C.Spec. concepts and other analysis and reporting methods. Baseline plans can be stored and compared. Project management packages will now typically interface with widely used databases and standard management information systems (such as Oracle), and many project management packages come with powerful self-contained databases of their own.

- Partial integration, through the use of output files produced by one module as input for one or more other modules. Higher-end project management packages, for example, can now accept input directly from the ubiquitous Microsoft Project (which itself has improved beyond all measure from its modest beginnings).

- Files, input and output data and tables used by each system, although not integrated, are produced by a file manager or database package using the same type of format. Database management systems, the simplest of which is a simple file manager, can be used to set up data input screens, file and table structures, and output reports, without necessarily linking all the modules in one large database. All modules use data and text in a tabular form. Such files are made up of records (that is, rows in a table) typically with one record for each activity, work package, cost account, purchase order or drawing. Within each record, columns or fields hold data for that item, such as the scheduled completion date, vendor code, person's name or actual labour cost (to give just a few of hundreds of possible examples). Creating, maintaining and organizing such files on an independent module basis is relatively easy with such packages. Thus the use of a file manager or database package to set up and operate individual modules is of value in itself, even without considering how it facilitates particular communication between modules and total integration into a database system.

- The next step is, of course, to move to a relational database approach that links all the modules into an integrated project management information system (IPMIS). The widespread availability and ease of use of these database packages have made the adoption of an IPMIS a reality, not a dream. Inter-company integration is now easy, either through the Internet or through private dedicated links. The primary modules in such systems generally cover the factors described below.

Structure and coding

The structuring of the project into its WBS and OBS elements, cost accounts, and work packages, together with the coding of these, establishes the essential framework for integrating the project and its information systems. All the information modules (not just planning and cost control) should use the same structure and coding.

Although it might not be possible to establish the full structure and coding of the project in its earliest stages, at least the first few levels of structure and coding can be established at the start, both in the work and organizational dimensions. This can be expanded later into the lower-level elements, cost accounts and work packages as the project develops.

In addition, if different coding systems must continue to be used elsewhere for any reason (such as for a customer's drawing numbers) these must always be related to this structure and coding, preferably automatically in the software. This structure and coding module is very much the organizational module for the project and its information systems and, as such, is central to the design of the IPMIS.

Basic project, WBS and OBS codes were introduced in Chapter 8 and Figure 8.9 (p. 114) is particularly relevant. However, in projects many more items are typically given codes, such as resource types, alternative calendars and, especially, activities in network diagrams. Codes are sometimes used, perhaps in addition to general passwords, to determine levels of access permitted to a computer system or to the data held in it. For example, those with the highest code level of 1 might have access to all data and be trained to the point where they can make changes to the system itself without corrupting its operation. At access code level 2, perhaps, people will be allowed access to all the data, and may change or enter data, but will have no access for making changes to the system. Those at the very lowest level of access coding will have very limited access – perhaps only sufficient to view data directly related to their own group.

Project design

Although the planning and control of the design phase is part of the project planning, the detailed planning and control of design involves a large amount of data, which is normally handled in the design module. The planning and control of design may thus be carried out totally in the planning module, shared between the planning and design modules, or done in the design module alone. This planning will involve the normal sequential type of development of the design plan. The design module may thus contain three elements:

1 an interface with any computer aided design (CAD) system
2 the detailed planning and control of the design phase, interfaced with the planning module
3 output data and information to be used in other modules.

The design module thus takes information from any CAD modeller used, or from the general design process, and generates detailed information. The output data to be used in other modules will include the following:

• equipment registers
• drawing registers
• material take-offs or bills of materials
• descriptions and specifications.

The detail used extends to individual pieces of equipment and drawings, so detailed design planning and control will generally be based on a tabular presentation of milestone-type schedules, using a standard planning template for each item. As such, it takes the form of, or is integrated with, design and documentation control and the drawing register. This maintains the records of documents and drawings, persons responsible for the drawings, dates required, dates produced, the work package or cost account to which it belongs, the list of people to receive the drawing, and other data pertaining to the design and the drawing.

Output information will be structured and coded to the level of the work package wherever possible. If structuring and planning have not progressed to that level, then it should be linked to whatever stage structuring and coding have reached. However, every effort should be made to reach the cost account stage of coding in the design phase to ensure that the following are identified for each cost account:

- the equipment required for its completion
- the relevant drawings
- the material requirements
- descriptions, specifications and any special requirements.

Change control

Change control can be a separate module or form part of one or more of the other primary modules. In any case it has links with all the information modules (see Chapter 18).

Estimating

Although some project estimates are usually established very early, before the design stage starts, the detailed estimates needed for planning and control can usually be made only after all or most design is complete, possibly extending into the early part of the materials management stage. In addition, during the design and estimating stages, structuring and coding can be extended to cost account level and often also to the work or planning package level.

The estimating module will take information from the design, and possibly also the materials management module. It will hold the estimated cost for the whole project and for its component parts. Whether or not the estimating process is computer-assisted, the estimating data will also include the estimated man-hours for each labour category, materials requirements, and the manufacturing or construction equipment usage for the work to be done on each cost account or work package, planning package or cost account. It will therefore produce much of the basic data for the planning database or cost–time–resource catalogue – that is, the following data for each work package, planning package or cost account:

- man-hours for each category of labour
- labour rates and costs
- materials usage
- materials rates and costs
- overheads
- equipment usage and costs
- services required.

Materials management system

Innumerable projects are delayed through the late delivery of materials or equipment. Yet many project schedules show only a single network activity or Gantt chart bar entitled

'Delivery of equipment and materials'. The planning and management of this phase of a project is vital – at least as important as any other project phase, irrespective of the project size.

The materials management information module must extend to cover all firms supplying materials and equipment to the project, so that they can be included in the global project control system. These suppliers are no different in importance than the other contractors, subcontractors or functional departments working on the project, and are part of the overall project organization. Delivery delays can be kept to a minimum, and unpleasant surprises avoided, by ensuring effective and well-organized planning and control.

The materials management information module is thus a critical part of any PMIS. It must extend from the equipment specifications and material take-offs from drawings at the design stage, to the issue and usage of this equipment and materials on the job. It interrelates with all the other primary modules and could be considered as an alternative central element of the project's information system. It covers both of the following items:

- equipment – discrete items such as pumps, motors, computers, and so on used on individual work packages
- materials – bulk quantities common to several work packages, such as structural steel, piping or cable.

These categories are not necessarily clear distinctions. For example, one kind of pump might be purchased in quantities for use on more than one work package. This means that the identification and quantification of common items might be a requirement of the management information system, made possible by the use of appropriate equipment codes or part numbers.

The procurement of these materials can be represented by a standard planning template which can be displayed as a Gantt chart or network module for each purchase order, but is generally contained in a milestone table, purchase order control schedule or file in a similar fashion to drawing registers. An example of the format is shown in Figure 17.3. Entries for each of the milestones include 'Scheduled', 'Actual' and 'Forecast' data. Other information can be included in the file, or in related files, such as prices, quantities and details of vendors for each purchase order or requisition.

Various reports in the materials management or procurement cycle can be produced from these files as required, including, for example, individual supplier performance, late invitations to tender, tenders requiring further information from design, variations between forecast delivery dates and dates required on site, and the identification of all purchase orders issued for one cost account.

Nowhere is reporting by exception more important than in these procurement reports. A full, unedited, report on all purchase orders, or work package information on a large project would be as thick in hard copy as a large book. Although such reports must be produced and reviewed at times, particularly when the project is archived on completion, it is more likely that, in the office of a busy manager, they would soon find their way unread into the waste paper bin. Therefore, procurement reports, as with most project reports, need to be structured so that individual managers receive only the information relevant to their area of responsibility. They should also be structured so that exceptions can clearly be recognized.

The materials information module will thus have linkages to all the primary modules, as follows:

Equipment/materials milestone schedule

Project name: Project X

Report date: 28 August 2009

Requisition number	Description	Cost a/c Work pkg	Drawing number	Design complete	Spec./Matl take-off	Enquiry sent off	Quote received	Order placed	Interim inspection	Final inspection	Fabrication complete	Received on site	Required on site
0013897	Elec. motor	42–321	EM24649	29 May 09	27 Apr 09	4 May 09	19 May 09	25 May 09	6 Jul 09	17 Aug 09	28 Aug 09	14 Sep 09	25 Sep 09

Figure 17.3   Typical format for an equipment/materials milestone schedule, or purchase order control schedule

Cost/performance report

Project name: Project X design

All figures £000s

Report date: 29 May 2009

A Item	B Cost code	C Original budget	D Approved budget changes	E Current budget C + D	F Actual cost to date ACWP	G Achievement to date BCWP	H CPI=G/F	J Estimate to complete ETC =(E - G)/H	K Estimate at completion EAC = F + J	L Variance E - K
Design	4–31	150	25	175	132	140	1.06	33.01	165.01	– 9.99

Figure 17.4   Popular format for a cost account or full-project cumulative cost/performance report

1 *Design*. Design provides the initial input regarding equipment, drawings, purchase specifications, and bills of materials or material take-offs.

2 *Estimating*. Materials management provides information on actual materials and equipment prices, to be used either in the definitive estimate or for comparison with previously estimated prices.

3 *Planning*. Planning provides information on 'required by' or 'required on site' dates, whilst materials management provides planning with feedback information on actual receipt dates. As changes occur in both these modules, such as slippage on progress at the workplace and delays in the delivery of materials, information must be exchanged between these two modules.

4 *Cost management*. Estimating and materials management provide input on estimated materials and equipment costs for each cost account and work package to the cost management or budgeting module. When compared with schedule information, this gives the time-phased expenditure budget for these elements of the CBS. Materials management also provides information on commitments and cash flow.

5 *Job cards*. Information for job cards (or their equivalents) for each work package, activity or task is produced from the materials information system. For example, in addition to the drawings and specifications required, purchase order numbers and the requirements specific to each job card or work package will be produced from this module.

6 *Data acquisition*. Information on actual prices and materials usage is fed back, not only to the cost management module, but also to the materials management module to monitor actual usage against estimated, ordered and stock. Many projects run out of stock or use more than ordered, and stock usage and availability must be controlled. The system must be responsive to changes in requirements – for example, when there are project changes or contract variation orders. Damaging errors will obviously occur if such changes are not taken into account in the ordering system.

7 *Analysis and reporting*.

Cost management or budgeting

All projects have some form of cost management information system, but not all of these are integrated with the project schedule and resourcing. Sometimes the methodology used does not include budgeting – that is, time-phased expenditure plans for work packages, activities or cost accounts and so on. An expenditure budget for the elements of the CBS is essential for the financial control of the project, and this cost budget must be integrated with the project schedule and the resource budget. Without expenditure budgets for the project activities, work packages, cost accounts and WBS/OBS systems, it would not be possible to carry out performance analysis, be in control of costs, or be fully in control of the project as a whole.

The project information systems should include a budgeting or cost management module that takes the estimating, purchasing, subcontract, schedule and resource information and produces a time-phased expenditure budget for all elements of the project. The budgeting module may be stand-alone or part of the planning module. Most project planning packages have simple labour cost facilities linked to their scheduling and resourcing, but these do not usually include all the elements of the CBS, except through some modification of the available fields.

Some of the better project management packages (for example, Artemis, Open Plan and Primavera) come with cost management modules or in-built capabilities with C.Spec. analysis and reporting facilities to varying levels of sophistication. They can thus include full WBS, OBS and CBS structure) structuring, with cost accounts and their coding plus C.Spec. analysis and reporting. Nevertheless, it must be emphasized once more that structuring and coding must not only apply to planning and cost management, but must also pervade all the project systems and information modules.

Quality management

Quality is a significant consideration for any project and, just like any other element, it must be planned and managed. The quality management module is an integral part of any project's system, whether it is simply a file containing inspection reports or clerk of works reports or a system module fully certificated in accordance with the ISO 9000 series of quality systems. In addition to a higher-level quality statement and quality procedures, a quality management system will contain formal checklists and test procedures to be followed for each materials delivery, each job according to its discipline and each subsystem. Depending on the nature of the project and the industry in which it exists, some quality functions will be defined by the client, and there might also be an external inspecting authority to satisfy. The quality management module will contain the data on all inspections, work sign-offs, inspection and test certificates, and so on. If job cards are in use, these will only be shown as completed when the final inspection is signed off.

Data acquisition

Without effective data acquisition, any management information system is dead from the start. Without fast, accurate and correctly assigned data on what has actually been accomplished, together with information on the time, cost and resources actually used, project control is impossible.

There are often problems in obtaining information, as it must come from many sources, not all of which are under the direct control of the project manager. Some data might be dependent on accounting systems where the codes and collection methods are not project-oriented. This can limit the number of cost centres over which project cost analyses can be made and, in the extreme case, there might be only one possible cost centre that can be monitored, which is the project itself. Collaboration between the accounts manager and the project manager has always been important, not least for gathering data and for arriving at mutually compatible collection and analysis methods.

C.Spec. analysis and reports, particularly when these are processed by unforgiving computer systems, are prone to wild errors even if only small parts of the required data are not collected. Indeed, it is extremely difficult to set up and maintain this particular function. It only takes one manager to fail to submit data at the expected time for enormous errors to appear in the output. This is an area where manual methods, which allow for commonsense human intervention, can often succeed where the computer cannot. Figure 17.4 (p. 238) shows headings for a popular performance analysis report which, although based on C.Spec. principles can often be produced quite easily in this format from manual records, or at least with only partial assistance from the computer.

Costs are often spread over work in such a way that they cannot be accurately assigned to individual jobs or work packages. For example, the use of a hired crane in a work area may be difficult to assign to individual work packages, or even to cost accounts. Similarly, people may go from one work package to another during the course of their working day, making the assignment of their time to different cost codes at the end of, say, each week difficult and often a matter of judgement.

The design of the monitoring or data acquisition system must take into account any collection difficulties for which no practicable or economic solutions can be produced. In the worst-case scenario, these problems may even limit or determine the structure and coding system used.

Three types of data need to be collected:

1 *Actual values*. These include, for example, costs, man-hours, actual job start time, actual finish time, and so on.
2 *Earned value*. This is expressed as the percentage complete, or the budgeted cost of work performed (in terms of money or man-hours) or the measured quantities of work done on site (particularly for construction contracts). Sometimes great approximations are made here, such as counting every short-duration job that has started as being 50 per cent complete, or assessing design achievement by dividing the number of drawings issued by the total number of drawings required for the particular activity.
3 *Non-quantifiable information*. This includes, for example, textual reports, comments, reasons, and even remarks relating to suspected problems ahead (or hunches).

In addition to the information collected in other modules, such as design and materials management, the principal sources of data include the following:

1 *Accountancy, payroll and timekeeping systems*. These systems will collect the man-hours and other direct cost information, the value of commitments, invoices and cash flows. Some of these data must be collected at the point of work, perhaps through direct input to the company's computer network. Other input will be required from other modules – for example, from the planning module for the timing of cash flows in cash flow schedules produced by the cost management module.
2 *Progress measurement systems*. Measurements of work done will include quantity surveyors' valuations (for construction projects), other measures of work completed such as the actual finish dates for activities, records of milestones achieved and estimates of work completed. The use of estimates should be kept to the unavoidable minimum if errors are to be kept low. Data collected by progress measurement systems need to be consolidated and allocated to the structures and coding in use before being communicated to the other system modules, particularly analysis and reporting.

Analysis and reporting

The analysis and reporting module is the interface between management and the project control system. As such, the methods by which analysis is carried out, and the contents, distribution and timing of reports, can determine the effectiveness of project control. The use of superficial status and progress reports is one of the many possible causes of project failure.

Thus, conscious thought and care must be given to the design of the analysis and reporting modules.

Although some modules, such as design and materials management, will contain their own analysis and reporting facilities, particularly of detailed activities, the principal analysis and reporting functions are generally incorporated in the planning and cost management modules. However, the analysis and reporting functions take data from all the other information modules and analyse them to produce reports on progress and performance, both for the past and as projections for the future. Although emphasis in the literature tends to be on the quantitative and graphical output, written reports, comments on fears, hunches and other non-quantitative information are just as important.

The analysis must make use of the following three sets of data produced by the planning and data acquisition modules:

1 the baselines for control (the baseline schedule, resources and expenditure budgets)
2 the actual schedule progress, resource usage and expenditure
3 the earned value obtained by this resource usage and expenditure.

The system must use these three sets of data to extract information for decision-making and action, using both variance analysis and performance analysis, based on earned value.

No matter how sophisticated the analysis is, it must also be remembered that one cause of project failure is insufficient use of status/progress reports. Senior managers do not always read project reports, or fully understand the implications of what they *do* read. Urgently needed recognition of problems and the appropriate corrective actions are therefore delayed until too late to be effective. Panic and firefighting measures can then result. Thus the way in which information is presented to management can make a significant difference to understanding it. It should therefore have the following characteristics:

• It should be easy to understand.
• It should be presented in as simple a form as possible.
• It should highlight problems (exception reporting).
• It should be relevant and meaningful.
• It should be timely.
• It should cover period-to-period analysis.
• It should be cumulative to date.
• It should identify trends and project these trends into the future.
• It should be consolidated, but also allow problem causes or sources to be traced.
• It should be personalized for the recipient.

The personalization of analysis and reports is important to reinforce personal accountability, motivation and the contractor–consignee concept. Each manager of a cost account, WBS and OBS element, as well as the project manager, should receive reports on their own and the group's progress and performance, and how it affects the project as a whole. Without this personalization, the whole concept breaks down. With it, performance can improve significantly. This personalization is made automatic, and requires relatively little human effort, when the project is structured and coded in two or more dimensions.

Planning and scheduling

Computer project management software packages have been evolving since the 1960s and continue to grow in terms of the numbers available and their individual capabilities. There is now a bewildering array of software packages available. Unfortunately there is no standard approach to all aspects of project management planning and control in all these packages, and a review of them would need a complete book that would probably be out of date before it could be written and published. Comparative tables are, however, published from time to time in journals, particularly in *Project Manager Today*. There is also some general advice on choosing and using project management software in Lock (2003).

The planning and scheduling capabilities of software varies, but very poor systems no longer proliferate as they once did. However, the better systems schedule using precedence network analysis with activity on node networks. There are no systems currently available that schedule from activity-on-arrow diagrams. Systems at the lower end of the market present a blank Gantt chart screen when the program is opened, but this is usually based on a linked chart that is almost the equivalent of a precedence network diagram. The weakest systems, although they may claim to be 'powerful', do not allow sufficient structuring and, especially, flexibility and choice in coding all necessary dimensions.

18 *Managing Project Changes*

Changes are one of the most common identifiable causes of project delays, increased costs and low labour productivity. Changes can ruin a project that started with high expectations among all the stakeholders. It is quite common for changes to add anything up to 50 per cent to project costs and not unusual for them to add even more. Thus one of the most important, but unfortunately unpleasantly tedious and troublesome, functions of a project manager is to control all the changes to a project.

Changes that are not changes

Quite often, project work that has been started or even finished must be scrapped, and the job restarted. Perhaps a designer has spent a week or two slaving over a hot computer only to discover that the approach is completely wrong, so that work must be scrapped and everything has to begin again. Construction workers use facing bricks from the wrong pile, and the mistake is only discovered after a few courses have been laid. Someone has carried out an over-volt test on an electrical transformer with 10 000 volts by mistake when 1000 volts was the specified test voltage, so that the charred and smoking transformer must be stripped out and replaced.

These occurrences, and others like them, certainly represent serious setbacks to the project. They will cause changes, both to the schedule and to the project costs. But they are not in themselves changes, because they are unintentional, rectifiable occurrences that will not change the final as-built project.

One useful definition of a change is that it is *any occurrence in a project which causes a drawing, specification, purchase order or other executive document to be reissued with changed details or instructions after a previous version has already been issued with authority to trigger expenditure and work on the project.* Thus the scrapping of an architect's designs on the drawing board before issue would be a setback, but changes to the design once the drawings had been released for construction would constitute a change.

Good supervision and motivation can reduce the number of setbacks, but there can really be no formal system of setback control. People will always make mistakes. Changes are different, because they are more likely to stem from deliberate mind changes that could affect the originally intended scope and build of the project.

Unfunded changes

One of the most depressing aspects of project changes is the diverse number of ways in which they can be caused. The need, or at least apparent need, for a change can happen anywhere in the project organization and at any time during the project life cycle. Changes of any kind that occur at or near the very beginning of the project will cause delays but their effects are likely to be far less serious than changes later in the project life cycle when there will be far more potential for scrap and rework, disgruntled workers and the loss of sunk costs. The consideration and treatment of a proposed change will differ to some extent according to the nature of its origin and its timing in the project life cycle.

From the contractor's point of view, the least distressing changes will come from the customer or client, because at least these bring with them the probability that the project price will increase and the possibility of compensation for any scrap and rework caused. Internal changes are quite different, because the contractor must fund any additional costs and be prepared to explain resulting delays to the customer. Generally speaking, internal changes must be subjected to closer scrutiny before approval than those requested by the paying customer.

SOME ORIGINS OF UNFUNDED CHANGES

Internal unfunded changes can arise from many causes, including the following:

- A design error might be discovered after the issue of drawings and specifications. This kind of change should result in a formal change request from the design engineers (see Figure 18.1). Such forms have many different names but, for convenience, they will be referred to throughout this chapter as an engineering change request.
- Workers on a project at any level might have an idea for a project improvement that, if accepted, would change the issued manufacturing or construction instructions. Many companies have suggestion boxes that, when the ridiculous or downright rude suggestions have been weeded out, can produce worthwhile changes. Anyone should be allowed to make such a request because there might be a potential for significant improvement to the project or to the company's processes in general. However, for most such changes to a current project, the disruption that they cause will outweigh the potential advantages. The same engineering change request form used for design errors (Figure 18.1) will be suitable for controlling suggestions that have passed initial screening.
- A problem might arise during construction or manufacture where the workers and their supervisor cannot understand the instructions contained in the drawings or specifications. Some formal but simple system for reporting these difficulties back to the designers should be in place. If work is held up, such queries need to be dealt with quickly. If they were the result of design errors, then emergency instructions such as signed marked-up drawings can be issued, but these must be followed up by a corresponding engineering change request so that the change can be approved retrospectively and incorporated in the as-built project documentation.
- Sometimes an item fails to pass a prescribed inspection or test, but the non-conformances listed are only just outside the previously stated tolerances. This can give rise to the issue of a manufacturing or construction concession, which might mean simply signing off the inspection report and allowing the work to proceed or, alternatively, the issue of a formal concession document. In some cases the original tolerances might be considered unnecessarily and unreasonably tight, resulting in the issue of changed drawings or test specifications. In some industries where reliability and public safety are particular concerns, any such change to a drawing must be requested formally on an engineering change request.

Engineering change request

ECR number:

Project title: Project number:

Details of change requested (use continuation sheets if necessary):

Drawings and other documents affected:

Reason for request:

Originator: Date:

Emergency action requested (if any):

Effect on costs: Cost estimate ref:

Will customer pay, yes ☐   no ☐   If yes, customer authorization ref:

Effect on project schedule?

Change approved ☐   **Approved with restrictions** ☐   **Rejected** ☐
Point of embodiment, stocks, work in progress, units in service, special restrictions etc.:

Authorized by: Date:

Figure 18.1   A change request form for engineering projects

Requests for concessions can arise under any circumstances where, retrospectively, it is found that manufacture or construction has not taken place strictly in accordance with the issued drawings and specifications.

- Occasionally, the manufacturing or construction managers will request prior permission to depart from the issued instructions contained in the drawings. Perhaps cadmium-plated bolts of a particular size cannot be obtained but galvanized bolts are available from stock. In many companies, a formal production permit system will be in place so that such departures from the designer's intentions can be formally considered and the approval recorded.
- After a project has been delivered or handed over, problems can be discovered which are the result of shortcomings or design errors by the contractor. These can result in retrospective change action that, again, must be recorded using the formal change request procedure, so that proposed rectification measures are properly considered and the true as-built nature of the project remains on record.

PAYING FOR UNFUNDED CHANGES

Although changes that are not to be funded by the client are usually called 'unfunded' changes, this description is not strictly accurate because the changes must be funded somehow. There are two principal funding methods for 'unfunded' changes:

1 The changes must be paid for out of the project's potential profits, in which case the authorized budget cannot be increased. The changes will simply be seen as amounts overspent against the baseline budget. They will have the effect of depressing the cost performance index and increasing the estimated cost of the project at completion.
2 Many project estimates and proposals include contingency sums which are held as hidden reserves against unforeseen setbacks or changes. These sums will vary according to the amount of competition faced when the project was initially costed. If the competition is light, there might be the opportunity to add a significant percentage of the original cost estimates as a contingency allowance. When there are sufficient funds in the contingency reserve, a suitable amount might be 'drawn down' when an internal, otherwise unfunded change is authorized. The authorized budgets for the cost accounts and organizational units affected can then be increased to allow for the change, and the increase can be consolidated (rolled up) into the total project budget.

Client-funded changes

A project contractor that has won a contract for a large commercial project will almost certainly have done so against fierce competition. The contractor will, often at considerable expense, have prepared and submitted a formal proposal as a result of receiving an invitation to tender. The project client, on the other hand, should benefit from the competitive bidding environment in which all the potential contractors have been placed.

When the client, for any reason, asks for a change to an existing contract, the bargaining advantages pass decisively from the project purchaser to the contractor. The other potential contractors who tendered for the original contract have long since left the scene and there is now effectively no price competition. In theory (although, fortunately, this is not often

Contract variation

CVO number:
Project number:
Issue date:

Project title:

Summary of change (use continuation sheets if necessary):

Originator: Date:

Effect on project schedule:

Effect on costs and price: Cost estimate ref:

Customer's authorization details: Our authorization:

Distribution:

Figure 18.2   One form of a contract variation order

followed in practice) the contractor could name any price, however high, for each proposed change. There is a general belief, not without foundation, that some contractors price their original contracts low and expect to make all or most of their profit from the higher profit margins that can be obtained from the inevitable project changes. A project where the client, for whatever reason, has failed to specify all the requirements in the first place can be a financial calamity for the purchaser but a money-spinner for the contractor.

In construction contracts, the most usual form of change request from a client will be a contract variation order, perhaps along the lines of that shown in Figure 18.2. The contracts for many manufacturing projects and some subcontracts for any kinds of project are made using standard purchase order forms, in which case every change must be authorized by the issue of a purchase order amendment. The procedures for purchase orders and their amendments are well known and need not be illustrated here.

The receipt of a contract variation order or purchase order amendment can often trigger the internal change control procedure, a typical version of which is described in following sections of this chapter.

Non-commercial factors of project changes

Every company of significant size that handles projects as part of its normal business should have an established procedure for originating, administering, considering and implementing proposed changes. Quite apart from the potential commercial impact of changes on work in progress, and on time and costs generally, there are also questions of reliability, safety, interchangeability and traceability to be considered. Some companies set up a 'change committee' or 'change board' to consider all these questions and decide whether or not a particular change should be allowed.

RELIABILITY AND SAFETY

Changes must be considered in terms of their possible effects on reliability and safety. If the company employs a reliability engineer, that person might need to be consulted when each change is considered. Many changes are introduced for the expressed reason of improving reliability and safety. But a change to one part of the project might, unknown to the originator of the change, produce adverse effects elsewhere in the project.

INTERCHANGEABILITY

Some projects, especially engineering projects, might require the design and building of a number of identical components. If a change occurs partway through the project life cycle, some components manufactured early in the project may not be interchangeable with later versions of the same component. This can have important implications for operating, maintenance and the provision of spares. There is a sensible rule which says that, if a component is changed to the extent that it is no longer interchangeable with earlier versions, then the new component must not be given merely a new revision number to its previous part number, but must instead be given a new part number.

TRACEABILITY

Suppose that crash investigators find the cause of an aircraft crash to be a design fault in a component, or that a railway locomotive became derailed through the fracture of bolts in the undercarriage assemblies. The responsible statutory bodies and the travelling public will expect that all similar aircraft or trains built with the same components will be withdrawn from service, and not allowed to carry passengers again until the faults have been put right. But this means being able to trace all other aircraft or locomotives that actually have those particular components. Similar considerations apply to a number of industries, including those producing defence weapons, for instance.

Traceability in this sense is achieved though a number of procedures. The first requirement is that every aircraft, locomotive, weapon or other product should have both a part number and a unique serial number. Then the initial build status can be recorded using documents that are sometimes called build schedules, which simply list all the drawings and specifications used in the manufacture and assembly of the product. When a change is introduced, the build schedule will change, so that each version of the build schedule will relate to a batch of one or more serial numbers. The most common occurrence of this is seen in the automobile service industry, where the local repair garage will search a computer record to find the particular version of a component that must be replaced on a car of a particular type and chassis or engine number.

Complete traceability is not possible without a change control system. In industries that place a particularly high emphasis on reliability and safety, the system should record and be able to trace not only design changes, but also concessions and production permits that were allowed during manufacture. When taken to its full extreme, traceability will extend downwards through all parts of the WBS, and all purchasing and production records, so that the particular supplier and batch of a faulty item can be tracked down in the event of problem or failure.

As with so many other project management systems, coding is a vital part of traceability. Without the existence of identifying codes, no part or batch could be traced or positively identified. Coding (in the form of document serial numbers) is just as important for all change documents.

Change administration and approval procedures

CHANGE ADMINISTRATION

Change control procedures can involve considerable administrative effort, and all but the smallest companies must appoint someone to follow through each change request to ensure that it is dealt with expeditiously and effectively. Each change request has its small life cycle, from request, through consideration and approval to implementation, integration and final documentation.

Some companies have a sufficient number of changes to warrant the appointment of one or more change clerks, whose job is simply to carry out change administration. In other cases, this might be a part-time role performaned by a technical clerk or similar person, who also carries out other administrative functions on the project. Another possibility, which is often to be recommended, is to place responsibility for change administration with the project support office, the functions of which are described in Chapter 19.

Change register				Project number:	Approved? Y/N/R*	Date signed off	Sheet number:
ECR number	Originator		Date requested	Brief details or title	Approved? Y/N/R*	Date signed off	Budget change (if any)
	Name	Dept.					

* Y = change approved   N = change not approved   R = approved subject to restrictions

Figure 18.3   A project change register

The duties of the change administrator are simple to describe, but vital. They include:

1 Receive each change request from the originator.
2 Register the request and allocate a serial number. A suitable form of register sheet is illustrated in Figure 18.3.
3 Bring the change request to the attention of the change committee, change board or other appointed arbiter for approval or rejection. Some very urgent requests might mean actually visiting the change committee members with the request to secure their immediate decision.
4 Keep the originator of the change informed of progress and decisions.
5 Follow up to ensure that all the approved changes are implemented, integrated and documented.

The change committee (see the next section) or its individual members will, from time to time, need support from specialists such as a reliability engineer, a cost and estimating engineer or a planning engineer. Since cost and planning engineers are often found in a project support office, that would seem to be a sensible place in which to employ the administrator or change control clerk.

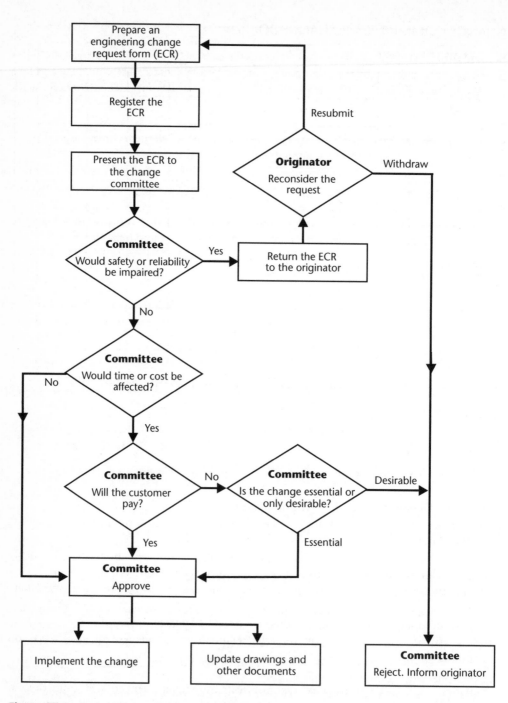

Figure 18.4   Basic steps in a change control procedure

CHANGE COMMITTEE OR CHANGE BOARD

Because the typical project change can affect many different aspects of the project, not all of which might be foreseen by the originator, a committee of experts can be convened regularly to consider changes, either individually or in batches. A typical committee might include the following:

- a senior engineering manager, or chief engineer, to consider all the technical aspects of the proposed change – in some cases, known as the 'design authority'
- a senior representative of the construction or manufacturing team, to consider the effects of the change on work in progress and whether or not the change will be practical to carry out
- a quality manager or chief inspector, sometimes called in this context the 'inspecting authority', to assess the effects of the change on quality, safety and reliability
- a commercial manager or contracts manager to consider the implications of additional costs and programme delays.

A typical sequence of events in the process of change consideration and approval is shown in Figure 18.4.

CHANGE COMMITTEE'S DECISION

From any sample of a project change request, one of the following decisions might typically result:

- Send the change request back to the originator for clarification or for an alternative solution.
- Approve the change and order its immediate implementation.
- Approve the change with reservations. For example, give approval for future work, but not for work in progress, or give temporary approval for work urgently affected but request that a better solution be sought for work not yet started.
- Reject the change unequivocally, giving reasons.

Change implementation and integration

Since a change can affect baseline plans and budgets in several cost accounts and organizational elements, the changed budget and schedule implications must be input to the database, first by rescheduling the project with the changed activities substituted. Hence-forth all the earned value calculations and forecasts to completion will be affected, and these must be reflected in subsequent reports.

It is important to ensure that the necessary, but usually unprofitable, task of updating all drawings, parts lists, plans, bills of material, specifications, calculations, build schedules and other documents is undertaken so that these always reflect the true as-built project. Such records will be found convenient for many post-project purposes, such as dealing with operating and maintenance difficulties, as a source of proven designs for re-use on future projects, or even as evidence in possible legal proceedings.

Less formal procedures for change control

Described below are two examples where the full rigour of a change control system, complete with change committee, can be avoided whilst still maintaining effective control.

A FIXED-CHARGE TARIFF FOR CHANGES

An electronic systems company was working as subcontractor to an aerospace company as the provider of specially designed, trailer-mounted automatic test equipment for complete aircraft systems. The commissioning engineers were working at an airfield some 200 miles distant from their parent company to prove the prototype trailer, and they had to deal with many day-to-day requests from the aircraft company's engineers to make small changes to the test routines and measurement values. Each change required a simple temporary wiring change followed by a quick test check.

An amicable agreement was reached between these two companies for the control of all such small changes. A simple request form was devised that allowed each change to be described both in words and as a simple circuit diagram sketch. Triplicate pads of these forms were prepared using NCR (no carbon required) paper, and with each triplicate set printed with a serial number. Thereafter, each change was written on the special form, signed by a senior on-site commissioning engineer from each of the two companies. The changes were implemented immediately using temporary patch wiring. One copy of each request form was sent to the engineering office of each company, which allowed for the changes to be incorporated in the final as-built drawings from which the final production versions of the trailers would be built.

Rather than estimate the cost of each change, a fixed-price tariff was agreed (which at the time was £10 per change), so that invoicing each month was simply a question of totting up the number of changes made. Although simple, the procedures ensured both fair payment and adequate control and recording of every change.

DAYWORKS

This chapter should not end without mention of dayworks. These are typically a feature of construction work where the client has frequent access to the site, or particularly where work is carried out on the client's existing premises.

Dayworks sheets are simple documents that record and authorize small additional work items requested by the client at the project site. These additional items might not even affect the main project. One example is a request for skips to be provided for purposes other than the disposal of rubbish caused by the project. The client, seeing painters at work, requests them to paint areas outside the scope of the original project. Or the client asks glaziers working on the project to replace a few cracked panes in a part of the premises not included in the project works.

These are, in effect, changes to the scope of the contract and, as such, they need to be controlled. But they do not justify formal requests to a change committee or even special pricing and quotation by the contractor. What happens in practice is that the site foreman will, on receiving a request for additional work, issue a dayworks sheet. This dayworks sheet will allow space for the extra job to be described, and will allow for collection of the time and materials involved.

There might be hundreds of such dayworks sheets on a large project, each of which must be authorized by a senior on-site representative of the client. The idea is that all the dayworks sheets raised in a particular accounting period are priced, with the relevant amounts invoiced to the client as extras to the original contract.

Not all contractors invoice promptly or accurately. In one City of London contract, a reputable contractor carried out a series of building alterations, extensions and renovations for a large company. Many dayworks sheets were raised during the process, for all kinds of additional jobs ranging from the fixing of gates and fences to the collection and disposal of non-project rubbish. Unfortunately, the contractor did not invoice the client for the final project costs, which included all the dayworks, until a year after the project had been finished. It took a firm of quantity surveyors two months, at additional cost, to sort out and certify all the additional work. All this could have been avoided if the client had filed its copies of the dayworks sheets more carefully and analysed their cumulative effects in advance.

19 *Centralized or Decentralized Planning and Control*

All managers of significant projects need specialist support, not only for the specialist functions associated with the technology of the project, but also for project management administration, estimating, planning, purchasing, cost accounting and information handling. The way in which such specialist project administration and management support is provided and organized varies greatly from company to company and from project to project. For example, one large project might have its own legal department, whilst in other cases the project manager will need to refer to a centralized legal or commercial management department, or to an external solicitor for advice on contractual and legal issues. A company handling a number of different projects simultaneously might entrust the planning and scheduling of those projects to the individual project managers or it might provide a central planning and scheduling office. That central planning and scheduling group might be part of a larger project services office, staffed not only with planners but also with cost engineers, progress control and contract administration clerks, a local cost accounts clerk and even, in some cases, a small purchasing group. So, companies obviously have profound differences of opinion about the centralization or distribution of project support services. This chapter examines some of the roles that a project support office might fulfil, together with some of the advantages and disadvantages of centralization of the project planning and control function.

Possible functions and forms of a project support office

The principal purpose of a project support office, or project services group, should always be to provide assistance to the project manager; it should take upon itself the drudgery of project administration, providing expert help in the use of sophisticated project management software, planning methods, the application and standardization of project management systems, report preparation, change control administration and so on. However, in addition to its supporting role, a central project support office can also take on a regulatory function, ensuring that project managers conform to the company or project procedures. For example, when a project manager is expected to write or contribute to a progress report, he or she is likely to be under pressure from the support office to meet the report deadlines. A central office can also help to ensure standardization in the use of project management procedures and coding and numbering systems.

A company that carries out a large number of small projects in a coordination matrix organization (the weakest form of the matrix) might have a central project services group, perhaps reporting to the engineering manager, that can even take on the role of project coordinator, so that the senior design engineers appointed as project leaders are free to deal only with the technical aspects of their projects.

POSSIBLE ROLES FOR A PROJECT SUPPORT OFFICE

A project support office or centralized project services can perform a large number of roles, from planning to purchasing, from contract administration to cost control, and many others. Here are some of the more usual functions of a large project support office:

- Project administration:
  - maintaining the register of current and past projects
  - allocating project serial numbers
  - issuing project authorization notices
  - recording and progressing contract variations (see also change control and administration)
  - issuing project closure notices.
- Planning and scheduling:
  - assisting at planning meetings
  - operating sophisticated computer software packages
  - plotting and issuing network diagrams and Gantt charts
  - preparing work-to lists
  - preparing resource schedules
  - developing standard networks and templates
  - advising or choosing project management software.
- Cost management:
  - cost estimating
  - timesheet administration
  - project cost collecting
  - preparation of cost reports
  - preparation of cash flow schedules.
- Programme management:
  - assessing resource availabilities and creating/updating the computer resource file
  - multi-project scheduling
  - analysing and consolidating project data to corporate level
  - 'what-if?' analysis for the effect of new projects
  - exception reporting
  - supporting strategic planning
  - manpower planning and draft recruitment schedules.
- Progress and performance management:
  - collecting progress data
  - updating plans and schedules
  - exception reporting
  - earned value analyses and reports.
- Subcontract administration:
  - monitoring and checking claims for payment
  - progressing and expediting.

- Change control and administration:
  - change registration
  - change progressing, through all stages of consideration and approval up to full implementation
  - change integration, updating schedules budgets, and earned value statistics
  - maintaining records of client liability for the costs of changes.

All companies have departments that support projects in a number of ways, and, rarely, some roles such as health and safety, engineering standards, specialized purchasing and materials management functions, legal services, document distribution, filing and archives, project cost accounting and so on might be located in a central project services office. However, most of the functions performed by the average project services office are to do with planning and control.

Degrees of centralization for planning and control

It is neither possible nor desirable to centralize all project services. For example, although the project support office might produce summary plans and schedules, individual department managers must still control the day-by-day, week-by-week and even month-by-month allocation of jobs to staff under their control. Despite the temptation to interfere, project managers should not attempt to schedule the internal activities of suppliers and sub-contractors. One can imagine the responses that might be generated by such actions. There are circumstances, however, when clients and purchasers need to be reassured, in general terms, that their suppliers do have adequate planning and control measures in place.

There is usually a strong case for centralizing those functions that help to maintain consistency and standardization of procedures and the PMIS. Centralization is also to be recommended where it removes routine administrative chores from the busy project manager's daily round.

Arguments for the centralization of planning and control

In the early days of project planning, planning had to be centralized because knowledge of the specialist planning techniques was limited and computing was centralized on a mainframe computer. So all processing of original plans and their subsequent updates had to be channelled through those familiar with the particular computer system. Strong arguments for the centralization of planning remain in today's world, provided that the planning logic and data are under the ultimate control of the project manager. Arguments for providing a centralized planning and control service to the project manager include the following:

- There is a need for the standardization of systems and methodology across all groups and elements of the project.
- Planning needs to be coordinated and integrated across the project.
- Project managers have a central role in the planning and control of their projects, and planning must be under their direct control.

- There should be a top-down approach to planning a project. This means that the project manager or central group undertakes the planning, so that it is not left to uncoordinated and unskilled group and element managers in a bottom-up approach.
- Grouping planners together in a functional staff group brings all the benefits of functionalization.
- The management, planning and control of a portfolio or programme of projects requires centralized planning, so that the projects can be managed and resourced, in effect, as one large project.

Arguments for decentralized planning

There can be strong arguments for decentralized planning. These include:

- human factors
- encouraging individual accountability
- the fact that planning cannot be considered in isolation from other factors
- problems of centralized planning in large, multi-company projects.

HUMAN FACTORS

Unless the people responsible for the preparation of a plan have made a thorough and logical analysis, that plan will not be realistic or practicable. Similarly, unless the people responsible for executing the plan work in accordance with the information outlined in it, nothing will have been achieved by producing the plan in the first place.

Centralized planning tends to emphasize the role of the specialist planner, and the techniques used, to the detriment of the human factors involved. When plans are made by centralized planners acting on their own there is a high probability that they will be unrealistic, because it is just not possible for those planners to be fully informed and to exercise critical judgement on what is practicable in the many areas and functions of a project. More importantly, the plans will be unlikely to be carried out as intended because, human nature being what it is, most managers have their own preferred ways of doing their job. They dislike being told in detail how to do it.

Effective planning requires the involvement of all those concerned, both to ensure the best possible correctness of the plan and to obtain the commitment of everyone to it. If this participation and commitment is not achieved, plans are unlikely to be realistic and they will not be used.

ENCOURAGING INDIVIDUAL ACCOUNTABILITY

If planning is completely centralized, then control and reporting also tend to be centralized. Centralized planning and control are not compatible with an emphasis on individual accountability, responsibility and the contractor–consignee concept. The managers of each cost account, group and higher-level WBS and OBS element must at the very least be involved in, but preferably carry out, the planning and control of their individual responsibilities. Control must start at the individual managers' level: they should each control their own area of responsibility.

MODE OF PLANNING AND ORGANIZATION

Whether planning and control are centralized or decentralized is only one facet of the decision. If planning is centralized, the organization and management of the project or portfolio of projects will usually also be centralized, with all that entails. This may be effective for the smaller project but will incur many problems in the larger project, as discussed previously.

MULTI-COMPANY LARGE PROJECTS

The concept of totally centralized planning in a multi-company large project is, of course, not practical, partly because of the large numbers of activities and groups involved. A more significant difficulty is that each company will tend to have its own methodology, systems and techniques with which it is familiar. In those, typical, circumstances it will simply not be possible to have totally centralized planning and control.

Distributed, but integrated, project control

Project control should be neither centralized nor decentralized. Put differently, it should be neither a top-down approach nor a bottom-up approach: it has to be a combination of both. The function of project planning and control does need to be integrated, but it also needs to be distributed. Individual managers should plan and control their individual areas of responsibility, but they can be assisted by staff planners who might come from a central group. These individual plans should be integrated into the overall project control system. The terms 'distributed' and 'integrated' are more appropriate than decentralized or central-ized. It is useful to note here that several of the more sophisticated project management packages can reside in a central server and accept and integrate planning data from individual managers who plan their own areas of work using somewhat simpler and more user-friendly software, such as Microsoft Project.

Planning and control should be a combination of the top-down and bottom-up approaches, with the emphasis changing as the form of organization evolves through the project life cycle. Thus on a large project, the emphasis will be on centralized planning and control at the early and later stages of the life cycle, with an emphasis on distributed planning and control in the middle, work-intensive stages. In the hierarchical multi-level approach, the level 1, and possibly the level 2, plans may be made centrally, but the level 3 and 4 plans may be made on a distributed basis.

Distributed planning requires the establishment and use of standardized methodology, systems and techniques, either throughout the project or at the top two or three levels of planning. This will mean training all the managers involved in their application and use. This is not to say that these busy managers need be expected actually to do all the work in the planning process. They are unlikely to have the time available, or the same skills and speed in the use of the systems as the specialist planners. Specialist planners, who perhaps reside in a project support office, have an important role in assisting with planning or assembling the plans, but the plans made must be based on those made by the individual managers, prepared within the framework of the level 1 or level 2 plans, structures and coding.

In a large multi-company project, complete standardization of methodology, systems and techniques is seldom possible. This is where the hierarchical, multi-tiered WBS and

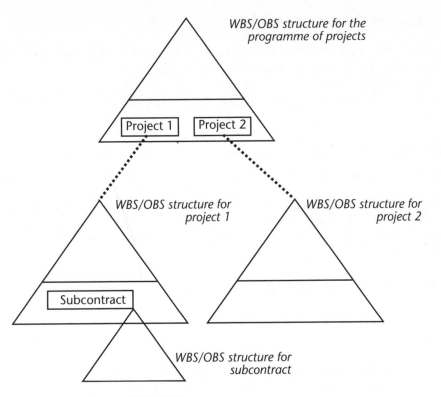

Figure 19.1   Multi-tiered WBS/OBS structures

CTR methods are applicable. When the overall project organization is divisionalized and has multiple organizational units, each perhaps using a different contractor, the WBS/OBS framework becomes multi-tiered. Each project division or organizational unit will be responsible for an individual major or minor WBS element that will have its own dedicated OBS or organizational structure.

Within the overall project WBS/OBS framework, each division or unit will have its own WBS/OBS framework for the element in the overall structure for which it is responsible. This concept, illustrated in Figure 19.1, can easily be extended to include the common situation where the client company has a mirror-image organization spanning all the WBS/OBS frameworks, where each separate structure is that of a separate contract. This is, in fact, multi-dimensional structuring, and it can be implemented using database principles. This permits the integration of structures into one system, with project data completely traceable through the hierarchy of structures. It allows multiple contractor structures to be mapped, chained and merged into one project-wide WBS and gives great flexibility in the use of alternative structures for integration, planning, control and reporting. The main advantage of this approach is that it can handle multiple company control using the inevitable diversity of different structures, methodologies and techniques, yet can integrate the data from these into one system. Standardization and integration are possible at levels 1, 2 or even 3 in the overall WBS, and this integrates the distributed planning and control.

In this database approach, the key components are as follows:

- *Control elements*. These are the elements of the work that make up the project – for example, work breakdown elements, cost accounts or work packages.
- *Relational data*. This defines the relationships between the control elements – that is, the parent–child relationships. This may involve multiple coding references, each of which might belong to a separate hierarchical structure.
- *Control data*. These data are the usual control data, such as cost.
- *Project structure hierarchy*. This is the set of parent–child relationships used for summarizing control elements (Calnan, 1988).

Thus, both on the smaller and the larger project, distributed, but integrated, planning and control is feasible and should be used to combine most of the advantages of both centralized and decentralized planning in a modern methodology of structured project management, planning and control.

20 *People in Projects*

So far, this book has been concerned with the organization of projects and project management systems. But one important system has yet to be covered. This is the 'people system', without the effective working of which all the other systems will fail. Management has been described as 'obtaining results through people' and the way in which the project manager deals with people, and how these people deal with one another, can make or break project performance. Effective organization, a structured methodology for project planning and control and good human relations are all necessary for good performance on projects but none of these is sufficient on its own. In addition to professional skills in organizing, planning and controlling a project, to be successful, a project manager must develop his or her skills in managing people.

Critical areas

There are five critical areas of human behaviour in which a project manager must have expertise:

1 leadership
2 achieving power in a fluid situation
3 motivation of individuals and groups
4 developing teams and teamwork
5 managing conflict (discussed in Chapter 21).

The project manager needs these skills to handle the human problems that arise because the normal patterns of human behaviour are characteristically accelerated and accentuated in project work and because of the particular problems associated with the forms of project organization used. One of the problems that adversely influence human behaviour is the forms of project organization which are necessary to manage a project; they are specialized, often complex, handle multi-discipline, multi-company undertakings and conflict with conventional organization theory in many ways.

Other branches of management in well-run companies follow most of the textbook principles of organization theory:

1 The structure is hierarchical.
2 The lines of authority are based on superior–subordinate relationships.
3 Each subordinate has only one superior (unity of command).
4 There is a division of labour by task specialization.
5 Each manager has a limited span of control.

6 There is a division between line and staff.
7 There is parity between responsibility and authority.

Project organization forms often ignore these so-called principles of management and break the rules. Disregard for these long-accepted principles means that the project organization is complex and has an inherent tendency for conflict. However, in large projects involving different departments and companies, there is a new set of circumstances. In order to bind these diverse elements into one organization, committed to complete a project to its time, cost and performance objectives, and effectively to manage it, a new set of ground rules has had to evolve.

Managing people working on projects requires a modification of the conventional human relations approach. In this, many of the cherished beliefs taught in business schools and preached by human behaviour consultants have to be reconsidered, and the approach used must be based on the harsh reality of the project environment. The remainder of this book is devoted to the principal points, strategies and tools that a project manager can use to manage the human side of projects. As such, it endeavours to take an applied and realistic approach to the specialized nature of human problems in the project setting.

Leadership

The quickest way to change the performance of an organization is to change its leader. Leadership is critical to high performance on projects, as it is with almost any human endeavour. There is some debate over whether there is a difference between management and leadership, or between managers and leaders. One of the problems stems from the definitions used for these factors. The conventional definition of management is 'the achievement of results through people'. The definition of leadership is not so well established, but most definitions follow the general lines of that given below:

> The human behaviour process by which the activities of one person influence the behaviour of others to support goals desired by the leader.

There is very little difference between these definitions for management and leadership. However, it has been argued, not surprisingly, that managers and leaders are very different kinds of people. They differ in motivation, personal history and the ways in which they think and act.

The problem arises from the conventional definitions of leadership, in that it is much more than merely 'getting followers to follow'. Leadership involves the following important factors:

- a mission, or vision, of a future state of nature, or set of goals, normally involving change
- a high personal commitment and drive to these goals
- actions to achieve these goals, normally involving a conceived strategy
- mobilizing, inspiring and maintaining commitment by others to the achievement of these goals.

Thus maintaining the status quo – expressed, rather unfairly, as the ongoing management of operations – may not require much leadership, but changing the status quo does. Managing an existing planning system or an organizational unit requires less leadership than the introduction of a new methodology of project control, or the development of teamwork among a group of managers starting work on a new project. Thus emphasis on leadership is far higher in the management of change (which includes project management) than in the management of ongoing operations. This is the prime difference between management and leadership. Some types of management and some situations require more leadership than others.

Leadership is critical to the successful completion of a project, and indeed to the effective introduction or improvement of project management. A leader can lift the performance of an organization to a new level if he or she conceives and believes it is possible, is totally committed to it, takes actions to achieve it and inspires the people in the organization to this higher level of performance: that is, if he or she makes the followers believe it is possible and makes them committed to this vision. Leadership, or management style, is how the project mobilizes this commitment, but this vision is as much, if not more, the defining characteristic of leadership than merely getting others to follow.

Leadership style

Leadership style has been the subject of considerable research, much of it originally carried out in the context of manufacturing organizations. Conventional belief identifies two independent dimensions to a manager's leadership style or behaviour. These two dimensions go under many names, including those listed in Figure 20.1.

The project manager who is *task-oriented* is characterized as a strong, competent, dominant leader who centralizes decision-making, problem-solving, planning and control. Conventional theory indicates the following results from such a leader:

Task-oriented	Employee-oriented
Initiating structure	Consideration
Autocratic	Social orientation
Despotic	Human behaviour approach
Directive	Participative
Production-centred	Team-oriented
Concern for production	Concern for people
Dictator	Democratic
Strong leadership	Socio-emotional orientation
Managing	Non-directive, permissive
Theory X	Theory Y

Figure 20.1 Different leadership styles

- Production or goal attainment will be higher than with the employee-oriented approach, at least in the short term.
- Decisions will be made more rapidly, although their implementation may be slower.
- Emergencies and crises will be tackled more effectively.

However, in addition:

- Personal needs and interests of employees will have low priority.
- Employee morale may be low.
- Hostility may be high.
- Employee creativity and initiative may be stifled.
- It the strong leader leaves, the organization will tend to fall apart.

The *employee-oriented* project manager is characterized by a high emphasis on participation and teamwork in decision-making, problem-solving, planning and control. Conventional theory indicates that, with such a leader, the following will result:

- Personal needs and the interests of employees will have a high priority.
- Production and goal achievement will be higher in the longer term than with the task-oriented approach.
- Employee creativity and initiative will be increased.
- Morale and employee satisfaction will be high.
- Commitment will be strong.

However, in addition:

- Decision-making will take longer, but implementation may be faster.

Thus both the task-oriented and employee-oriented approaches have advantages and disadvantages. Theories of leadership style tend to integrate the two dimensions that were defined by Blake and Mouton (1964) in their managerial grid (Figure 20.2). They used the terms 'concern for people' and 'concern for production' to describe the two dimensions, each of which they ranked on a scale of 1–9. The managerial grid identifies the four following principles or extremes of management style:

1 the highest concern for people and the lowest concern for production – the 1,9 manager (employee-oriented)
2 a low concern for people and a high concern for production – the 9,1 manager (task-oriented)
3 a low concern for both production and people – the 1,1 manager
4 a high concern for both production and people – the 9,9 manager.

Between these extremes, managers can be anywhere in the grid, depending on the balance between their concern for people and production. The principal focus of the theory, and the most recommended leadership style is the 9,9 style, sometimes termed the 'Hi-Hi' leader, who combines a high task orientation and a high employee orientation. This is identified by Blake and Mouton as the ideal leader, who can get the best results and can flexibly use both dimensions of leadership.

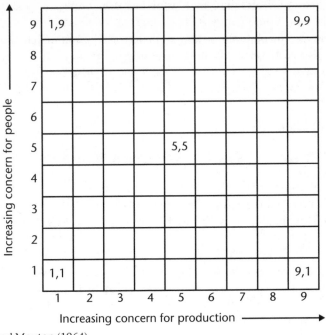

Source: Blake and Mouton (1964).

Figure 20.2   Blake and Mouton's managerial grid

Other behavioural researchers and theorists find problems with this concept. Hunsaker and Cook (1986, p. 309), for example, wrote: 'Despite abundant testimonials about the effectiveness of such "ideal" style as 9,9 however, empirical research does not necessarily support the claims.'

Care must therefore be taken when applying conventional beliefs and theories to applied situations, such as project management. Fortunately there is a body of applied research relevant to project management that does give some practical guidelines to an effective leadership style.

EMPLOYEE-ORIENTED APPROACH

Research work to determine those factors that contribute to the success or failure of projects reveals the following:

- The lack of project team participation in decision-making and problem solving strongly affects the perceived failure of projects.
- Project team participation in determining schedules and budgets is associated with project success.
- The lack of team spirit and sense of mission within the project team also strongly affects the perceived failure of projects (see Wilemon and Baker, 1983, p. 633).

Therefore it can be concluded that participation and teamwork – both factors that are given high emphasis in the employee-centred approach – contribute to preventing project failure and achieving success.

However, research also reveals that participation increases employee satisfaction, but not necessarily performance. Despite conventional belief, no direct link has been established after decades of research. The objective of the employee-oriented approach appears to make people happy and satisfied at work, but not necessarily to obtain high performance in the achievement of the task. High performance is supposed to arise naturally out of the job satisfaction, but it does not necessarily do so.

TASK-ORIENTED APPROACH

Applied research in project management has also drawn the following conclusions with regard to leadership style:

The most effective project managers are non-directive, human relations-oriented leaders as opposed to directive, managing, task-oriented leaders ... [is] mostly false. (Baker *et al.*, 1983, p. 677)

In very favourable or in very unfavourable situations for getting a task accomplished by group effort, the autocratic, task controlling, managing leadership works best. In situations intermediate in difficulty, the nondirective, permissive leader is most successful. (Fiedler, 1965, p. 18, cited in Baker *et al.*, 1983, p. 677)

The project manager must have a high task orientation and a competent autocrat does get results. Nevertheless, the manager will not achieve high performance in the attainment of a project's goals if people are alienated, demotivated, and uncommitted to the project's goals, and there is not at least a cooperative working relationship.

The project manager's prime objective must be the effective achievement of the project's targets through high performance, and not just to make people happy and satisfied at work – except in so far as this contributes to achieving the project manager's task. Thus the employee-oriented dimension of leadership style is essentially supportive to the task-oriented dimension of project leadership. It must also be recognized that motivation, commitment and teamwork can be achieved by the directive, task-oriented leader in many ways, and the participative human behaviour approach is only one of these.

This concept of a high task-oriented style with a social back-up has to be moderated in the matrix and multi-company setting. It can be effective when the project manager is in charge of a dedicated project team (or organizational unit) where the individuals and groups are directly responsible to the project manager. Yet it is more than likely to bring about conflict with those over whom the project manager has limited or indefinite authority, which is the case in the weak or balanced matrix form of organization.

This is particularly relevant in the multi-company case, where the project manager's power is defined by the contracts and the manager's personal and political power. Acting directly with those people who do not recognize one's authority can be counterproductive and lead to serious conflict. Therefore, the leadership style that can be used is contingent on the project manager's power and the particular circumstances.

Thus, to summarize on the subject of leadership:

• The project manager must have a high task orientation that, in terms of the managerial grid, can be expressed as a 9,? manager.

- As a means towards achieving the project's objectives the contribution should also encourage participation and teamwork, but as supportive to the task orientation. In managerial grid terms the project manager should be something like a 9,6 or 9,7 manager.
- This must be modified by the amount of power the project manager has and the particular circumstances. The lower the power, the higher must be the participation emphasis.

Power

With the simplest definition of management in mind (obtaining results through people) the simplest definition of power is 'the ability to get people to do what you want them to do'. Therefore management can be redefined simply as 'the use of power to obtain results'.

Power is thus essential to management. Without it, the manager cannot manage. Whether power belongs to an individual, a group or is widely dispersed does not change the fact that it is power that gets things done. Thus it is power that:

- takes decisions
- commits resources
- controls
- takes actions
- rewards
- punishes
- sways minds
- generates enthusiasm
- gets others to follow
- changes the course of events.

Power is essential to all achievements, to management and to leadership. It is no wonder that insufficient authority and influence strongly affect the perceived failure of projects. For example, in an emergency or crisis or, more particularly, when small signs point to the beginning of an adverse trend requiring urgent corrective action of which others are unconvinced, which of the following will get the fastest results?

- requesting action as a plaintiff
- from a position of weakness, trying to persuade others to take action
- negotiating for agreement with equals
- giving instructions (directing or requesting action) as a superior who must be obeyed.

The level of the project manager's power influences the leadership styles that can be used. The higher the level of power, the more task-oriented the manager can be. Conversely, the lower the level of power, the more participative the manager must be. The level of power, or more particularly in this case, the level of authority also interacts with the organization structure used. The form of matrix is determined by, or determines, the authority of the project manager. In the functional or weak matrix this authority is low. In the balanced matrix, authority is somewhere between high and low, and is often uncertain. It is highest in the strong forms of the matrix, such as the project matrix or secondment matrix.

In the multi-company project, the project manager typically has limited and insufficient authority to give directions to all those involved. Thus, as noted earlier, in the matrix and multi-company organizations there exists an authority gap, where the project managers' responsibilities exceed their authority. Yet project managers need some measure of power over all those concerned if they are to manage the project and exercise leadership to achieve the project objectives. Thus project managers' power must be considerably in excess of their positional authority.

It is important to understand the difference between power and authority. Authority is often termed 'legitimate power', but this is a misnomer as it wrongly implies that all other forms of power are illegitimate. Authority is, in fact, the legal power which pertains to a manager's position in the organizational hierarchy to give subordinates instructions that they must follow or else be disciplined. It thus also includes the power to reward or punish, sometimes termed 'coercive power'. Authority is, however, only one source of a manager's power. The many sources of power available to a manager can be viewed on three levels, as follows:

1 Positional superior–subordinate power, including the following:
   a) Legal authority: the superior has the right to give instructions to subordinates, and they accept that they have a duty to carry out those instructions.
   b) Reward power: the superior has the power to offer financial rewards, promotions and attractive jobs. The subordinate does what the superior wants in order to obtain these rewards.
   c) Coercive power: the superior has the power to punish or discipline the subordinate, even to the extent of dismissal. The subordinate does what the superior wants to avoid punishment.
   d) Contract authority: a special case of positional power that arises from contracts and purchase agreements in multi-company or even matrix organizations. These agreements give the client some measure of authority over the other party, and often this works both ways.
2 Personal power, which includes the following:
   a) Expert power: people do what the power-holder wants because he or she is recognized as having special knowledge or expertise.
   b) Referent power: people do what the power-holder wants because of admiration, loyalty, friendship, respect, attraction or other forms of personal relationship (for example, charismatic leadership).
3 Political power: power based on the power-holder's skill in, and use of, the many activities of politics to gain power.

Positional superior–subordinate power is unidirectional, operating directly downwards through the hierarchical pyramid. It is thus exercised by superiors over their subordinates. All other forms of power are multi-directional, and can be exercised down, up, sideways and diagonally across the hierarchical tree. For example, a subordinate can have real power, often termed influence, over a superior.

Positional superior–subordinate power, or more specifically authority, can also operate diagonally downwards but this can lead to problems and conflict. In other words, someone of higher position in the hierarchy can give instructions to a person occupying a lower position who is employed in another manager's group. However, if the instructing manager relies only on positional authority, the subordinate need not necessarily carry out the instructions, and the subordinate's own superior may resent the perceived interference.

The term 'level of power' is used deliberately in these circumstances because, as in other spheres (the martial arts, for example) the manager tends to progress to higher levels of power as his or her experience and abilities increase. For example, a newly appointed manager might at first have only positional power but, with increasing experience, expert power may develop, along with referent or leadership power. However, at the lower levels of management, the level of political power is generally also lower. It is only when managers start to climb the hierarchical tree that they become players in the arena where politics play a part, and they may gain political skills or power. Political power is the highest form of managerial power and (to return to the martial arts analogy) can be considered management's 'black belt'.

Any manager who relies solely on superior–subordinate authority is of very limited effectiveness, particularly at the more senior level. It is only necessary to have seen a succession of two or more different people holding the same management position in an organization to realize what a difference varying levels of personal and political power can make to a manager's effectiveness.

The positional power of project managers is always limited in multi-company and most matrix organizations, and therefore they must rely on their personal and political power. The new project manager in a first appointment in that role has little personal power and must make a conscious effort to develop this in the years ahead. The successful experienced project manager can have considerable personal power, which may have been enhanced over the years by rewarding subordinates through the use of upward influence. The successful project manager therefore tends to attract loyal followers, who prefer to move with the manager from project to project. However, such personal power has to be complemented and enhanced by political power.

POLITICAL POWER

Politics has a negative image and has acquired a bad name over the centuries. Few managers will freely admit to being skilled political operators, or are willing to talk about the extent of politics in their organizations. Yet the *Collins English Dictionary*, in its Millennium edition, includes the following among its many definitions of politics:

> The practice or study of the art and science of forming, directing and administering states and other political units … .
> Any activity concerned with the acquisition of power … .

Thus there need not be anything immoral about activities aimed at achieving power, and politics need not necessarily lead to ill-feeling, double-dealing or conflict. In reality, the art of achieving power (in other words, politics) is just as much a function of management as planning, decision–making and controlling. It is necessary and normal in management. This is because straightforward superior–subordinate authority is very limited and totally inadequate by itself for achieving results in the larger hierarchical organization.

Although the term 'politics' has become associated in many people's minds with underhand activities, this only represents the dark side of politics, which in turn is usually associated with conflict. The light side to power and politics is similar to socialized power

1. *Gaining support from a higher power source or sources*

- Sponsorship
- Lobbying
- Co-option

2. *Alliance or coalition-building (gaining support from near peers)*

- Exchange of favours (IOU)
- Bargains
- Bribery (in one form or another)
- Establishing a common cause
- Combining for mutual support or defence

3. *Controlling a critical resource*

- Money
- People
- Expertise
- Reporting
- Centrality or gatekeeping
- Information

4. *Controlling the decision process*

- Selection of criteria of choice and constraints
- Selection of the alternatives shortlist
- Controlling the information about alternatives

5. *Controlling the committee process*

- Agenda content
- Agenda sequence
- Membership
- Minutes
- Chairmanship
- Calling of meetings
- Pre-agenda negotiations

6. *Use of positional authority*

- Rewards
- Coercion

7. *Use of the scientific element*

- Planning
- Control

8. *Deceit and deception*

- Secrecy
- Surprise
- Hidden objectives
- Hidden agendas
- Two faces
- All things to all people

9. *Information*

- Censoring or withholding
- Distorting

10. *Miscellaneous games*

- Divide and rule
- Whistle-blowing
- In the same life boat
- Red herring game
- White knight game

Figure 20.3   The political manager's toolkit

motivation. In this the manager uses power and politics to achieve results for the benefit of others, the organization and the common good (which includes achieving project success to the satisfaction of all the stakeholders).

Inhibitions, ethics or scruples restrain the negative use of power and the type of political activities used. Teamwork, participation, and 'theory Y' (McGregor, 1960) concepts can coexist with the light side of power and politics. This is just as well, because this light side of politics is an essential complement to a manager's superior–subordinate authority. This means that, in project work, the project manager's political activities are generally directed towards the achievement of the project's objectives and not towards self-advancement.

The project manager thus must be able to use all those activities which make up politics, as shown in the political toolkit of Figure 20.3, with the exception (we hope) of deceit and exception. The project manager should be in a strong position to use all of these activities because of his or her central place in the project organization. The tools are available and are important in enabling the manager to manage the project (Harrison, 1988). In particular, one of the most important and strongest tools to achieve power in matrix and multi-company organizations is the project planning and control system.

The project plan – that is, the total plan including the work schedule, resource and expenditure budgets – is an important source of power for the project manager. The planning process is an effective way of obtaining the participation of people in other groups and companies, and of obtaining their commitment to achieving the targets contained in the plans. This commitment can be achieved, even if participation is limited, provided that the plans are 'accepted' by those concerned. Plans commit the people involved to achieving their time targets, with the resources specified, at or below the budgeted cost. Once the plans have been accepted, the project manager has the implicit power to hold all those responsible for the activities to their commitments, and to take action if those commitments are not met.

Similarly, the application of the contractor–consignee concept and of distributed accountability and responsibility gives the project manager power to hold other managers accountable for the achievement of their goals, which are clearly specified. Even more importantly, these other managers normally then accept their commitment to meeting these goals, and they recognize the role of the project manager in this process. In essence, they concede a measure of power to the project manager, either knowingly or unknowingly.

The PMIS is also a source of power for the project manager. It enhances the project manager's planning power and, since the project manager is responsible for reporting progress to higher management, this gives him or her the ear of these higher power sources, thereby enhancing his or her personal power. The project manager is also at the centre of the information system and has the power to call, chair and minute meetings. These factors are recognized sources of power. Thus the planning and control system can give the project manager the greater source of political power over all the diverse individuals, groups and companies working on the project – provided that he or she knows how to use it as such.

Motivation

The performance of individuals is a function of both their ability and their motivation. Motivation can influence a person's performance both positively and negatively and many theories have been advanced on motivation in the organizational setting. Some of these are philosophies, some of them are very popular, most are very moralistic and sometimes they are not backed up or confirmed by applied research carried out in actual, hard managerial situations. What is certain is that the organizational person is a complex being and no single stereotype or motivational factor applies to all of the people for all of the time.

The following discussion provides a brief outline of some motivating theories and factors which have been supported by applied research and are of practical use in the management of projects:

- participation – the project itself as a motivator
- expectancy theory – the reward system
- achievement, goal theory and target-setting.

PARTICIPATION

At one time, participative management based on organizational behaviour concepts was very much the fashion and was considered to represent good practice. Those who did not adopt these concepts were looked down upon pityingly, and were considered to be old-fashioned or even immoral.

The participative approach to management and motivation could be said to have evolved as a reaction to the adverse effects of early scientific management. The scientific approach to management – especially the 9,1 manager in managerial grid terms – involves an emphasis on planning, direction, control and work study. It includes theory X concepts of human behaviour (McGregor, 1960) and has been found wanting over the years.

As its name implies, participative management involves the subordinate in decision-making and a reduction in the use of direct authority. Subordinates or groups set (or largely contribute to setting) their own objectives. The senior manager does not take decisions unilaterally or autocratically. Instead, the manager meets with the group, shares the problem with them and encourages them to participate in determining the solutions. This emphasizes the role of the senior manager as less of an autocratic boss and more of a teacher, professional helper, colleague or consultant. In turn, this approach assumes that each individual can then derive job satisfaction from performing a job effectively and have a high level or motivation.

The concept of a manager as a teacher, professional helper, colleague and consultant does hold some validity. In intergroup and intercompany relationships, authoritative management is often difficult, if not impossible and there must always be an element of participative management in project work. However, in the late 1970s and 1980s, people raised doubts about the validity of the human behaviour approach as an all-embracing philosophy of management. Although it was recognized that these concepts can and do represent relationships between some individuals and groups, it was questioned whether the fully participative approach leads to high performance and whether it is applicable, in its basic form, to the reality of people, to life, and to the hierarchic organization. The following comments were made at that time:

In discussion of this concept, two of its propositions should be clearly distinguished. One, of a factual – that is, testable – nature is that participation leads to increased productivity: 'Involve your employees and they will produce more', management has been told by a generation of industrial psychologists. ... it is interesting to note that the factual proposition has not held up in much of the research. Studies by Fiedler (1965) and others have indicated that participation is not necessarily correlated with satisfaction or productivity. These relationships depend on the work situations in question. (Mintzberg, 1983a)

If the human behaviour, participative approach is implemented on its own, there are no guaranteed results in terms of task achievement, and it is results that must count. Thus there is a danger that implementing this approach can result in a well-adjusted, happy and contented organization, but not necessarily one which will produce the best results. Thus the participative human behaviour approach (the 1,9 manager in managerial grid terms) has also been found wanting. Nevertheless, participation can increase employee creativity, initiative, morale and satisfaction, and can generate commitment to the project and its goals.

Commitment can be defined as a strongly held attachment to, personal association with or belief in something, such as values, a cause, a person, or a project and its objectives. Commitment is an emotional state and can motivate people to extreme self-sacrifice. Thus although participation on its own does not necessarily increase performance, it is a motivating factor that project managers should use to achieve their objectives.

People need meaning in their organizational life, to feel that they are part of events and to have some influence over them. If people are treated as children, they will behave as naughty children. Treat people as adults, and they might behave like responsible adults. People do generally work better if they are given respect, are involved with decisions that affect their life and work, and are treated in a participative manner (although this does not apply to everybody and not for all of the time). Participation, when combined with a task-oriented approach, is an effective motivator. This is not the weak style of management that could result from the early participative movement, but a combination of leadership with the scientific and human sides of management.

Participation can be used to build a strong commitment to the project, to the extent that it almost becomes a living entity to which people owe loyalty and to which they are committed. Some professional and supervisory people feel alienated by the nature of their work and by their failure to see how it fits into the bigger picture of the company or the project. The many layers of management that can exist in a large organization leave those at the lower and middle levels feeling a sense of powerlessness and remoteness from decision-making, and it is difficult for them to equate their personal needs with those of the organization. This leads to a loss of involvement and commitment to the project and its objectives.

Participation, when combined with the delegation of authority to contractor–consignee cases, cost account, WBS and OBS element managers and a structured approach to project control, can overcome these problems and lead to a high level of personal commitment and satisfaction. Everyone on the project can become associated with its success or failure. They can see how their personal contribution fits into the complete picture. If they work a little harder, they can see the effect on the progress of a job.

This commitment to the project can lead to the development of what could be termed a 'project' attitude of mind, in which people's interests are subordinated to the project and they associate themselves with it. This attitude is a way of thinking that penetrates throughout the organization and unites all those involved towards accomplishing the project objectives. An acceptance develops that it is no longer enough to say 'our department's effort was satisfactory: the project was delayed because of someone else'. No single individual's or group's effort is satisfactory unless the project is a success, with every effort made to assist other organizational elements to carry out their tasks successfully. This involves removing departmental blinkers and cooperating by helping one another to complete the project successfully in terms of all its objectives. Thus participation can generate commitment to the project, and the project itself can become a strong motivator.

EXPECTANCY THEORY AND THE REWARD SYSTEM

Most managers in the project setting have personal goals and are ambitious. They want to advance their careers. As a result, they will exert considerable effort if they believe that their efforts will lead to promotion, more money and perks, power, recognition, praise, more scope, or a better assignment. This applies to all levels of management, although the actual personal goals may vary with the individual and the level of management.

This describes expectancy theory, in which the individual is motivated by the belief that increased effort will result in higher performance, which in turn will be rewarded by the fulfilment of personal goals. The expectancy theory of motivation does not apply to all individuals in all types of organization, and is subject to several constraints. However, applied research on expectancy theory, as expressed by the reward system, has confirmed that it is an effective motivator to some of the people, for some of the time.

In general, the reward system can motivate individuals to higher performance if the following are true:

- The individual values highly such rewards as advancement, more money, more scope, power, a good assignment and a good assessment.
- The individual believes that a high level of personal or team performance will be recognized, produce results and bring these rewards.
- The individual has an opportunity to perform.

Thus expectancy theory can be made to work through the reward system, particularly when it is linked to clear-cut individual objectives and performance measurement. This motivational factor can be combined with an emphasis on individual accountability and responsibility, as expressed in the contractor–consignee principle, cost account, WBS and OBS element managers, and structured and personalized project planning and control.

The equity of the reward system is also important. Nothing demotivates people faster than inequity. If promotions, pay increases and other rewards are seen to be fair and just, then motivation is increased. If they are based on nepotism, fawning and favouritism, then all but the chosen few are demotivated.

ACHIEVEMENT, GOAL THEORY AND TARGET-SETTING

McClelland's achievement motivation theory is a long-established concept which states that the need to achieve is a strong motivator (McClelland et al., 1976). It is generally accepted that achievement is a strong motivator for most of the kind of people who are engaged in project work. Indeed, project work is designed for achievement: 'Look everyone, I built that!' In addition it has been established, both in theory and in practice, that setting people specific difficult, but achievable, targets can motivate many people to a higher level of performance than just the simple admonition to 'do your best'. Achievement and target-setting can be combined with the project planning and control system to give an extremely effective motivator in project work.

A large amount of research has shown that if people are set difficult targets they will exert themselves to achieve them. The 'acceptance' by people of the reasonableness of these targets and feedback on performance are critical factors in the effectiveness of these motivational factors. Whether or not these targets are set participatively or autocratically appears not to be critical, as long as they are accepted by the individual. Participative target-setting will, of course, facilitate acceptance but tends to result in easier targets being set. Targets that are set autocratically are often accepted because of respect for positional authority, but if the targets are viewed as being too difficult they will not be accepted or achieved.

In practice, this describes the planning process, where involvement of those who are to carry out the work is crucial to the acceptance of, and commitment to, the plan. Therefore one of the objectives of the project manager is to use the planning process as a motivational tool. Again the contractor–consignee principle, cost account, WBS and OBS element managers, and the structured and personalized planning and control system can be used to establish personal targets for each manager and group, and to motivate them to a high level of performance.

Research has also shown that knowledge of how a person is performing can enhance the motivational effects of target-setting. Thus feedback on performance is essential. In other words, project control information is another motivator, but it must be related to the individual and to each individual's personal targets. At this stage the recognition of achievement is important, through praise, rewards and positive reinforcement – that is, expectancy theory.

One of the dangers inherent in target-setting for motivation is that individuals will focus completely on their own targets to the detriment of cooperation with others and the overall project targets. Thus it is essential that the individual's target must be a building block in the overall project's targets, and joint responsibilities must be defined and targeted. This is what planning is all about. The matrix of responsibilities – an example of which was shown earlier in Figure 5.4 (p. 68) – also defines individual and joint responsibilities. The overall structured plan integrates the individual's plans and targets.

SUMMARY

Thus in the project setting, participation, the project as motivator, expectancy (as expressed by the reward system), achievement and target-setting can all be used to increase motivation. These factors interact with the organization structure of the project and the structured methodology of project planning and control, such that a synergy is created between the scientific and human sides of project management that effectively motivates individuals and groups to achieve higher performance and the project objectives.

Team development

When individuals, groups and companies interact and are independent, as in project work, overall organizational performance depends not only on how these organizational elements perform as individual entities, but also on how effectively they work together. This is largely determined by the nature of the interpersonal relationships between these elements, which are described by such terms as conflict, cooperation and teamwork.

THE CONFLICT–TEAMWORK DIMENSION

When there is interdependence between individuals and groups, there must always be some degree of cooperation between them. However, the nature of this cooperation can vary considerably and it is this that, to a large extent, determines the performance of the organizational unit. At one extreme, the nature of this cooperation or, in other words, the relationship between the individuals and groups, can be very hostile, which means conflict. At the other extreme, the relationship can be very friendly and supportive, which means teamwork. By definition, conflict and teamwork cannot coexist, and between these two extremes there can be varying degrees of cooperation. Thus the different possible relationships between individuals and groups can be considered to lie on a continuum or single dimension, at one end of which is extreme conflict and at the other teamwork. Between these two extremes the nature of relationships or the degree of cooperation can vary through hostile, neutral and friendly cooperation as shown in Figure 20.4.

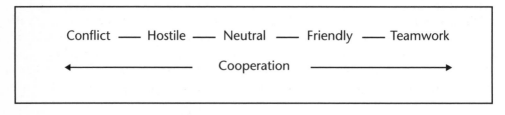

Figure 20.4   The conflict–teamwork dimension

Initially when people come together, relationships lie somewhere between the two extremes of this dimension. The exact initial position is dependent on the people themselves, the nature of their previous relationships and a number of structural causes of conflict. In an ideal world, relationships would start at the cooperation point and then move on to teamwork. This is the phase theory of team development, which has been identified by many researchers.

In practice, the relationships between those involved in a project organization can move back and forth between both extremes of the conflict–teamwork dimension. In most organizations relationships tend to be grouped somewhere near the middle ground in some form of cooperation, and the full benefits of teamwork are not achieved. However, in a significant number of project organizations, relationships between individuals and groups approach or reach the conflict extremity.

The term 'team' is often used to describe any group of individuals, or managers of groups or departments (for example, management team or project team). This is often misleading as there are differences between a collection of individuals or managers comprising a group or organizational unit and a 'team'. For example, the term 'team' describes the characteristics of the relationships within the group, and not all groups are teams. This is best understood by looking at the factors that characterize teamwork, and the lack of it, between individuals, groups and companies who make up an organizational unit (see Figure 20.5).

When there is interaction and interdependency between individuals, groups and companies involved in a joint undertaking such as a project, cooperation is essential to efficient working. The more this cooperation approaches teamwork, the more effective the organization is likely to be. Conversely, the more this cooperation approaches conflict, the

Teamwork	Conflict
• Group members are committed to the group's/project objectives.	• Group members have divergent objectives.
• Communication is open.	• Communication is guarded, censored or withheld.
• There is mutual trust between members.	• Distrust and negative stereotyping are typical.
• Mutual support exists between members.	• When one group member has problems, other members stand aside or take advantage of that member's predicament.
• People express feelings and ideas.	• Feelings are hidden and ideas are withheld.
• Disagreements are expressed and worked through.	• Disagreements lead to power struggles and win–lose battles.
• The group atmosphere is relaxed, comfortable and informal.	• The atmosphere is cold, strained, unpleasant and formal.

Figure 20.5   Characteristics of teamwork and conflict

less effective the organization will be. Therefore one objective of the project manager should always be to lead the individuals, groups and companies that make up the project organization towards total teamwork.

Developing teamwork in a small group is much easier than developing teamwork between groups and in a larger organizational unit. Often, small groups form effective teams within themselves and are committed to their individual group objectives, which may or may not be the project's objectives. At the same time, they are hostile to other groups outside the 'ring fence' that delimits their team's boundaries. The larger the organization (or, more precisely, the larger the organizational unit) the more difficult it becomes to develop total teamwork throughout the organization and the more likely there is to be conflict between groups.

Developing teamwork requires first of all that those individuals who interact together, are interdependent and form a distinct group, be identified and a group 'entity' established. This applies to the formal and informal organization, and includes the functional, mixed, matrix and horizontal groups that exist at all levels in the project organization. Once these 'family' groups are identified, team development can begin. It is also essential to identify key integrating superiors, whose functions are to lead, manage and integrate the groups, both in terms of work output and human relations.

However, in a large organization it is particularly important to apply team development to those individuals who have overlapping group membership. These include the formal group superiors, among others, and are what Likert (1961) termed 'linking pins'. These individuals link the groups together and, if teamwork can be established between the linking pins, then their respective subordinate groups will probably work together in the same manner. Conversely, if there is conflict between these linking pin senior managers, it is very likely that there will be conflict between their respective subordinates.

For example, in a construction project, if the client's representative, the architect and the construction manager work together as a team, then their respective organizations will also work together in the same manner. Similarly, if a project manager and the functional managers can work together as a team, the problems of the matrix organization are greatly reduced. Thus this linking pin concept is particularly relevant in the matrix and multi-company project situation. The relationships between the senior managers of the different groups, departments and companies involved in the project set the tone and nature of the relationships for all those working on the project.

TEAM-BUILDING

Team-building (or team development) remains very fashionable, with many exponents and specialist consultants. Team-building interventions may involve the following activities:

- role analysis and the psychological matching of team members
- team-building through organizational development, training courses, management games and, in particular, the use of problem-solving, team-building workshops.

The role analysis approach

The study of teams has shown that team members carry out various roles that facilitate the working of the team and its development. Traditionally, these have been divided into 'task roles', which help the team accomplish its objectives, and 'building and maintenance roles' which help establish and maintain the teamwork relationships between members (see Figure 20.6).

Task roles	Building and maintenance roles
Initiator	Harmonizer
Informer	Gatekeeper
Information seeker	Encourager
Clarifier	Compromiser
Summarizer/coordinator	Observer/commentator
Reality tester	Follower
Procedural technician	
Energizer	
Elaborator	
Consensus tester	

Figure 20.6   Teamworking roles

Research, such as that carried out by Belbin (1996) and Margerison and McCann (1990) has taken this concept a stage further and crystallized the roles required in an effective team. It also uses a battery of psychometric and other tests, which enables people's preferences for various roles, their mental ability, personality and character to be determined and 'measured', as detailed below:

- An individual's role preferences can be clarified, together with the expectations and obligations of these roles.

- Individuals can be counselled and matched to their preferred roles.
- Balanced teams can be designed on the basis of the roles required and by matching group members to their preferred roles.

Unfortunately, in a matrix or multi-company project organization it is difficult to design a balanced team based on preferred roles. Nevertheless an understanding of the different roles involved in teams, and of the role preferences of the project group members, are of use in tackling the difficult problem of team-building.

Stages of team development

It takes time to develop a team from a new group. It does not happen overnight. Such a group progresses through a number of phases in which mutual trust and respect grow as it develops into a team. This development may include the following phases:

- evaluation/immature group
- experimentation/risk-taking
- consolidation/intimacy
- mature team.

When a new immature group comes together on a project it is usually at the neutral cooperation stage in the conflict–teamwork dimension. There is then a period when people get to know and evaluate one another in relation to personalities, abilities, personal goals and the power structure. If these are found acceptable, there will be a period of experimentation when people start to expose their feelings and take risks in terms of more open communication and trust. If these experiments are successful, they respect the other members and feel they can trust them. They then move on to a group consolidation phase and there is more intimacy and the growth of friendly cooperation. At this stage, disagreements are aired more freely and attempts are made to work them through without emotions being raised. Once this stage is passed, they can move on to a mature teamwork phase, with all the characteristics of a team.

If an adverse reaction occurs at any stage, team development may stall and the group will remain at the stage of cooperation, revert to an earlier stage, or even start down the slippery slope to conflict. The process of team development can be accelerated by the use of organization development interventions on team-building and action-learning-type courses on teamwork.

Team-building through organization development

Organization development (OD) has been defined as 'the process of improving organization performance by improving the pattern of interaction between members of the organization' (Pass *et al.*, 1999). It tends to have the following characteristics:

1 An emphasis on the work team as the key unit for addressing issues and learning more effective modes of organizational behavior.
2 An emphasis, although not exclusively so, on group, intergroup and organizational processes in contrast to substantive content.
3 The use of an action research model.
4 An emphasis on the collaborative management of work team culture, including temporary teams.

5 An emphasis on the management of the culture of the total system, including intergroup culture.

6 Attention to the management system ramifications.

7 A view of the change effort as an ongoing process. (French and Bell, 1995, p. 22)

OD is not a quick-fix solution. Rather, it is a longer-term effort to improve the way in which people work together in a group or organization, and their effectiveness. Team-building is an important part of OD, and its activities are concerned with the following:

* diagnosis
* task accomplishment
* building and maintaining effective relationships
* understanding and maintaining group processes
* role analysis and negotiations.

OD emphasizes working with the total group of individuals who interact and are interdependent. This includes 'family' groups of a superior and his or her subordinates, and special groups such as task forces and groups of interlinking pins. The types of intervention used include the following:

* *Diagnostic meetings*. These involve an evaluation of the functioning of the group and the identification of any problems.
* *Sensitivity training*. This helps individuals to learn about themselves and the effects that their behaviour can have on others.
* *Team-building meetings*. These concentrate on how the group can develop teamwork. They generally involve problem-solving and team-building workshops.
* *Role analysis and negotiations*. This involves the processes defined previously and negotiations (or horse-trading) on roles, power distribution and behaviour.
* *Intergroup interventions and organizational mirror interventions*. These interventions are similar to the above, but are concerned with resolving problems between groups.

Team-building through OD can be effective over time, and can change the behaviour of managers and lead to effective teamwork.

Team-building courses

Many behavioural consultants and organizations run team-building courses and management games, which can be arranged either externally or run in-house. These courses generally concentrate on the following areas:

* developing team skills through action learning and personal experience
* sensitivity training
* problem-solving, team-building activities
* counselling, coaching and reviewing activities and behaviour observed in the process.

These courses can be effective, but are preferably run in-house. They should involve the total group, or linking pins, including in particular the senior manager or managers. Outward bound or wilderness survival courses are popular in this context.

APPLICATION TO PROJECT WORK

Unfortunately it is not generally possible, in the project setting, to design a balanced team based on role analysis, and there is insufficient time for the full OD approach. Individuals are assembled from different groups, departments and companies for a temporary undertaking, and teamwork must be developed quickly.

The project manager may have very little say in which people from the other departments in the company are allocated to the project, and no say at all on the people from other companies. However, an important tool in team-building is the problem-solving, team-building workshop, and the project start-up requirements are made to measure for this intervention. These workshops do lead to the development of teamwork, and they underpin both the OD approach and the team-building courses.

The concepts underlying the use of these workshops in team-building are best described by French and Bell (1995) as follows:

> When a team engages in problem-solving activities directed towards task accomplishment, the team members build something together. It appears that the act of building something together also builds a sense of camaraderie, cohesion and esprit de corps. (French and Bell, 1995, p. 145)

The main ingredients involved in a group 'building something together' are as follows:

Get the right people together for ...
1   a large block of uninterrupted time ...
2   to work on high priority problems or opportunities that ...
3   they have identified and they have worked on ...
4   in ways that are structured to enhance the likelihood of ...
5   realistic solutions and action plans that are ...
6   implemented enthusiastically and ...
7   followed up to assess actual versus expected results. (Bell and Rosenzweig, 1978, cited in French and Bell, 1995, p. 145)

At the time of project start-up, it is necessary to communicate the objectives of the project, its scope and the responsibilities of those involved. It is also necessary for people to come together to develop the project's organization structure, plans, communication channels and information systems. These requirements are often handled by an extended project start-up or 'kick-off' meeting, involving all the key people who will work on the project (the linking pins). This kind of meeting is invaluable not only for communicating the project requirements, but also for allowing people to get to know each other and for developing teamworking.

If time and money allow, the start-up meeting could be supplemented by a problem-solving, team-building workshop, with or without external consultants or other aspects of the team-building courses. Such a team-building programme would involve the key project members from the groups, departments and companies taking a three- to five-day residential break.

Before there is a chance of teamworking being developed, conditions conducive to teamwork must be created. All too often in project work the conditions created are more conducive to the creation of conflict. This subject is discussed in the following chapter.

21 *Conflict in Projects*

An underlying assumption of behavioural researchers is that individuals are well-balanced human beings who work unselfishly together towards a common objective. In practice, unless the project manager happens to be very fortunate, the reality of people and organizations will not live up to that ideal. Instead, the following conditions are more likely to be encountered:

• The level of trust, mutual support, respect and open communication is generally low.
• Teamworking, except in small groups, is rare.
• Hostility, even hatred, between individuals and groups is not uncommon.
• Conflict is widespread.
• Political manoeuvring to achieve power exists in almost every organization.
• Political conflict among senior managers is widespread.

These facts of life might seem to be a jaundiced and cynical view of management, but they do represent life in many organizations. Thus conflict between individuals and groups is a significant problem for the project manager who is attempting to establish participation and teamwork throughout the project organization. It is useless to attempt to develop teamworking in a project unless the prevalence of conflict can be overcome.

Consequences of conflict

Conflict is where, but for the restraints of civilization and society, blows would be struck. The depth of feelings or hostility that conflict can engender in the business setting is often astonishing. Conflict between individuals and groups prevents participation and makes it impossible to mould and maintain an effective team from those working in the project organization. Worse, the health or even lives of people have been put at risk through conflict in business organizations, especially where an individual feels isolated and collectively threatened. Not surprisingly, performance suffers under these conditions.

Even mild conflict leads to a lack of respect and trust between groups, disharmony and poor cooperation. Communications break down, with information being distorted, censored or withheld. Each group will tend to reject ideas, opinions and suggestions from other groups for no better reason than they come from a source that is perceived to be hostile. Feelings and emotions will run high, leading to a greater chance of mistakes being made by people whose judgement is clouded by stress. Some groups will tend to have unspoken objectives, different from those of the organization, such as to 'get' the other group, block anything that they propose, achieve dominance over them and show them in a poor light to senior management.

Instead of an 'all for one and one for all' atmosphere of cooperation, a damaging polarized 'we/they' attitude will exist. Decision-making and problem-solving will suffer, differences will not be worked through openly, and win–lose situations will lead to further hostility and conflict, lowest common denominator compromises, or the referral of disputes to higher levels of management for arbitration.

So, it is clear that conflict in general is detrimental to overall performance and will make the development of mutual commitment to the organizational objectives impossible.

There is an alternative argument that conflict between groups can actually enhance the cohesion and spirit within an individual group. Group loyalty will increase, internal differences will be buried within the group, and there will be a greater commitment to the group's objectives – but not necessarily to the objectives of the project or the organization. The group members will tend to close ranks against a common enemy – that is, the other groups.

Within challenged or threatened groups there is a more purposeful atmosphere, and probably more autocratic leadership patterns, more structuring and organization, more in-group loyalty and conformity for presenting a common front to the 'enemy'. Within itself the group tends to be more effective in achieving its own objectives, so long as coordination and interaction with other groups are not required. Although this may be advantageous for the individual group, it will prevent development of total teamwork and thus lead to poorer organizational performance.

Thus it is true that conflict between individuals and groups can give rise to increased performance in isolated groups. However, when those individuals and groups are required to be interdependent, conflict will always prevent participation and teamwork, and will consequently result in reduced overall performance. People, groups and organizations rarely achieve their true potential performance because of the damaging effects of conflict.

Disagreement or conflict?

A number of researchers have studied conflict in project management. For example, Thamhain and Wilemon (1974) identified the following ranking order for potential sources of conflict identified by a sample of 100 project managers:

1 schedules
2 project priorities
3 manpower resources
4 technical conflict
5 administrative procedures
6 cost objectives
7 personality conflicts.

Although disagreements over these factors are identified as the content of conflict, it can be argued that, in general, they are not the actual sources of conflict, except perhaps for the last factor, personality conflicts. A misconception about conflict is that it is caused by disagreement between people – in other words, disagreement over schedules, project priorities or, as Pfeffer (1992) calls them, 'heterogeneous beliefs about technology'.

It is almost impossible to have an organization without disagreements arising among its members and, indeed, it would be foolish to imagine that people and groups could work together without disagreement. Such disagreements lead to heated discussions and arguments. In fact, it is highly desirable that these differences and disagreements should exist

Problems with the organization structure

- Large organizations
- Large organizational units
- Tall hierarchies
- Bureaucracy
- Overcentralization
- Authority/power problems
- Complexity
- Uncertainty

- Temporary nature
- Large functional departments
- Problems of integration
- Clashes of cultures
- Functional orientation
- Confrontation of managers
- Dual subordination
- Defence of territory

People's self-interests

- Personal motivations
- Incompatible objectives
- Forms of contract

- Peer competition
- Competition for scarce resources
- Competition for survival

People problems: with 'normal people'

- Differences in personalities
- Differences in abilities
- Differences in motivation

- Dependency
- Lack of interpersonal skills
- History of conflict

People problems: with 'problem people'

- Extreme ineptness in interpersonal skills
- Insecurity and stress:
  - Peter Principle
  - Professional as a manager
- The managerial rogue

- Management style not conducive to teamwork:
  - Autocratic
  - Permissive
  - Administrator (1,1 on the managerial grid)
- Clashes of style

Figure 21.1   Sources of conflict

because, without them, performance would be low and the organization would be mediocre and complacent, or a collection of 'yes men'. Disagreement in a healthy organization is essential for efficient and effective problem-solving and decision-making. It need not, by itself, lead to conflict.

When there is teamwork, or at least a cooperative working relationship, disagreements can be worked through and good relationships between the individuals and groups maintained. However, as relationships move from cooperation to the early stages of conflict, disagreements tend to be resolved by bargaining and compromises are made. The danger then is that resentment about having to give up too much in the compromise will push relationships into conflict.

The important point is that such disagreements over issues are not the causes of conflict, but are what conflict is observed to be about. Differences and disagreements can occur over a million and one topics, and in one organization these can lead to raging conflict and major power struggles involving the whole workforce, whereas in another, these very same differences are worked through and teamwork prevails.

Where these disagreements do lead to conflict, they are not generally the root cause of that conflict but are merely symptoms of the underlying conflict 'disease' caused by other factors. They are therefore what conflict is about, but not the source of conflict. People in a healthy organizational relationship can walk away from disagreement and continue to cooperate or work as a team. Where conflict is endemic, this is not possible. Emotions are raised to high intensity. Disagreements are not limited to the subject involved but extend to everything proposed by the other party: if 'A' says something is white, 'B' will declare that it is black. The following factors differentiate conflict from disagreement about an issue:

- Intense emotion is generated and sustained over a long period.
- The disagreement or conflict extends beyond the issue concerned into all the interrelationships between the two parties.
- There are one or more underlying sources of conflict.

It is thus necessary to probe deeper to determine the source or sources of such conflict. It is not disagreement over the million and one possible topics that causes conflict: it is the breakdown of relationships between people and groups. Conflict occurs between people and is caused by people. There are many factors that either cause or accentuate conflict. These fall into three classifications, as shown in Figure 21.1:

1 factors primarily associated with problems caused by the structure of the organization (organization problems)
2 factors arising out of people's self-interests
3 factors primarily associated with problems caused by individuals (people problems).

Organization structure and conflict

The project organization structure can increase or decrease the potential for conflict and thus, conversely, the potential for teamwork between individuals and groups. Organization design is therefore of great importance. It can, on its own, impel people into conflict or into teamwork, despite individual attitudes or desires. Problems with project organizations that can accentuate the tendency for either conflict or teamwork were covered explicitly and implicitly in Part 2, but the following summary recapitulates the main characteristics of those factors which contribute to the generation of conflict.

SIZE AND SHAPE OF THE ORGANIZATION STRUCTURE

The larger the organization and its organizational units, the taller the management hierarchy, the more centralized it is, and the more bureaucratically it operates, the more likely there is to be conflict between the managers and groups involved. The size and shape of the organization structure used can impel people towards conflict because of uncertainty and complexity in the structure, problems with authority, the existence of large functional departments and the remoteness of key integrating superiors among other things.

PROBLEMS DUE TO WEAK, INADEQUATE OR UNCERTAIN POWER

Writers such as Pfeffer (1992) and Mintzberg (1983b) identify the dispersion of power as the principal factor leading to political game-playing in an organization. The same principle applies to authority gaps, weaknesses in the organization structure and weak superior power, whether this is positional, personal or political power.

Pfeffer's model is particularly applicable to the analysis of conflict and power in an organizational unit. It states that the following factors produce conflict in an organization:

- the environment
- interdependence
- heterogeneous beliefs about technology and differences over how to achieve goals
- differentiation – that is, functionalization
- scarcity of resources.

If this conflict concerns matters which management considers to be important and power is dispersed, then conflict escalates to the political level. In addition to the problems created by the authority gap of the project manager, a weak key integrationist superior in any position can exacerbate conflict since he or she will simply not have the power to prevent conflict occurring, or to manage it if it does. This is often coupled with a superior who has only positional power and who often has to exercise coercive power 'to maintain his or her authority'. The manager who is continually disciplining subordinates almost certainly lacks personal or political power. If this superior is also insecure for any reason, he or she will feel threatened by subordinates, peers and superiors and will tend to employ the 'dark' side of politics to strengthen his or her position and to weaken others involved in the conflict, purely for defensive reasons. Thus factors such as the authority gap of the project manager, combined with the nature and complexity of the organization structure, are strong sources of conflict in project management.

DUAL SUBORDINATION

The matrix organization has many of the above problems, not the least of which is dual subordination. Unless both project and functional managers accept the arrangement and deal with it sensitively, conflict will be exacerbated.

FUNCTIONALIZATION

The mere fact that separate groups are formed, reinforced by the specialist nature of those groups, creates divisions in the organization and sets people apart. These divisions can then lead to problems with large functional groups. These problems (described earlier in Part 2) include the following:

- accentuation and clashes of cultures
- difficulties in integration, both of work and people
- functional orientation
- confrontation between matrix and functional managers.

Problems caused by the existence of separate differentiated groups can lead to conflict. Not the least of these is the age-old concept of defence of territory. The urge to defend one's territory is a basic human motivator. A manager's sphere of influence, area of technical expertise, responsibilities and subordinates can be considered his or her territory. When another manager encroaches on this territory, the manager springs to its defence and conflict arises. This is an instinctive reaction, but is also stimulated by the fear that this encroachment might only be a prelude to a greater incursion or more permanent takeover of his or her territory.

This territorial problem exists with any hierarchical organization, but it is particularly prevalent in the matrix organization. The project manager must be involved in the management, planning and control of all the groups involved in the project. Functional managers may resent this invasion of their territory and the subversion of their subordinates, as they see it, and act defensively or counter-attack. The problem is compounded when responsibilities and authority are unclear. Thus this most primitive motivational factor can lead to conflict in organizations involving the highest technology work, and is exacerbated by the organization structure used.

The people factor

Although structural problems can influence people towards either conflict or teamworking, the people factor can dominate this influence. In other words, even if the form of organization structure is heavily biased towards teamwork between individuals and groups, problems between individuals can lead to conflict. Conversely, even if the organization structure is conducive to conflict, individuals and groups can still develop teamwork. People problems leading to conflict in project management can be classified under three headings:

- individual and group self-interests
- personality problems
- 'problem people'.

Individual and group self-interests

PERSONAL MOTIVATIONS

Behavioural theories tend to assume that all managers are social beings who are totally unselfish and primarily concerned with the interests of the organization. It would be nice if such a paragon of virtue could be called the 'normal' manager, but it is highly debatable whether this is so, and most of us will have encountered managers who are exceptions to this rule. None the less, it would be wrong to take the cynical opposite approach that all managers are cold, calculating beings concerned solely with self-interest.

Most managers are at least partially motivated by self-interest. It would be foolish to imagine otherwise. There is nothing intrinsically immoral about this, particularly if these self-interests are, or can be, aligned with the organization's interests. Even if a manager's interests are not aligned and are purely selfish, this is still understandable and very human. But conflict can be the result when managers' self interests differ or their objectives are incompatible.

INCOMPATIBLE OBJECTIVES

Often individuals and groups, both large and small, have their own objectives, which may be incompatible with those of other groups and of the organization. These objectives may be openly displayed but, during conflict, they are more often hidden. Typically, in such a case the objectives concerned are self-advancing or adversarial – for example, to gain dominance over, discredit or even eliminate another group.

Sometimes incompatible objectives arise from the difference in cultures in functional and project groups, but often they occur between large groups in projects because of the form of contract used. This can create conflict over time, cost and quality between the client, contractor or subcontractor and so on, unless the contract is designed to avoid this sort of problem. For example, the client will most probably want the lowest cost, fastest completion time and the highest quality, which are usually incompatible objectives in themselves. The contractor will usually expect to make a profit, which might mean claiming for all the extras and changes, thus increasing the cost to the client. The contractor will want to finish the project in the time that is most cost-effective for itself and will probably want the minimum quality to meet the contractual specification. At least, this is likely to be each party's view of the other's supposed objectives. The most extreme example of this is the (now relatively uncommon) cost-plus or reimbursable form of contract, where incompatible objectives, defence of territory and conflict are the norm.

Sometimes the problem is not so much that the objectives are incompatible but more that they are invisible. It is not unknown for organizations to fail to communicate their objectives adequately to all those involved and to neglect to break them down into individual and group objectives, coordinated with the objectives of the organization. Sometimes the organization's objectives are not accepted by individuals and groups as their own objectives. Occasionally, the organization even has no clearly defined objectives. Whatever the reason, when incompatible objectives exist in an organization, or when the objectives are unclear, do not exist or are not accepted, conflict is a likely consequence.

COMPETITION

People vary in the degree to which they are motivated by the 'desire to win' – that is, by competition. This may even be influenced by different national cultures. For example, the English might place value on being 'good losers' while another nation might emphasize winning at all costs. Whatever the accuracy of these stereotypes, the desire to win (or, in some cases, fear of losing) is a strong motivator for most people. Belbin (1996) describes such competitive managers as 'shapers', and comments on their proneness to aggression, producing reciprocal reactions from other group members, and the fact that they have no hesitation in pursuing their goals by illicit means. In business management and organizations winning is everything for many managers: to come second is to fail. Thus beating competitors becomes the 'name of the game'. Too often, coming second does in fact mean that the manager does not survive for very long in that organization.

Competition is a stimulus to performance in management, as it is in sport and athletics, spurring individuals, groups and organizations to higher performance and greater teamwork. Thus competition between groups will lead to greater teamwork within the group and (if the groups are independent and do not interact with each other) higher organizational performance. Conversely, however, if groups are interdependent and do interact with each other, competition between groups is likely to lead to conflict and lower organizational unit performance.

Three common areas of competition contribute to conflict in a project:

1 peer competition
2 competition for scarce resources
3 competition for survival in a harsh environment.

Human nature being what it is, there will always tend to be competition between peers for rewards, promotion, recognition, credit, 'glory', getting one's own way, power and dominance. In a healthy organizational climate this can lead to increased performance, but if any of the other sources of conflict exist, and particularly if there are people problems, this competition will severely exacerbate conflict. The higher this competition is found in the hierarchy, the more serious will be its effect.

When resources are scarce there will always tend to be competition for them, both in the interdependent and the independent situations. The two most common resources in this respect are money and people. If funds are limited, senior managers will compete and fight to get their share. Similarly, managers will compete to get 'adequate' staff for their projects, both in terms of numbers and quality. Empire building is a common facet of many organizations, and each manager may compete to build up his or her department or group. Managers will also compete for scope to expand, to achieve, and for the opportunity to perform.

Although most organizations experience scarce resources, the fiercest competition occurs when a firm is faced with a harsh environment in the shape of a project with a very tight schedule, lack of work so that too few projects are shared among too many project managers, or when rationalization, retrenchment or even closure is threatened. In such situations conflict is about survival and, almost literally, blood can flow. Which groups are to suffer redundancies or be eliminated, or be merged, who goes and who stays, and who is to become the new group's manager are all issues that, from the individual's point of view, are justifiable sources of conflict.

In less dramatic terms, this source of conflict occurs in the matrix organization where several projects or tasks are resourced by common functional groups. Each task or project manager is in competition with others to get the best people working on the project in sufficient numbers to meet the objectives. Conflict can thus arise between the task managers, and between them and the functional group managers, over the quality and quantity of human resources and facilities assigned to the individual project or task.

Thus people's self-interests, as expressed in what motivates them, incompatible objectives and competition amount to an understandable collective source of conflict. It is up to the project manager to ensure that people's interests are aligned with those of the project and that they are best served by cooperation rather than by conflict.

Personality problems

PERSONALITY DIFFERENCES

Conflict, almost by definition, involves raised emotions or ill-feelings. But, so far, the sources of conflict discussed here have been based on substantive self-interest or structural problems.

It has been presumed that, as two parties come into conflict over substantive issues, emotions become aroused and ill-feeling grows between them. However, this process also operates in the opposite direction.

Organizations are not staffed with rational, cognitive persons abstracted from such emotions as anger, hate, envy or pride. Emotions exist. Emotional ties do link individuals and groups in an organization, and they cannot be ignored. They may be positive and encourage teamwork, but they may also be negative and encourage conflict. Thus a significant source of conflict is that which is known generally as 'personality differences' – perhaps more appropriately termed 'people problems'. Conflict need not be based solely on substantive self-interest; it can be based on emotions or, rather, on ill-feeling experienced by one party or between two parties. The theorist would term this the 'socio-emotional relationship' between parties. The way in which people deal with one another is one of the most important sources of conflict and destroyers of teamwork.

In practice, when conflict is based primarily on emotions, substantive issues are brought into the conflict. But resolving them does not resolve the conflict because they are merely side-issues or symptoms, not the root causes. Thus conflict based on emotions and personality differences or 'people problems' is very difficult to deal with.

The term 'personality differences' is a rather inadequate description of the feelings or emotions generated by a breakdown of human relationships. It may cover the following emotions or reactions:

- aggression
- anger
- annoyance
- antagonism
- dislike
- envy

- fear
- frustration
- hate
- jealousy
- neurotic hostility
- resentment

Although, in the management setting, terms such as 'hate' might appear to be extravagant, it is unfortunately true that feelings can, and do, develop to this intensity. The ways in which people relate to each other can stimulate the full range of human emotions, often without any substantive self-interest being involved. Once one or more of the parties feels any of these emotions, relationships slide on to the slippery slope towards conflict.

It must be recognized that, even if every manager were a competent, well-balanced human being with no special likes or dislikes, there would still be problems with personality differences. Further, managers have their own share of human failings, likes and dislikes, variable competencies and motivations. Thus, to the personality differences and problems that arise with well-balanced human beings, it is unfortunately necessary to add the many causes of conflict deriving from personality, ability and motivational sources that arise with so-called 'normal' people. If this were not enough, it is also true that many organizations have their share of fools, incompetents, rogues, neurotics and other 'problem people', who multiply the sources of conflict. Just one such catalyst is sufficient to lead to conflict and the breakdown of teamwork.

Sometimes personality differences arise simply because one person takes an instant dislike to another. People are all different and sometimes clash for no apparent reason. Often the root cause of conflict is simply resentment at another person's actions, attitude, mannerisms, tone, expression or words. This resentment is followed by a reduction in, or withdrawal of, cooperation, at which point the relationship has then started to move away from teamwork and towards conflict.

DEPENDENCY AND HISTORY OF CONFLICT

Often the mere fact that these individuals and groups are interdependent leads to personality differences and conflict. Individuals and groups in an organizational unit depend on one another to achieve their objectives. Some people may simply resent being dependent on someone else and react against it. More commonly, when problems or setbacks occur, the tendency is to blame the other person or group involved. Sometimes this may be justified, sometimes it is not, but the net result is the same: antagonism, personality differences and conflict. A common result of this factor is 'negative stereotyping' in which each group comes to believe that the other group is composed of morons, fools and incompetents.

Negative stereotyping and conflict may arise from a history of conflict built up over a number of years. This source of conflict is very difficult to eradicate, as it may have been incorporated into each group's culture. Any new member, even a group leader, would find it very difficult to break with tradition and 'consort' with the enemy. This is the 'Hill Billy feud' or 'Montagues and Capulets' syndrome, which typifies many interdepartmental relationships.

DIFFERENCES IN ABILITY AND MOTIVATION

Varying ability and commitment can also contribute significantly to personality differences and conflict. Managers and their subordinates in an organizational unit may vary in their managerial and technical abilities. They may be good at some activities and less good at others. Their speed of working or understanding of new ideas may vary. Their motivation, energy and commitment to the organization's objectives might be different. When any such variation is significant, there is the potential for conflict.

The 'slower' or apparently less energetic or motivated individual might feel insecure and threatened and act defensively as a result, whereas the higher performing individual may feel superior and openly hold the others in contempt. The outcome could be an intellectual elite that forms a close-knit team and excludes those whom it perceives not to meet its standards.

LACK OF INTERPERSONAL SKILLS

Problems in interpersonal relationships that are not based on structural or substantive self-interest issues generally arise because of a lack of interpersonal skills in the otherwise competent manager. Many managers lack skill in dealing with interpersonal relationships and can quite unconsciously 'put people's backs up', cause offence and resentments, and set relationships on the path to conflict. It is surprising – or perhaps not so surprising – what a difference the choice between the following routes can make to interpersonal relationships:

1 The manager communicates with people with sensitivity and tact, and takes their feelings into account.
2 The manager is apt to use the wrong word, be somewhat abrupt when under pressure, does not listen, or shows his or her feelings through a glance or body language.

This is not to say that one need be soft or easy-going, or even participative. Consider the subtleties of the English language as applied to a strong leadership style. The dictionary or thesaurus associates 'strong' with 'hard', 'harsh', 'tough', 'firm', 'unyielding', 'callous' and so on, yet there is a world of difference between leadership styles based on these descriptions – for example, between strong and harsh.

Nevertheless, this lack of interpersonal skill causes many of the interpersonal difficulties in organizations. As a general style of management, sensitivity training (which aims to stimulate openness, break down inhibitions and develop the skill of honest feedback) is not the complete answer as it tends to develop ineffective theory Y managers. Yet, used selectively, it can improve the way in which managers deal with their fellow human beings. Thus specialized training can make a significant difference in reducing the incidence of this source of conflict. The same cannot always be said about personality problems caused by the actions of difficult or problem people.

Problem people

Although conflict through personality differences can occur with almost anyone, 'difficult' or 'problem' people are particularly common sources of conflict. Many organizations can identify managers who have problems in one way or another in their interpersonal relationships. They are generally not team players and they can generate interpersonal differences and conflict across the complete span of their relationships – with peers, subordinates and even their superiors.

These problem managers, in addition to having one or other of the problems already outlined, often have one of the following characteristics:

- extreme ineptness in personal skills, often deeply based in their personality
- insecurity and stress
- a management style not conducive to teamwork
- ruthlessness and lack of principles – the 'managerial rogue'.

EXTREME INEPTNESS IN INTERPERSONAL SKILLS

Although many managers have some deficiency in their interpersonal skills, there are some who are particularly inept in this area. This ineptness is due to, or has become part of, their personality. In such cases it is probable that no amount of training or psychotherapy is likely to change their manner of dealing with people. If this type of training is pressed too far, there is a risk of mental breakdown with this type of personality.

At first, it might be thought unlikely that any effective organization would have fools, incompetents or neurotics in its management. Yet it is not uncommon to have such problem people even at the highest levels and, if present, they act as a catalyst for interpersonal problems. However, the opposite can also apply, in that groups made up of extremely clever people, with high scores in mental ability, can be difficult to manage, prone to destructive debate, and have difficulties in decision-making.

INSECURITY AND STRESS

Insecurity and stress are related and can be sources of conflict. Most organizations have their share of managers who either feel or in fact are insecure. Insecure managers are generally afraid to expose themselves to the risk of failure, or of 'being found out'. They act defensively and resist change. Thus, in an interdependent situation where there is continuous change and where authority and responsibilities are unclear, the insecure manager is always likely to come into contact with the agent of change, who in our case is the project manager.

Sometimes this insecurity is entirely justified if the manager's survival is personally threatened. It may be that the project workload in the organization is falling and there is the danger of redundancy. The manager may be under threat of disciplinary action for some reason. He or she may be out of his or her depth with new methods and technology, or may be being stalked by a powerful enemy. The manager may have incurred a superior's displeasure and, especially if this superior is a rogue, his or her life might have been made very difficult.

More often the root of the insecurity lies in being unable, or feeling unable, to cope with the demands being made. Managers may be experiencing role conflict, be unhappy with ambiguity in their role or be out of their depth in a rapidly changing environment. Their greatest fear is being found out to be incompetent. They feel barely able to cope with the present situation and, if change should happen, they would be totally lost. This can occur with two phenomena that are common in management:

- the Peter Principle
- the professional specialist who has difficulties with the managerial role.

The Peter Principle was propounded, not without humour, by the American management writer Lawrence Peter. It declares that 'in a hierarchy every employee tends to rise to his level of incompetence' (Peter and Hull, 1969). Unfortunately this frequently applies to managers, who will thus tend to be insecure, act defensively, resist change and be a source of conflict.

Problems associated with the professional specialist as a manager are more complex. Many professionals encounter problems when they move from a role as a specialist technologist to that of a manager. This can happen in two stages:

1 when the professional specialist becomes a functional manager (such as a chief engineer) at the head of his or her own specialist discipline
2 on promotion to more general management or to project management.

Professional people are generally promoted on the basis of their technical or professional expertise, and not necessarily on their potential management ability. This can lead to problems related to their role identities and to conflict when they occupy functional management positions. The professional person will sometimes continue to identify more closely with his or her former specialist role than with that of a manager.

Such professional people often find it difficult to overcome problems caused by the lack of compatibility between their purely functional roles and the non-technical requirements of the managerial role. This can not only lead to difficulties in dealing with people, organizing, planning and controlling activities and in handling the financial aspects, but also to possible conflict with others and within themselves. When professional specialists move into general manager or project manager roles their problems are compounded unless they can shed most of their former professional background and culture, which is often difficult.

Insecurity and other personality problems as sources of conflict are made worse when the individual concerned cannot handle the stress involved in his or her job. Following Hans Selye and J.E. McGrath, Hunsaker and Cook define stress as:

> ... non-specific response of the body to any demand made upon it. It is manifest in the psychological, emotional and physiological reactions to internal or external environmental conditions to which the individual's adaptive abilities are perceived to be overextended. (Hunsaker and Cook, 1986, p. 232)

Stress can affect a person mentally, emotionally or physically. A degree of stress can stimulate a person to higher performance, but increasing stress will reduce performance, increase potential for conflict and can even kill. Of course, extra-organizational factors can cause stress in an individual, but within the organization there are two principal sources of stress:

- workload
- conflict and politics.

A heavy workload – that is, too great a volume of work to handle within the time available or work that is too difficult for the person's level of ability – can cause stress in a conscientious or insecure individual. However, the principal causes of organizational stress are found in the sources of conflict outlined in this chapter – in the conflict itself and in the power politics that arise from it. Thus a vicious spiral can be created, whereby stress can be caused by those conflict factors, which in turn leads to further conflict.

MANAGEMENT STYLE AS A SOURCE OF CONFLICT

The employment of a leadership or management style in dealing with subordinates, peers and near-peers in other groups that is inconsistent with the organization's culture, the people involved, the situation and the power of the manager can be a significant source of personality differences, a destroyer of teamwork and a creator of conflict. People associate an autocratic, despotic style of leadership or management with the generation of this type of conflict, and this does happen in many organizations. Take, for example, the arrogant misuse of power by the autocratic manager who 'treats subordinates like dirt'. The manager's attitude is 'I'm the boss and you are my subordinate, so when I say "Jump", you jump!'. Clearly, the explicit use of naked authority or power to enforce compliance can be counterproductive and is unlikely to generate willing commitment and teamwork. Fear is a poor motivator in these circumstances.

Yet it is the manner in which power is used that largely determines whether it results in enthusiastic commitment, passive compliance or resistance. Strong leadership, the exercise of authority and power, autocratic management and firm control need not stand in contradiction to participative management, motivation and teamwork but can actually complement them. It is the combination of these factors that leads to effective project management. To obtain the best results, power must be exercised in a manner that is more implicit than explicit, and that demonstrates respect for the individual.

People dislike living or working in an uncertain and disorganized world. They actually welcome leadership, accept legitimate authority and established power, and need control. People accept recognized authority and power not simply through fear, but through their respect for it. Thus the exercise of power need not break down participation or teamwork; in fact if it is not exercised uncertainty, confusion and conflict can be created. Also, autocratic management is accepted in appropriate circumstances – for example, when time is short, when decisions are critical, or where there is respect for the ability, power and leadership of the autocratic manager. The necessity or legitimacy of control is also recognized and accepted by most people, and control does perform essential monitoring and motivational functions in project work.

Nevertheless if a strong leadership style is employed, the leader must have the necessary power and the people involved must recognize and accept it. If these conditions are not met, as can occur in matrix or multi-company organizations, the management style must be tempered to suit the situation if conflict is to be avoided.

It is not only the autocratic manager who can generate such problems. The weak, indecisive manager and the bureaucratic manager can also be sources of conflict. If leadership is indefinite and the senior manager lacks or fails to exercise power, but instead uses a weak participative style, subordinates and others will feel that they are becalmed, rudderless and leaderless and will tend to try to establish their own power. This in turn leads to politics and conflict. The bureaucratic manager, who acts more as an administrator, who minutes everything in detail, who uses memos and e-mails to excess and copies them to all and sundry instead of engaging in face-to-face two-way communication, can also generate personality differences which lead to conflict.

A clash of management styles between the various groups and companies working on a project can also cause conflict. This can happen when two strong leaders compete for dominance, but can also be the outcome of different groups or companies with different management styles having to work together. Consider the simple case of individuals from four groups, or the groups themselves, working as one organizational unit and suppose that each group could be placed at a different corner of Blake and Mouton's managerial grid. One group is totally turned off (1,1); one is at the extreme of concern for people (1,9); one is at the extreme of concern for production (9,1); and the other combines task and people (9,9). Without a very effective and sensitive integrationist manager, misunderstandings, bewilderment and conflict will pervade the relationships between these individuals and groups.

THE MANAGERIAL ROGUE

Another source of conflict occurs with what could be termed the management 'rogue' who has a personalized power orientation. The term 'rogue' is used to describe a manager who is ruthless, unprincipled, determined to gain advancement by any means and has a strong personalized power motivation. Behavioural theorists identify two sides to power motivation:

- a light side, or socialized power motivation
- a dark side, or personalized power motivation.

Socialized power motivation can enhance the effectiveness of an organization, in that the senior manager uses his or her power to achieve results for the benefits of others and for the objectives of the organization. Social norms restrain the negative use of power, and it is still possible to have participation and teamwork.

This is not the case with personalized power motivation, which almost invariably leads to conflict. The senior manager with personalized power motivation tends to operate as a bully, has a strong detrimental effect on individual motivation, and conflict within and between groups is the norm. Personalized power motivation is characterized by a desire to dominate others, beat the competition, keep subordinates weak and dependent, practice divide-and-rule politics to maintain dominance, and use power for personal gain. Rogues exploit others for their own purposes and are very status-conscious. They have favourites, who act as spies, and manage using fear and force.

The impact of such managers on their organizations can be disastrous. Subordinates and other managers will endeavour, either formally or informally, to develop a power balance. Political in-fighting becomes endemic. The power-crazed manager becomes isolated, surrounded only by 'yes men' and favourites. Not only does he or she get minimal performance and compliance limited only to direct instructions, but there is also a risk of sabotage. Communication operates on a narrowly channelled one-to-one basis, new ideas are suppressed (either slapped down or simply ignored) and risk-taking is diminished. It is only because of the subordinates' inherent acceptance of positional power, their commitment to the organization's goals, their desire to survive and, admittedly, the ability and energy of the superior manager that the organization achieves any results. In addition, such managers are usually expert in the use of rewards and coercion to motivate subordinates.

However, fear being a poor motivator in management organizations, motivation is considerably reduced and participation and teamwork are non-existent within the manager's group. Outside the manager's positional power sphere, other managers reject his or her attempts to increase positional authority or power, and teamwork between groups is limited to isolated individuals – that is, to one-to-one relationships or very small groups.

The managerial rogue and political conflict

One of the unfortunate facts of life is that rogues tend to reach senior management positions and thus have a significant impact on the extent of dark politics within the organization. The hard working, head-down, straightforward manager who is not involved in politics will always tend to be trumped by the effective political operator. In some ways this is justified in that, as a manager advances to middle and senior management, involvement in the light side of politics becomes necessary if he or she is to be fully effective. Thus senior managers should be both effective managers and effective political operators.

The light side of politics may be employed to acquire the power to manage the organization more effectively or, to put it more bluntly, to get one's own way for the good of the organization. In the dark side of politics the manager is concerned with defeating the opposing forces to get his or her own way for personal or group objectives that are often unrelated to the good of the organization. Woe betide the organization when this conflict climbs the hierarchical tree and enters the political arena. Political conflict draws everyone to one side or the other, and management effort and ingenuity, instead of being employed in achieving the objectives of the organization and the project, is diverted towards achieving victory over the enemy.

Political conflict can be defined as a struggle between opposing forces combined with the activities of opponents to gain power to 'defeat the enemy'. Typically, the opposing individuals and groups build up alliances and coalitions until conflict extends throughout the organizational unit, and way beyond those originally involved in the struggle. Individuals who try to stand clear of this political conflict and support neither party usually end up by being treated unfairly by one or both of them.

The situation may deteriorate to such an extent that the two factions who are locked together in combat will concentrate all their attention on in-fighting to the extent that they ignore greater external threats to the organization's existence. The organization can fail or be taken over without these warring factions being aware of the threats until the very last moment. Typically, ethics or scruples are lost, political games dominate, divisive objectives are maximized, winning becomes all-important and deviousness, rather than teamwork, prevails. Unfortunately this struggle for power, particularly among senior managers, and the consequential organizational political manoeuvring appears to characterize many large hierarchical organizations.

How to manage the managerial rogue

Managerial rogues tend to be difficult to handle as subordinates, and almost impossible to work with as peers without conflict and politics. One such rogue in an organizational unit is enough to destroy teamwork and bring about political conflict. The higher such a rogue advances up the hierarchy, the more disruptive is the impact. Yet as superiors, particularly as chief executives or the head of an operational unit, they can sometimes be very effective because they are often hard-driving, personally competent autocrats. In managerial grid terms, they are 9,1 managers. In addition, so-called troublemakers may be classified as rogues when in fact they are individuals who do not accept the status quo. But, if managed correctly, this type of troublemaker can be a high performer.

Thus in deciding what action to take to deal with such rogues, it is first necessary to determine whether or not the individual's particular attributes are effective in, or counter-productive to, achieving the project's objectives. There are usually only two options:

1 Get rid of the rogue, if that is possible.
2 Manage the rogue and take the risk.

The management of rogues, as a subordinate, peer or superior, is a high-risk strategy involving the following:

- Gain the rogue's respect, if only as a dangerous person to cross or to have as an enemy. As Machiavelli (1540) stated, 'You have to be both a fox and a lion', or as the Scots would say 'Wha' dare meddle wi' me.'
- Align the rogue's objectives so that they are compatible with yours and the organization's. This involves using the 'lifeboat' strategy from the politician's toolkit – that is, ensure that you are both in the same lifeboat, so that the rogue knows that you will both sink or swim together. This is achieved by increasing the rogue's interdependency with you and those managers with whom he or she must interact, such that he or she becomes dependent on them for the achievement of personal goals.
- Decrease the rogue's interdependency, so that he or she is the head of a more or less independent organizational unit and does not have to interact or be interdependent with anyone who is not a direct subordinate (Mastenbroek, 1987).

This last strategy is by far the most effective way of using competent rogues to contribute to the project's objectives. Rogues are particularly suited to a troubleshooting role or managing a crisis. They are most effective in a short-term management-of-change role under pressure and least effective in the management of ongoing operations that require interaction with their peers. This may not be very pleasant for the rogue's subordinates, but it can result in high organizational unit performance.

The management of conflict

Traditional theory identifies five modes of managing conflict:

1 *withdrawal* – retreating or withdrawing from an actual or potential disagreement
2 *force* – exerting one's viewpoint at the potential expense of another, often characterized by competitiveness and a win–lose situation
3 *smoothing* – de-emphasizing or avoiding areas of differences and emphasizing areas of agreement
4 *compromise* – bargaining and searching for solutions that bring some degree of satisfaction to all parties in the dispute
5 *confrontation* – facing the conflict directly, which involves a problem-solving approach in which the affected parties work through their disagreements.

However, these modes of conflict resolution are more applicable to resolving disagreements than conflict, for the following reasons:

- Their use and success in resolving disputes is dependent on the nature of the existing relationships between individuals and groups.
- They tackle only the symptoms and not the underlying sources of conflict.

For example, the following modes of disagreement resolution are only applicable when the existing relationships are as shown:

Relationships	*Mode of resolution*
Conflict	Withdrawal
	Forcing
Cooperation	Smoothing
	Compromise
Teamwork	Confrontation

Withdrawal and force are used in the conflict situation. Although they resolve the differences, they increase the underlying sources of conflict. Smoothing and compromise are effective in the cooperative stage of relationships, provided that they are reasonably balanced. Confrontation works when there is teamwork – and only then. The management of conflict involves identifying and tackling the underlying causes, not the symptoms. The most effective cure for conflict is prevention. This can be achieved by the following means:

- Create conditions conducive to teamwork.
- Recognize the first signs of deteriorating relationships and take corrective action.

- Manage the organization in such a way that teamwork is encouraged and conflict is discouraged.

This is not always possible. Once conflict is recognized, it is necessary to identify the underlying sources, whether they be organization structure, personal self-interests, personality or people problems. This is achieved by auditing the relationships, the organization and the people involved and comparing them with the models outlined earlier in this text. Thereafter it is a case of eliminating the sources of conflict by restructuring the organization or taking other management action to improve the nature of the relationships, deal with problem people, create conditions conducive to teamwork and lead the people from conflict to cooperation and teamwork.

Conclusion: from conflict to teamwork

Leadership from the project manager and other senior managers is critical to achieving the high performance necessary to meet project objectives. Inevitably, this involves a high degree of task orientation; it is results that count, not simply making people happy and satisfied at work except insofar as this contributes to their motivation and achievement. The project manager must therefore be a professional in the 'scientific' aspects of project management – that is, in the organization, planning and control of the project combined with the necessary analysis and decision-making. He or she must also have a high personal motivation to succeed and possess both leadership and drive. To carry out this leadership, the project manager must be able to use all the available tools for enhancing his or her positional power through personal and political power.

However, unless project managers can also combine this scientific side of project management with the human side, they will be unable to motivate all those involved in the project to achieve high performance and will be in constant conflict with their peers and near-peers, particularly in matrix and multi-company organizations. Teamwork, or at the very least a cooperative working relationship, is essential in project work: it is the performance of the organization as a whole that is critical to success, not just individual or group performance.

Among the most important of the project manager's tasks is the combination of the following:

- leadership of the organization for task achievement
- motivation of individuals, groups and organizational units
- welding these entities to work as a team to achieve the project objectives
- management of conflict, or more precisely the moving of relationships in the conflict–teamwork dimension towards the teamwork extremity.

Therefore not only must the project manager exercise leadership in the achievement of the project objectives, but must also 'lead' the people and groups involved towards being an effective, highly motivated team.

The project manager needs the following attributes:

- a vision that teamwork is possible and desirable
- high personal commitment to that vision

- a conceived strategy for achieving it
- the ability to take the steps necessary to implement it
- the ability to create a climate in the organization by words and deeds that inspire the people involved to follow his or her example.

In this leadership, the project manager must recognize that whatever the shortcomings of the conclusions reached by human behavioural scientists, they contain a great deal of truth. Therefore the project manager should include the following steps in his or her strategy:

- Treat people as adults.
- Communicate with them.
- Vary management style to suit the circumstances, the people and your managerial power. In other words, use a contingency approach.
- Deal sensitively with the following issues:
  - dual subordination
  - defence of territory
  - insecurity and stress
  - professional specialists as managers
  - the Peter Principle.
- Deal with – that is, manage – rogues.
- Rotate people between functions to break down functional and cultural barriers.
- Establish close physical contact and social interaction in groups and linking pins: try, for example, to locate them in the same or adjacent offices.
- Align the objectives and create mutual self-interests. For example, do not write contracts designed to create conflict.
- Implement the following behavioural strategies:
  - Be aware of small warning signs indicating breakdowns in human relations.
  - Audit the organization.
  - Train the people and groups in human relations.
  - Implement team-building.
  - Encourage the establishment of the project itself as a 'super-ordinate objective'.
  - Avoid win–lose situations, if possible without sacrificing task accomplishment.
  - Do not make enemies needlessly.
  - Apply achievement, goal theory and target-setting.
  - Back this up with a reward system.

In carrying out these strategies the project manager must combine the organization structure, the structured methodology of project planning and control and the human aspect to provide effective means with which to achieve high motivation and teamwork. If he or she can achieve this, there are many management tools available for managing conflict, motivating individuals and groups, and building an effective, high-performing total team.

ORGANIZATION STRUCTURE

The project organization structure should be designed to create conditions conducive to motivation and teamwork. This involves taking the following steps:

- Avoid tall, monolithic, centrally controlled hierarchical organization structures.
- Avoid large, functional groups or departments internal to the project.
- Use mixed or small functional groups whenever possible, to avoid functional orientation and to facilitate teamwork.
- Emphasize flat, decentralized organization structures combined with a divisional structure and discrete organizational units in the larger project.
- Emphasize the delegation of personal accountability and responsibility to individual managers, groups and organizational units.
- Use the contractor–consignee concept with the in-company matrix organization.
- Clarify the overall project organization structure and, for individuals, groups and organizational units, clarify their:
  - authority
  - objectives
  - responsibilities.
- Identify formal, matrix and informal groups as discrete entities, and their key integrating managers. This establishes mutual self-interests, integration and facilitates teamwork.

PLANNING AND CONTROL

The structured methodology of planning and control is used to reinforce this delegation of accountability and responsibility:

1 Structuring the project in one, two or more dimensions clearly identifies the responsibilities of organizational and project element managers, group managers, and cost account or work package managers.
2 Planning and control are participative and personalized:
   - Each individual manager and group has specified their own unique goals, objectives, and planned baselines of schedule, cost and resources.
   - They have participated in actually setting these goals and objectives.
   - They know what they have to do to achieve good performance.
   - They each receive reports on progress and performance measured against their own goals and baseline objectives.
3 This is used to:
   - encourage commitment to the project and the development of a project attitude
   - give meaning to individual contributors to the project
   - facilitate motivation through achievement, goal theory and target-setting
   - give a basis for the supporting reward system.

References and Further Reading for Part 4

Atkinson, J. (2001), *Developing Teams Through Project-Based Learning*, Aldershot: Gower.

Baker, B.N., Murphy, D.C. and Fisher, D. (1983), 'Factors Affecting Project Success', in D.I. Cleland and W.R. King (eds), *Project Management Handbook*, New York: Van Nostrand Reinhold.

Belbin, R.M. (1996), *Management Teams: Why They Succeed or Fail*, Oxford: Butterworth-Heinemann.

Bell, C. Jr and Rosenzweig, C.H. (1978), 'Highlights of an Organization Improvement Program in a City Government', in W.L. French, C. Bell Jr and R.A. Zawaki (eds), *Organization Development: Theory Practice and Research*, Dallas TX: Business Publications Inc.

Blake, R.R. and Mouton, J.S. (1964), *The Managerial Grid 111*, Houston: Gulf Publishing Co.

Briner, W., Hastings, C. and Geddes, M. (1996), *Project Leadership*, 2nd edn, Aldershot: Gower.

Calnan, T.J. (1988), 'The Use of Structures in Today's Program Management Environment' in *From Conception to Completion*, Glasgow: IPMA 9th World Congress on Project Management.

Fiedler, F.E. (1965), 'Engineer the Job to Fit the Manager', *Harvard Business Review*, September–October.

French, W.L. and Bell, C.H. (1995), *Organization Development: Interventions for Organizational Improvement*, 5th edn, Englewood Cliffs NJ: Prentice Hall International.

Harrison, F.L. (1988), 'Conflict, Power and Politics in Project Management' in *From Conception to Completion*, Glasgow: IPMA 9th World Congress on Project Management.

Harrison, F.L. (1989), 'Structure and the Project Control and Information System, *Quantity Surveyors, Computers and Project Management Conference*.

Hartman, F.T. (2000), *Don't Park Your Brain Outside*, Newtown Square, PA: Project Management Institute.

Huczynski, A. and Buchanan, D.A. (2001), *Organizational Behaviour: An Introductory Text*, 4th edn, Hemel Hempstead: Prentice-Hall.

Hunsaker, P.L. and Cook, C.W. (1986), *Managing Organization Behavior*, Reading MA: Addison Wesley.

Kliem, R.L. and Ludin, I.S. (1992), *The People Side of Project Management*, Aldershot: Gower.

Likert, R. (1961), *New Patterns of Management*, New York: McGraw-Hill.

Lock, D. (2003), *Project Management*, 8th edn, Aldershot: Gower.

McClelland, D.C., Atkinson, J.W., Clark, R.A. and Lowell, E.L. (1976), *The Achievement Motive*, 2nd edn, New York: Irvington.

McDaniel, N.A. (chair) and Bahnmaier, W.W. (ed.) (2001), *Scheduling Guide for Program Managers*, Fort Belvoir, VA: Defense Systems Management College Press.

McGrath, J.E. (1976), 'Stress and Behavior in Organizations', in M.D. Dunnette (ed.), *Handbook of Industrial and Organizational Psychology*, Chicago: Rand McNally.

McGregor, D.M. (1960), *The Human Side of Enterprise*, New York: McGraw-Hill.

Machiavelli, N. (1540), *The Prince*, trans G. Bull (1961), Harmondsworth: Penguin Books.

Margerison, C. and McCann, D. (1990), *Team Management*, London: W.H. Allen.

Mastenbroek, W.F.G. (1987), *Conflict Management and Organization Development*, New York: Wiley.

Mintzberg, H. (1983a), *Structure in Fives: Designing Effective Organizations*, Englewood Cliffs, NJ: Prentice Hall.

Mintzberg, H. (1983b), *Power In and Around Organizations*, Englewood Cliffs, NJ: Prentice Hall.

Pass, C., Lowes, B., Pendleton, A. and Chadwick, L. (1999), *Unwin Hyman Dictionary of Business*, 2nd edn, Glasgow: Harper Collins.

Peter, L.J. and Hull, R. (1969), *The Peter Principle*, New York: William Morrow and London: Souvenir Press.

Pfeffer, J. (1992), *Power in Organizations*, 2nd edn, London: Harper Collins.

PMI, (2000), *A Guide to the Project Management Body of Knowledge (PMBOK® Guide) 2000 Edition*, Newtown Square, PA: Project Management Institute.

Project Manager Today (11 issues per year), Hook, (Hampshire), Larchdrift Projects Ltd.

Randolph, W.A. (1991), *Getting the Job Done: Managing Project Teams and Task Forces for Success*, Hemel Hempstead: Prentice Hall.

Stewart. R. (1999), *Gower Handbook of Teamworking*, Aldershot: Gower.

Thamhain, H.J. and Wilemon, D.L. (1974), 'Conflict Management in Project-Oriented Work Environments' in *Proceedings of the Project Management Institute*, Newtown Square, PA: Project Management Institute.

Webb, A. (2003), *Using Earned Value: A Project Manager's Guide*, Aldershot: Gower.

Wilemon, D.L. and Baker, B.N. (1983), 'Some Major Research Findings Regarding the Human Element in Project Management', in D.I. Cleland and W.R. King, *The Project Management Handbook*, New York: Van Nostrand Reinhold.

Bibliography

Andersen, E.S., Grude, K.V. and Haug, T. (1998), *Goal Directed Project Management: Effective Techniques and Strategies*, 2nd edn, London: Kogan Page.

Atkinson, J. (2001), *Developing Teams Through Project-Based Learning*, Aldershot: Gower.

Backhouse, C.J. and Brookes, N.J. (eds) (1996), *Concurrent Engineering*, Aldershot: Gower (in association with The Design Council).

Bartlett, J. (2000), *Managing Programmes of Business Change*, 3rd edn, Hook: Project Manager Today.

Briner, W., Hastings, C. and Geddes, M. (1996), *Project Leadership*, 2nd edn, Aldershot: Gower.

Burke, Rory (1999), *Project Management: Planning and Control*, 3rd edn, Chichester: Wiley.

Chapman, C.B., Cooper, D.F. and Page, M.J. (1987), *Management for Engineers*, Chichester: Wiley.

Churchhouse, C. (1999), *Managing Projects: A Gower Workbook*, Aldershot: Gower.

Cleland, D.I. (ed.) (1998), *Field Guide to Project Management*, New York: Van Nostrand Reinhold.

Cleland, D.I. and King, W.R. (1998) *Project Management Handbook*, New York: Van Nostrand Reinhold.

Devaux, S.A. (1999), *Total Project Control: A Manager's Guide to Integrated Planning, Measuring and Tracking*, New York: Wiley.

Gray, F.G. and Larson, E.W. (2002), *Project Management: The Managerial Process*, 2nd edn, Singapore: McGraw-Hill.

Hamilton, A. (1997), *Management by Projects*, London: Thomas Telford.

Hartman, F.T. (2000), *Don't Park Your Brain Outside*, Newtown Square, PA: Project Management Institute.

Healey, P. L. (1997), *Project Management: Getting the Job Done on Time and in Budget*, Oxford: Butterworth-Heinemann.

Holroyd, T. (1999), *Site Management for Engineers*, London: Thomas Telford.

Kerzner, H. (2000), *Applied Project Management: Best Practices on Implementation*, New York: Wiley.

Kerzner, H. (2001), *Project Management: A Systems Approach to Planning, Scheduling and Controlling*, 7th edn, New York: Wiley.

Kliem, R.L. and Ludin, I.S. (1992), *The People Side of Project Management*, Aldershot: Gower.

Kor, R. and Wijnen, G. (2000), *50 Checklists for Project and Programme Managers*, Aldershot: Gower.

Lester, A. (1991), *Project Planning and Control*, 2nd edn, Oxford: Butterworth-Heinemann.

Lewis, J.P. (2001), *Project Planning Scheduling and Control: A Hands-on Guide to Bringing Projects in on Time and on Budget*, New York: McGraw-Hill.

Lock, D. (ed.) (1993), *Handbook of Engineering Management*, 2nd edn, Oxford: Butterworth-Heinemann.

Lockyer, K.G. and Gordon, J. (1996), *Critical Path Analysis and Other Project Management Techniques*, 6th edn, London: Pitman.

Loftus, J. (ed.) (1999), *Project Management of Multiple Projects and Contracts*, London: Thomas Telford.

Mantel, S.J., Meredith, J.R., Shafer, S.M. and Sutton, M.M. (2001), *Project Management in Practice*, New York: Wiley.

Maylor, H. (2002), *Project Management*, 3rd edn, London: Financial Times/Pitman.

Meredith, J.R. and Mantel, S.J. Jr (2000), *Project Management: A Managerial Approach*, 4th edn, New York: Wiley.

Morris, P.W.G. (1997), *The Management of Projects*, London: Thomas Telford.

O'Neill, J.J. (1989), *Management of Industrial Construction Projects*, Oxford: Heinemann Newnes.

PMI, (2000), *A Guide to the Project Management Body of Knowledge (PMBOK® Guide) 2000 Edition*, Newtown Square, PA: Project Management Institute.

Randolph, W.A. (1991), *Getting the Job Done: Managing Project Teams and Task Forces for Success*, Hemel Hempstead: Prentice-Hall.

Reiss, Geoff (1995), *Project Management Demystified: Today's Tools and Techniques*, 2nd edn, London: Spon.

Reiss, Geoff (1996), *Programme Management Demystified: Managing Multiple Projects Successfully*, London: Spon.

Rosenau, M.D. Jr (1998), *Successful Project Management*, 3rd edn, New York: Wiley.

Shtub, A. and Bard, J.F. (1994), *Project Management: Engineering, Technology and Implementation*, Englewood Cliffs, NJ: Prentice Hall.

Simon, P. *et al.*, (eds) (1997), *Project Risk Analysis and Management Guide: PRAM*, High Wycombe: APM Group.

Stevens, M. (ed.) (2002), *Project Management Pathways*, High Wycombe: Association For Project Management.

Stewart, R. (1999), *Gower Handbook of Teamworking*, Aldershot: Gower.

Teale, D. (2001), *Project Risk Assessment*, London: Hodder & Stoughton.

Turner, J.R. (1998) *Handbook of Project-based Management: Improving the Process for Achieving Strategic Objectives*, 2nd edn, Maidenhead: McGraw-Hill.

Turner, J.R. and Simister, S.J. (2000), *Gower Handbook of Project Management*, 3rd edn, Aldershot: Gower.

Webb, A. (2000), *Project Management for Successful Product Innovation*, Aldershot: Gower.

Webster, G. (1999), *Managing Projects at Work*, Aldershot: Gower.

Index

If you have found this book useful you may be interested in other titles from Gower

Gower Handbook of Project Management 3ed
edited by J. Rodney Turner and Stephen J. Simister
0 566 08138 5 (hbk) 0 566 08397 3 (CD-ROM)

The Relationship Manager:
The Next Generation of Project Management
Tony Davis and Richard Pharro
0 566 08463 5

Project Management 8ed
Dennis Lock
0 566 08578 X (hbk) 0 566 08551 8 (pbk)

The Project Manager's Guide to Handling Risk
Alan Webb
0 566 08571 2

Project Management for Successful Product Innovation
Alan Webb
0 566 08262 4

The Project Management A-Z
A Compendium of Project Management Techniques and
How to Use Them
Alan Wren
0 566 08556 9 (hbk) 0 566 08557 7 (Looseleaf)

For further information on these and all our titles visit
our website – **www.gowerpub.com**
All online orders receive a discount

GOWER

Join our email newsletter

Gower is widely recognized as one of the world's leading publishers on management and business practice. Its programmes range from 1000-page handbooks through practical manuals to popular paperbacks. These cover all the main functions of management: human resource development, sales and marketing, project management, finance, etc. Gower also produces training videos and activities manuals on a wide range of management skills.

As our list is constantly developing you may find it difficult to keep abreast of new titles. With this in mind we offer a free email news service, approximately once every two months, which provides a brief overview of the most recent titles and links into our catalogue, should you wish to read more or see sample pages.

To sign up to this service, send your request via email to info@gowerpub.com. Please put your email address in the body of the email as confirmation of your agreement to receive information in this way.

GOWER